THE SAT IS A TEST
IT IS *ONLY* A TEST

If it were an actual indicator of your intelligence, you wouldn't be able to prep for it. But you can, and this book is a great place to start.

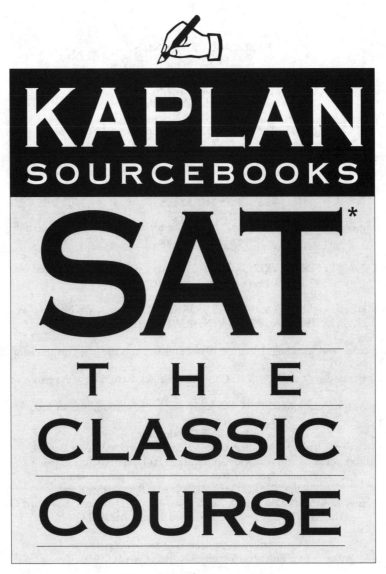

KAPLAN
SOURCEBOOKS
SAT*
THE
CLASSIC
COURSE

BY THE STAFF OF
STANLEY H. KAPLAN EDUCATIONAL CENTER, LTD.

Bantam Doubleday Dell

*SAT is a registered trademark of the College Entrance Examination Board, which does not endorse this book.

KAPLAN SOURCEBOOKS™
Published by
Bantam Doubleday Dell Publishing Group, Inc.
1540 Broadway
New York, NY 10036

A Seth Godin Production
Design: Charles Kreloff, Seth Godin. Editors: Tom Dyja, Joyce Bermel.
Production: Martin Erb, Vic Lapuszynski, Lisa DiMona, Chris Angelilli.
Layout: Julie Maner. Project Management: Megan O'Connor.
Copyediting: Patricia Goff, Michelle Eldridge, Jolanta Benal.
Cartoons: Holly Kowitt, Joe Dator, Rick Parker, Gary Larson, Dan Piraro and Frank Cotham.
Thanks to Robert Leinwand, Richard Ticktin, Michael Cader.

Manufactured in the United States of America
Published Simultaneously in Canada

January 1994

10 9 8 7 6 5 4 3

Library of Congress Cataloging–in–Publication Data
SAT, the classic course/by the staff of Stanley H. Kaplan Educational Center Ltd.
      p. cm.   (Kaplan sourcebooks)
      ISBN 0-385-31156-7
      1. Scholastic aptitude test--Study guides. 2. Universities
      and colleges--United States--Entrance examinations--Study guides.
      1. Stanley H. Kaplan Educational Center Ltd. (New York, N.Y.)
      11. Series.
      LB2353.57.S2675   1994
      378.1'662--dc20

                                       93-23315
                                           CIP

From the day she was born, Emily's parents *knew* she'd do well in school.

TEN WAYS YOU CAN BOOST YOUR SCORE

GET FAMILIAR WITH THE TEST

The SAT is one of the most predictable experiences you'll have in your life: before going into the test, you should know what to expect on every section; what the rules for each question type are; and what topics are covered. See pages 7 - 9 for this information.

MAKE THE STRUCTURE OF THE TEST WORK FOR YOU

Most of the SAT is multiple choice. That means that the answer is right in front of you. No one cares how you got the answer; only whether you got it. You can make the test format work to your benefit. See pages 1 - 6.

LEARN THE ANALOGIES THAT COME UP ALL THE TIME

Although baffling at first, SAT analogies really test the same basic relationships over and over again. By becoming familiar with these "classic bridges," you can know what types of relationships to expect on the test. These bridges are explained on pages 32 - 35.

KNOW WHAT TO LOOK FOR IN SENTENCE COMPLETIONS

Many sentence completions test your ability to understand the structure of sentences. By focusing on clue words, you can unwrap the meaning in seconds. See the list of clue words on page 47.

READ ACTIVELY

Critical reading on the SAT forces you to think about what you read. We show you how to unpack what the author says, pay attention to tone and make inferences. See pages 78 - 79.

BUILD YOUR VOCABULARY

Sooner or later, you're going to run into words you don't know. No one is expected to know all the words on the SAT. But don't worry — there are lots of techniques for finding the meanings of strange words, and for using what you do know about words to answer the question. See these strategies on pages 22 - 24.

DO QCS QUICKLY AND EFFICIENTLY

Quantitative Comparison questions appear on the math sections of the SAT. Difficult at first, they repay time spent practicing with them and are a good source of quick points. See the strategies on pages 112 - 122.

UNDERSTAND THE TOP 10 MATH TRAPS

What makes some SAT math questions hard? It's not the numbers, and not always the concepts. Often, they're hard because of a trap: something the testmaker hopes you'll fall for. We'll show you the most common traps and teach you how to avoid them on pages 173 - 191.

LEARN TO USE YOUR CALCULATOR

You can use your calculator on the new SAT. That means that thousands of students nationwide will be wasting their time using calculators on questions that are simple to solve with just a little thinking. We'll show you when to use your calculator and when not to on pages 96 - 98.

DON'T PANIC

People panic because the test is unfamiliar to them. Throughout this book, we show you the classic problems and how to solve them, so that there's no need for you to panic on test day.

FOREWORD

Midway through the exam,
Allen pulls out a bigger brain.

"**Y**ou can't prep for the SAT."

Some people wanted to believe that. For nearly fifty years the Educational Testing Service (ETS), the company that writes the SAT, and the College Board worked hard to make people believe it. Some myths die hard, and a few years ago, ETS and the College Board finally had to give it up.

More than fifty-four years ago, a young man named Stanley H. Kaplan knew that he could raise scores on the test. He perfected many special techniques and developed a course. Word spread, a business started, and eventually more than a quarter of a million high school students learned that you *could* increase your scores on the SAT. There were examples by the busload of students' scores increasing by 150, 200, 300 points or more. Finally, in the late 1980s, the College Board quietly inserted a change in the SAT information bulletin noting that it *was* possible to increase one's SAT score through formal and informal preparation.

There are other examples of Stanley Kaplan being ahead of his time. For decades he argued that the Scholastic *Aptitude* Test should be renamed the Scholastic *Assessment* Test, because the SAT was not an intelligence test. In 1993 ETS finally changed the official name of the SAT to the Scholastic Assessment Tests.

Other myths surround the SAT. Some people believe that it measures high school achievement and is an absolute predictor of college performance. Again, not true. Despite the fact that female students score about 52 points lower than male students on the SAT (on the 400-1600 combined scale), females tend to earn higher grades than males in both high school and college.

So the SAT doesn't test intelligence, it may not be the best predictor of college success, and it doesn't necessarily reflect high school grades. But it is used in the college admission process, and preparation can improve your score!

ETS claims their test "measures the verbal and mathematical abilities you have developed over many years both in and out of school." In describing the 1994 changes in the SAT, the testmakers have stressed that the new test places more emphasis on critical reasoning and the ability to apply concepts in different contexts. These are admirable goals. But still the SAT is a test, and the thing the SAT measures best is how well you take the SAT.

Can you zero in on the hidden question behind the question? Can you work confidently, even when you've got five minutes and seven problems left? Can you relax and pace yourself while taking a test that feels like the three most important hours in your life? These are some of the skills the SAT rewards. Without them you can be intimidated, confused, maybe even panic-stricken. With them you control the test. You are equipped for your own peak performance.

Feeling in control and making the SAT your own is the most valuable thing you can do for yourself as a test taker. And it's exactly what we've been doing for students over the last 55 years.

Kaplan is the largest test preparation company in the United States, preparing more than 150,000 students annually for more than 20 standardized tests. We spend millions of dollars each year in research, development, and teacher training so that our books and courses reflect even subtle changes in the tests. Most importantly, we raise scores. That's our business. If you want more extensive preparation than a book can offer, call 1-800-KAP-TEST to learn more about our SAT classes that are offered at over 750 locations around the U.S. and the world.

We want to acknowledge the hard work by the team of dedicated Kaplan teachers and researchers who contributed to this book.

Jeff Barton	Daniel Kane	Sam Nisson
Maureen Blair	Chris Kent	James Pervin
Linda Calzaretta	Gary Krist	John Polstein
Mike Cantwell	Jon Krupp	Donna Ratajczak
Fred Danzig	Dianne Lake	Robert Reiss
Craig Davis	Audrey Lee	Joe Rosch
Kenny Dinkin	Merideth Lee	Amy Sgarro
Gordon Drummond	Jason Levitis	Bob Stanton
Lee Fitzgerald	Rich Lowenthal	David Stuart
Kate Foster	Joyce Lupack	Chris Woods
Robert Greenberg	Kate McCarthy	Susan Yanovich
Chris Hobson		
Kate Holum		

Best of luck with the SAT and the college admission process. And remember, what you know is not as important as how well you think.

Stanley H. Kaplan
Chairman

Gregory Rorke
President & CEO

CONTENTS

CHAPTER 1

SAT MASTERY

To perform well on the SAT, you need to draw on a set of skills that the College Board does not mention in any of their materials. You need to be a good SAT test taker.

Acquiring this ability, and the confidence it produces, is what this book is about.

THREE SIMPLE PRINCIPLES OF SAT MASTERY

There are three simple things you need to master the SAT.

You need to have a basic understanding of SAT content.

You need to hone the thinking and testing skills that underlie the SAT.

You need to know the nature of the SAT.

Content and skills are obviously important. You can't do well without them. But understanding the nature of the SAT, its set-up, its structure, and the tricks it often lays for you, will allow you to gain points on the test that you might not otherwise have gotten.

USING THE STRUCTURE OF THE SAT TO YOUR ADVANTAGE

The SAT is different from the tests that you're used to taking. On a school test, you probably go through the problems in order. You spend more time on the hard questions than on easy ones, since this is where you get more points. And you often show your work since the teacher tells you that how you approach a problem is as important as getting the answer right.

None of this works on the SAT. You can benefit from moving around within a section, the hard questions are worth the same as the easy ones, and it doesn't matter *how* you answer the question — only *what* your answer is.

To succeed in this peculiar context, you need to know some fundamentals about the overall structure of the SAT.

A DIFFERENT KIND OF TEST

The SAT's not like the tests you take in school. In school, you might need to get about 85 or 90% of the questions right to get a decent score. On the SAT, you sometimes need little more than 75% of the questions right to get double 600's — a very solid score.

1. THE SAT IS HIGHLY PREDICTABLE

Because the format and directions of the SAT remain unchanged from test to test, you can learn the set-up in advance. On test day, Analogies, QCs, Grid-ins—or the set-up of any other question type or section—shouldn't be new to you.

One of the easiest things you can do to help your performance on the SAT is to understand the directions before taking the test. Since the instructions are always exactly the same, there's no reason to waste your time on test day reading them. Learn them beforehand, as you go through this book, and skip them on test day.

2. MOST SAT QUESTIONS ARE ARRANGED BY ORDER OF DIFFICULTY

You've probably noticed that not all the questions on the SAT are equally difficult. Except for the Critical Reading problems, the questions always get tougher as you work through a set.

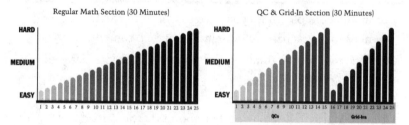

Questions get harder as you move through a section

Here's how to use this pattern to your advantage. As you work, you should always be aware of where you are in the set. When working on the easy problems, you can generally trust your first impulse—the obvious answer is likely to be right.

As you get to the end of the set, you need to become more suspicious. Now the answers probably won't come easy—and if they do, look again because the obvious answer is likely to be wrong. Watch out for the answer that just "looks right." It may be a distractor—a wrong answer choice meant to entice you.

3. THERE'S NO MANDATORY ORDER TO THE QUESTIONS

You're allowed to skip around within each section of the SAT. High scorers know this. They move through the test efficiently. They don't dwell on any one question, even a hard one, until they've tried every question at least once.

When you run into questions that look tough, circle them in your test booklet and skip them for the time being. Go back and try again after you have answered the easier ones if you have time. On a second look, troublesome questions can turn out to be amazingly simple.

If you've started answering a question and get confused, quit and go on to the next question. Persistence may pay off in school, but it usually hurts your SAT score. Don't spend so much time answering one tough question that you use up three or four questions' worth of time. That costs you points, especially if you don't get the hard question right.

4. THERE'S A GUESSING PENALTY THAT CAN ACTUALLY WORK IN YOUR FAVOR

The testmakers like to talk about the guessing penalty on the SAT. This is a misnomer. It's really a *wrong answer* penalty. If you guess wrong you get penalized. If you guess right, you're in great shape.

The fact is, if you can eliminate one or more answers as definitely wrong, you'll turn the odds in your favor and *actually come out ahead* by guessing.

Here's how the penalty works:

- If you get an answer wrong on a Quantitative Comparison, which has four answer choices, you lose 1/3 point.

- If you get an answer wrong on other multiple-choice questions, which have five answer choices, you lose 1/4 point.

- If you get an answer wrong on a Grid-in math question, where you write in your own answers, you lose nothing.

The fractional points you lose are meant to offset the points you might get "accidentally" by guessing the correct answer. With practice, however, you'll learn that it's often easy to eliminate *several* answer choices on some of the problems that you see. By learning the techniques for eliminating wrong answer choices you can actually turn the guessing "penalty" to your advantage.

5. THE ANSWER GRID HAS NO HEART

It sounds simple but it's extremely important: don't make mistakes filling out your answer grid. When time is short, it's easy to get confused going back and forth between your test book and your grid. If you know the answer, but misgrid, you won't get the points.

To avoid mistakes on the answer grid:

Always Circle the Questions You Skip
Put a big circle in your test book around any question numbers you skip.

KAPLAN RULES

DON'T GUESS, unless:
- You can eliminate at least one answer choice.

DON'T SKIP IT, unless:
- You have absolutely no idea.

CIRCLE BEFORE YOU SKIP

A common cause of major SAT disasters is filling in all of the questions with the right answers—in the wrong spots.

Every time you skip a question, circle it in your test book and be double sure that you skip it on the answer grid as well.

TRANSFERRING YOUR ANSWERS

You need to be careful at the end of a section when time may be running out. You don't want to have your answers in the test booklet and not be able to transfer them to your answer grid because you have run out of time.

When you go back, these questions will be easy to locate. Also, if you accidentally skip a box on the grid, you can check your grid against your book to see where you went wrong.

Always Circle the Answers You Choose

Circling your answers in the test book makes it easier to check your grid against your book.

Grid Five or More Answers at Once

Don't transfer your answers to the grid after every question. Transfer your answers after every five questions, or at the end of each reading passage. That way, you won't keep breaking your concentration to mark the grid. You'll save time and you'll gain accuracy.

These fundamentals apply to every section of the test. But each question type also has its own structural peculiarities that make them easy to prep for. Some examples: On Grid-ins, the grid cannot accommodate five-digit answers, negatives, or variables. If you get such an answer, you know you've made a mistake and need to re-do the problem.

Analogy answer choices are always ordered with the same parts of speech; this helps you determine if you're building an appropriate bridge.

Critical Reading questions with line references, "Little Picture" questions, can often be done quickly and don't require you to read the entire passage. You can do these first in a later reading passage if you're running out of time.

We'll show you lots of these structural elements, and the strategies you can use to take advantage of them, throughout this book.

APPROACHING SAT QUESTIONS

Apart from knowing the set-up of the SAT, you've got to have a system for attacking the questions. You wouldn't travel around a foreign city without a map and you shouldn't approach the SAT without a plan. Now that you know some basics about how the test is set up, you can approach each section a little more strategically. What follows is the best method for approaching SAT questions systematically.

1. THINK ABOUT THE QUESTION BEFORE YOU LOOK AT THE ANSWER

The people who make the test love to put distractors among the answer choices. Distractors are answer choices that look like the right answer, but aren't. If you jump right into the answer choices without thinking first about what you're looking for, you're much more likely to fall for one of these traps. In most cases, you've got to know what you're shopping for before you enter the store. The SAT is no different.

2. USE BACKDOOR STRATEGIES IF THE ANSWER DOESN'T COME TO YOU

There are usually a number of ways to get to the right answer on an SAT question. Most of the questions on the SAT are multiple choice. That means the answer is right in front of you — you just have to find it. This makes SAT questions open to a lot of ways of finding the answer. If you can't figure out the answer in a straightforward way, try other techniques. We'll talk about specific Kaplan strategies such as backsolving, picking numbers, and eliminating weak analogy bridges, in later chapters.

3. GUESS WHEN YOU CAN ELIMINATE AT LEAST ONE ANSWER CHOICE

You already know that the guessing "penalty" can work in your favor. Don't simply skip questions that you can't answer. Spend some time with them to see if you can eliminate any of the answer choices. If you can, it pays for you to guess.

4. PACE YOURSELF

The SAT gives you a lot of questions in a short period of time. To get through a whole section, you can't spend too much time on any one question. Keep moving through the test at a good speed; if you run into a hard question, circle it in your test booklet, skip it, and come back to it later if you have time.

To the right are recommended average times per question. This doesn't mean that you should spend exactly 40 seconds on every analogy. It's a guide. Remember, the questions get harder as you move through a problem set. Ideally, you can work through the easy problems at a brisk, steady clip, and use a little more of your time for the harder ones that come at the end of the set. One caution: don't completely rush through the easy problems just to save time for the harder ones. These early problems are points in your pocket, and you're better off not getting to the last couple of problems than losing these easy points.

5. LOCATE QUICK POINTS IF YOU'RE RUNNING OUT OF TIME

Some questions can be done quickly: for instance, some reading questions will ask you to identify the meaning of a particular word in the passage. These can be done at the last minute, even if you haven't read the passage.

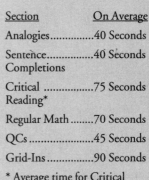

RECOMMENDED TIMING

Section	On Average
Analogies	40 Seconds
Sentence Completions	40 Seconds
Critical Reading*	75 Seconds
Regular Math	70 Seconds
QCs	45 Seconds
Grid-Ins	90 Seconds

* Average time for Critical Reading includes time to read the passage. Spend about 30 seconds per question.

- How to take advantage of the SAT's structure
- How to approach SAT questions systematically

On most Quantitative Comparisons, even the hardest ones, you can quickly eliminate at least one answer, improving your chances of guessing correctly. When you start to run out of time, locate and answer any of the quick points that remain.

When you take the SAT, you have one clear objective in mind: to score as many points as you can. It's that simple. The rest of this book will help you do it.

CHAPTER 2

INSIDE THE NEW SAT

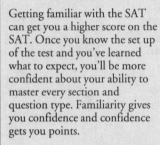

After giving the same test for years, they've decided to change the SAT. The test your parents took is gone forever.

Don't panic. Despite the changes, you can still prepare for the SAT with the solid strategy and content review you'll find in this book.

Even the new SAT is predictable. Because it's a standardized test, you can feel safe in knowing that the structure, contents, and questions on *your* SAT will be pretty much what you should expect after working your way through this book.

In this chapter, we will walk you through the structure of the new SAT. When you sit down to take the test, you should already know what kind of questions you'll find, what the instructions say, how the test will be scored, and how you will be timed. Until further notice, these things won't change again.

KAPLAN RULES

Getting familiar with the SAT can get you a higher score on the SAT. Once you know the set up of the test and you've learned what to expect, you'll be more confident about your ability to master every section and question type. Familiarity gives you confidence and confidence gets you points.

THE NEW SAT

What's the Difference?

Here are the biggest ways in which the spring 1994 SAT differs from the old test.

• No more antonyms.

• No more Test of Standard Written English (TSWE).

• Critical Reading now comprises about half of the verbal questions.

• One double passage: a pair of Critical Reading passages in which you'll be asked comparative questions.

• Calculator use permitted.

• 10 math Grid-ins: a new, non-multiple choice question type in which you fill in your own answer.

STRUCTURE OF THE TEST

There are six types of questions on the SAT: three verbal and three math. The likely number of questions you'll see of each type is listed below.

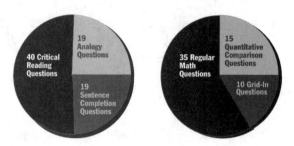

Verbal

- **19 Analogies** — Analogies test your ability to see relationships between words.

- **19 Sentence Completions** — These test your ability to see how the parts of a sentence relate. About half will have one word missing from a sentence; the rest will have two words missing. Both types test vocabulary knowledge and reasoning ability.

- **40 Critical Reading questions, in four separate sets** — Critical Reading tests your ability to read and understand a passage. The passages are long (400-850 words), and at least one passage contains two related readings. Some reading questions test your understanding of the content of the passage; others will require you to draw conclusions. Some will also explicitly test vocabulary.

Math

- **15 Quantitative Comparisons** — QCs, as they're called, give you two quantities and ask you to compare them. You have to determine if one quantity is larger, if they're equal, or if you don't have enough information to decide. They test your knowledge of math, your ability to apply that knowledge, and your reasoning ability. They're also designed to be done quickly, making them a good source of quick points.

- **35 Regular Math** —These are straightforward multiple choice math questions, with five answer choices.

- **10 Grid-ins** — These questions are open-ended, with no answer choices. Instead, you enter your response into a small grid. These questions test the same math concepts as the other types of questions.

SECTION BREAKDOWN

The SAT is divided into seven sections, which can appear in any order.

• Two 30-minute Verbal sections with Analogies, Sentence Completions, and Critical Reading.

• One 15-minute Verbal section with Critical Reading.

• One 30-minute section with QCs and Grid-ins.

• One 30-minute section with Regular Math.

• One 15-minute section with Regular Math.

There is also one 30-minute Experimental section. This section does not affect your score and is used to try out new questions. It can show up anyplace and it will look like any other Verbal or Math section. Don't try to figure out which section is experimental so you can nap during that period. First of all, you'll lose your momentum in the middle of the test. Second, and more important, you might be wrong.

SCORING

You get 1 point for each correct answer on the SAT, and lose a fraction of a point for each wrong answer. (Except for Grid-ins — but we'll go into that later.) If you leave a question blank you neither gain nor lose points. The totals are added up for all the Verbal and Math questions, and that produces two raw scores.

These numbers aren't your SAT scores. The raw scores are converted into scaled scores, each on a scale of 200 to 800, and these are the scores that are reported to you and the colleges you choose. (The reports include subscores as well, but most colleges focus on the two main scores.)

SAT TIMING

The new SAT:

• is three hours long.

• includes two 10-minute breaks (after sections 2 and 4).

There are some rules about how you can and cannot allocate this time:

• You are not allowed to jump back and forth between sections.

• You are not allowed to return to earlier sections to change answers.

• You are not allowed to spend more than the allotted time on any section.

• You can move around within a section.

• You can flip through your section at the beginning to see what type of questions you have.

You'll get more familiar with the format and set-up of the SAT as you work your way through this book. For now, just remember the basics we covered in Chapter 1: the SAT is predictable, there are elements built right into the test that allow you to prep for it, and you need to develop an approach to answering the questions.

Reading is important. It helps you find out what's on TV.

CHAPTER 3

INTRODUCING SAT VERBAL

Imagine yourself driving through Guadalajara, Mexico. As you approach an intersection, you see a red octagonal sign with the word "ALTO" on it. Even though you don't speak a word of Spanish, you come to a stop and look down the crossroads before driving on through the city.

ALTO You didn't learn Spanish just by being in Mexico. More likely, you took the information given to you — the shape, color, and location of the sign — and related it to what you already know. You may also have noticed, maybe subconsciously, that "alto" sounds something like "halt." From those connections, you made a very practical, and accurate, deduction: "Alto" means "stop."

The skills you displayed by making this deduction are skills of inference. To do well on SAT Verbal, you need to apply these same skills. The SAT does not test spelling or grammar. It does not test your knowledge of English literature or literary terms. It will never ask you to interpret a poem. SAT Verbal covers a fairly predictable, fairly limited body of skills and knowledge: vocabulary, verbal reasoning, and reading skills.

There are three scored Verbal sections on the new SAT. The breakdown of the questions will go something like this:

> **SAT VERBAL:**
> **WHAT DOESN'T MATTER**
>
> Your score on the Verbal section is based on your ability to do the following:
>
> • Solve analogies by finding two words that are related in the same way as the two words they give you.
>
> • Fill in the blanks in sentences that are missing one or two words.
>
> • Read a passage and answer a bunch of questions about it.
>
> You don't need to know pronunciation, antonyms, foreign languages, creative writing, spelling, or anything about literature.

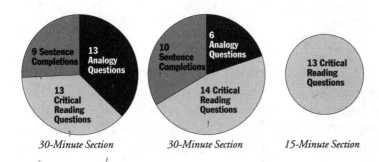

9 Sentence Completions / 13 Analogy Questions / 13 Critical Reading Questions

30-Minute Section

10 Sentence Completions / 6 Analogy Questions / 14 Critical Reading Questions

30-Minute Section

13 Critical Reading Questions

15-Minute Section

RULE OF THUMB

Work through the Sentence Completions and Analogies quickly and efficiently. Make sure you get all the points you can there, and then move on to Reading.

- one 30-minute section with 9 Sentence Completions, 13 Analogies, and 13 Critical Reading questions;
- one 30-minute section with 10 Sentence Completions, 6 Analogies, and 14 Critical Reading questions;
- one 15-minute section with 13 Critical Reading questions.

The Sentence Completions and Analogy sets are arranged by order of difficulty. The first few questions in a set are meant to be fairly straightforward and manageable. The middle few questions will be a little harder and the last few are the most difficult. Keep this in mind as you work and move through the early questions a little more quickly to leave yourself more time for the difficult ones.

Critical Reading is *not* arranged by difficulty. Any time you find yourself beginning to spend too much time on a question, you should skip it and return to it later.

HOW TO APPROACH SAT VERBAL

To do well on SAT Verbal, you need to be systematic in your approach to each question type and each of the three Verbal sections. Sentence Completions and Analogies are designed to be done relatively quickly. That means you can earn points fast, so you should do these first. Critical Reading takes a lot longer, so you can't just leave yourself five minutes to do a passage. Remember, you earn just as many points for an easy question as you do for a hard one.

TAPPING YOUR SAT VERBAL SKILLS

Although the test materials never explain this, a big key to doing well on the verbal part of the SAT is sharpening your verbal critical thinking skills —skills that you already use every day.

If you get to a movie ten minutes late, do you give up and walk out, deciding you'll never understand what's going on? Probably not. Instead, you use your inference skills—the ability to draw valid conclusions from limited information—to catch up and enjoy the rest of the film.

If you have a sudden urge for a tub of popcorn, do you leave during the climactic scene? More likely, you use your ability to distinguish important concepts from minor details to pick a dull moment to make your move.

When your younger brother asks you what the movie was about, do you take two hours and twelve minutes to explain it to him? You probably use your paraphrasing skills—the ability to condense complex ideas into a few words—to give him the highlights in a few minutes before you go back to ignoring him.

KNOW WHAT TO EXPECT

Doing your best on SAT Verbal comes from knowing what to expect, and knowing that you have the skills to handle it. You use words every day. You make your own ideas clear and you understand and respond to those of others. In all of these cases—talking with friends or talking with teachers, reading a textbook or reading a billboard, listening to lyrics or listening to your SAT proctor's instructions—you take limited information, process it through your own intellect and experience, and make sense of it. If you can learn to make the most of these skills on test day, you'll be well on the road to a much improved Verbal score.

> ## HIGHLIGHTS
>
> • The Verbal set-up
> • Tapping your Verbal skills
> • Know what to expect

F·A·S·T P·R·E·P

✍ CHAPTER CHECKLIST ✍
Once you've mastered a concept, check it off:

VOCABULARY

❏ A VOCABULARY BUILDING PLAN
❏ DECODING STRANGE WORDS

📣 PANICPLAN 📣

If you have a month or less to prep for the SAT, here's the best way to spend your time:
Go straight to the section called "Decoding Strange Words on Test Day" and try to master those skills.

CHAPTER 4

VOCABULARY

You know how to read. You can explain the relationship between "kitten" and "cat" to a three-year-old. You can finish a friend's sentence when she sneezes in the middle. So what makes the Verbal section such a challenge? Vocabulary. You may have a solid understanding of a Critical Reading passage but then get thrown by one tough vocabulary word. You may know the relationship between the original pair of words in an Analogy, but have a tough time finding the answer because all the choices have words you've never seen before. You may know precisely what kind of word to fill in on a Sentence Completion, and then find that all the answer choices look like they're in a foreign language.

All three Verbal question types — Analogies, Sentence Completions, and Critical Reading — depend upon your ability to work with unfamiliar words. You won't be asked to define words on the SAT. But you'll need to have a sense of their meaning in order to answer the questions.

TWO TYPES OF HARD WORDS

There are two types of hard SAT words:

- unfamiliar words;
- familiar words with unfamiliar meanings.

Some words are hard because you haven't seen them before. The words "scintilla" or "circumlocution," for instance, are probably not part of your everyday vocabulary. But they might pop up on your SAT.

Easy words, like "recognize" or "appreciation," may also trip you up on test day because they have secondary meanings that you aren't used to. Analogies and Critical Reading in particular will throw you familiar words with unfamiliar meanings.

To get a sense of your vocabulary strength, below is a representative list of words you might find on the SAT. Take a couple of minutes to look

---

WHO CARES?

Somewhere in the process of studying for the Verbal section, you'll decide that knowing the difference between *taciturn* and *tenacious,* between *obdurate* and *obloquy,* and even *plaudit* and *pusillanimous* is among the silliest things you've ever done. After all, no one on television talks that way.

It turns out that your vocabulary says a lot about your ability to express yourself, as well as giving some valuable hints as to how well read you are. Colleges like students with big vocabularies, so humor them. Learn some new words.

The single best way to do well on SAT verbal is to read as much as possible. Read newspapers and magazines to see words in use. Underline the ones you need to look up. If you recognize the words you see on the exam, you'll be on your way to acing the SAT.

through it and see how many you know. Write your answer right in the book. Give yourself one point for each word you know. Answers on p. 20.

irritate _____

truthful _____

conquer _____

passionate _____

inactive _____

eliminate _____

benevolent _____

elocution _____

irk _____

pragmatic _____

breadth _____

rectify _____

duplicity _____

impartial _____

abandon (n.)_____

vie _____

overt _____

august (adj.)_____

laud _____

voluble _____

flag (v.)_____

perspicacity _____

maladroit _____

sonorous _____

doleful _____

serpentine _____

rail (v.)_____

quiescence _____

idiosyncrasy _____

kudos _____

Turn the page for the definitions of the words in this list.

irritate	to annoy, bother
truthful	honest, straightforward, trustworthy
conquer	to defeat, overthrow
passionate	emotional, ardent, enthusiastic
inactive	not active, not moving
eliminate	to get rid of
benevolent	generous, kind
elocution	the study and practice of public speaking
irk	to irritate, anger, annoy
pragmatic	practical; moved by facts rather than abstract ideals
breadth	broadness, wideness
rectify	to correct
duplicity	deception, dishonesty, double-dealing
impartial	fair, just, unbiased, unprejudiced
abandon (n.)	total lack of inhibition
vie	to compete, contend
overt	apparent, unconcealed
august (adj.)	dignified, awe-inspiring, venerable
laud	to praise, applaud, honor
voluble	speaking much and easily, talkative; glib
flag (v.)	to droop; lose energy
perspicacity	shrewdness, astuteness, keenness of wit
maladroit	clumsy, tactless
sonorous	producing a full, rich sound
doleful	sad, mournful
serpentine	serpent-like; twisting, winding
rail (v.)	to scold with bitter or abusive language
quiescence	inactivity, stillness
idiosyncrasy	peculiarity of temperament, eccentricity
kudos	fame, glory, honor

If you scored ten points or less, you should probably work on building your vocabulary. The techniques and tools in this chapter will help you improve your vocabulary and make the most out of what you do know about words.

STRANGE WORD ORIGINS

Learning the derivation of words can often help you remember the meaning of words. Did you know...

jovial (joyful) comes from the Roman deity Jove, who was known for his pleasant disposition.

sardonic (characterized by bitter mockery) comes from sardinia, a mythical plant from the island of the same name. Ingestion of the plant caused convulsive laughter leading to death.

maudlin (overly sentimental) comes from Mary Magdalene, whose name sounds close to maudlin when pronounced by many Europeans.

If you scored between 10 and 20 points, your vocabulary is average. If you're willing to put in the time, using these techniques and tools can help you do better.

If you scored 20 points or more, your vocabulary is in great shape. You can polish it further, but you don't have to. If time is short, learn the strategies in Decoding Hard Words and concentrate on other aspects of the SAT that you find difficult.

A VOCABULARY BUILDING PLAN

A great vocabulary can't be built overnight, but you can develop a better SAT vocabulary with a minimum of pain.

Here's a plan:

1. Learn Words Strategically
The best words to learn are words that have appeared often on the SAT. The testmakers are not very creative in their choice of words for each test; words that have appeared frequently are likely bets to show up again.

The word list in the back of this book gives you a jump on some common SAT words. Learn a few words a day from this list, spreading them over the time remaining before the SAT. Keep reviewing those you've already studied.

The word list groups words into the common meaning families. For example, loquacious, verbose, and garrulous all mean "wordy, talkative." Taciturn, laconic, terse, concise, and pithy all mean "not talkative, not wordy." Instead of learning just one of these words, learn them all together — you get eight words for the price of one definition.

> *HINT— Be strategic. How well you use your time between now and test day is just as important as how much time you spend prepping.*

2. Work With Word Roots
Most SAT words are made up of prefixes and roots that can get you at least part way to a definition. Often that's all you need to get a right answer.

Use the Root List in the back of this book to pick up the most valuable SAT roots. Target these words in your vocabulary prep. Learn a few new roots a day, familiarizing yourself with the meaning.

3. Personalize Your Vocabulary Study
Figure out a study method that works best for you, and stick to it.
- Use Flash Cards — Write down new words or word groups and run through them whenever you have a few spare minutes. Put one new

---

PERSONALIZE YOUR HOME STUDY

- Use flash cards.
- Make a vocabulary notebook.
- Make a vocabulary tape.
- Look for hooks or phrases that lodge a new word in your mind.

YOU KNOW MORE ABOUT WORDS THAN YOU THINK YOU DO

Chances are, you won't come across too many words on the SAT that are completely unfamiliar. You can usually figure out something about the word — a root, prefix, or the "charge" of the word — to help you decode it.

Some "good sounding" words

> *Philanthropy*
> *Beneficent*
> *Euphonious*

Some "bad sounding" words

> *Curmudgeon*
> *Insidious*
> *Chasm*
> *Cacophonous*

word or word group on one side of a 3 x 5 index card and a short definition on the back.

- Make a Vocabulary Notebook — List words in one column and their meaning in another. Test yourself. Cover up the meanings, and see which words you can define from memory. Make a sample sentence using each word in context.

- Make a Vocabulary Tape — Record unknown words and their definitions. Pause for a moment before you read the definition. This will give you time to define the word in your head when you play the tape back. Quiz yourself. Listen to your tape in your Walkman. Play it in the car, on the bus, or whenever you have a few spare moments.

- Think of hooks that lodge a new word in your mind — Create visual images of words.

- Use rhymes and other devices that help you remember the words.

It doesn't matter which techniques you use, as long as you learn words steadily and methodically. Doing so over several months is ideal.

DECODING STRANGE WORDS ON TEST DAY

Trying to learn every word that could possibly appear on the SAT is like trying to memorize the license plate number of every car on the freeway. It's not much fun, it'll give you a headache, and you probably won't pull it off.

No matter how much time you spend with flash cards, vocabulary tapes, or word lists, you're bound to face some mystery words on your SAT. No big deal. Just as you can use your basic multiplication skills to find the product of even the largest numbers, you can use what you know about words to focus on likely meanings of tough vocabulary words.

GO WITH YOUR HUNCHES

When you look at an unfamiliar word, your first reaction may be to say, "Don't know it. Gotta skip it." But, not so fast. Vocabulary knowledge on the SAT is not an all-or-nothing proposition.

- Some words you know so well you can rattle off a dictionary definition of them.

- Some words you "sort of" know. You understand them when you see them in context, but don't feel confident using them yourself.

- Some words are vaguely familiar. You know you've heard them somewhere before.

HINT— If you think you recognize a word, go with your hunch.

1. Try to Recall Where You've Heard the Word Before

If you can recall a phrase in which the word appears, that may be enough to eliminate some answer choices, or even zero in on the right answer.

EXAMPLE

Between the two villages was a —— through which passage was difficult and hazardous.
(A) precipice
(B) beachhead
(C) quagmire
(D) market
(E) prairie

To answer this question, it helps to know the word **quagmire.** You may remember **quagmire** from news reports referring to "a foreign policy **quagmire**" or "a **quagmire** of financial indebtedness." If you can remember how **quagmire** was used, you'll have a rough idea of what it means, and you'll see it fits. You may also be reminded of the word **mire,** as in "We got **mired** in the small details and never got to the larger issue." Sounds something like "stuck," right? You don't need an exact definition. A **quagmire** is a situation that's difficult to get out of, so (C) is correct. Literally, a **quagmire** is a bog or swamp.

2. Decide if the Word Has a Positive or Negative "Charge"

Simply knowing that you're dealing with a positive or negative word can earn you points on the SAT.

Look at the word "cantankerous." Say it to yourself. Can you guess whether it's positive or negative? Often words that sound harsh have a negative meaning while smooth sounding words tend to have positive meanings. If "cantankerous" sounded negative to you, you were right. It means "difficult to handle."

You can also use prefixes and roots to help determine a word's charge. Mal, de, dis, un, in, im, a, and mis often indicate a negative, while pro, ben, and magn are often positives.

Not all SAT words sound positive or negative; some sound neutral. But if you can define the charge, you can probably eliminate some answer choices on that basis alone.

> **EXAMPLE**
>
> He seemed at first to be honest and loyal, but before long it was necessary to —— him for his —— behavior.
> (A) admonish..steadfast
> (B) extol..conniving
> (C) reprimand..scrupulous
> (D) exalt..insidious
> (E) castigate..perfidious

You don't need an exact definition of the words that go in the blanks. You just need to know that negative words are needed in both blanks. (See Chapter 6 for more about Sentence Completions.) Then you can scan the answer choices for a choice that contains two clearly negative words. (E) is right. Castigate means "punish or scold harshly," and perfidious means "treacherous."

3. Use Your Foreign Language Skills

Many of the roots you'll encounter in SAT words come from Latin. Spanish, French, and Italian also come from Latin, and have retained much of it in their modern forms. English is also a cousin to German and Greek. That means that if you don't recognize a word, try to remember if you know a similar word in another language.

Look at the word carnal. Unfamiliar? What about carne, as in chili con carne? Carn means meat or flesh, which leads you straight to the meaning of carnal — pertaining to the flesh. You could decode carnivorous, meat-eating, in the same way.

You can almost always figure out something about strange words on the test because SAT words are never all that strange. Chances are that few words on the SAT will be totally new to you, even if your recollection is more subliminal than vivid.

4. When All Else Fails

Eliminate choices that are clearly wrong and make an educated guess from the remaining choices.

- A wrong answer won't hurt you much.
- A right answer will help you a lot.

HIGHLIGHTS

- How to expand your vocabulary
- How to decode strange words

F·A·S·T P·R·E·P

✍ CHAPTER CHECKLIST ✍

Once you've mastered a concept, check it off:

ANALOGIES

❑ THE FORMAT
❑ BUILDING BRIDGES
❑ KAPLAN'S 3-STEP METHOD
❑ TEST YOUR ANALOGY SMARTS
❑ CLASSIC BRIDGES
❑ HOW TO FILL VOCABULARY GAPS
❑ PRACTICE SET

🧠 PANICPLAN 🧠

If you have a month or less to prep for the SAT, here's the best way to spend your time:

1: Learn the Kaplan 3-Step Method for Analogies (p. 28 - 29).

2: Do the practice set on pp. 39 - 40.

3: If you miss an answer, review pp. 35 - 38.

CHAPTER 5

ANALOGIES

Analogies may seem frightening at first because they don't look like anything you've ever done before. Once you get familiar with the format, however, you'll find there's a simple method for mastering this question type. In fact, prepping often gains you more points on Analogies than any other Verbal question type. With practice, you can even learn to get the Analogy right when you don't know all of the vocabulary words involved.

THE FORMAT

There are 19 Analogies in all on the SAT. You'll probably see one set of 13 and one set of 6. Each 30-minute Verbal section contains a set of Analogies. A question looks like this:

EXAMPLE

FLAKE:SNOW::
(A) storm:hail
(B) drop:rain
(C) field:wheat
(D) stack:hay
(E) cloud:fog

The two words in capital letters are called the stem words. The instructions will tell you to choose the pair of words from the five answer choices that is related in the same way as this pair. In this example, the answer above is (B). A FLAKE is a small unit of SNOW, just as a drop is a small unit of rain.

BUILDING BRIDGES

In every Analogy question, there exists a strong, definite connection between the two stem words. Your task is to identify this relationship, and then to look for a similar relationship among the answer pairs.

> ### ANALOGIES ARE PART OF YOUR LIFE
>
> Analogies can seem strange at first, until you realize that you speak and think in analogies all the time.
> Anytime you say "my sister is like a slug" you're drawing an analogy between your sister and slugs—perhaps your sister is as gross as a slug, or perhaps she always falls asleep in bowls of beer. That may not be the kind of relationship that will appear on your SAT, but the way of thinking is the same.

What's a strong, definite relationship?

- The words "library" and "book" have a strong, definite connection. A library is defined as a place where books are kept. LIBRARY:BOOK could be a question stem.

- The words "library" and "child" do not have a strong, definite connection. A child may or may not have anything to do with a library. LIBRARY:CHILD would never be a question stem.

The best way to pinpoint the relationship between the stem words is to build a bridge. A bridge is a short sentence that relates the two words. Often, a bridge reads like a definition of one of the two words. For instance: "A LIBRARY is a place where BOOKS are kept."

The ability to find bridges is fundamental to Analogy success. Your bridge needs to capture the strong, definite connection between the words.

KAPLAN'S 3-STEP METHOD

The Kaplan Method for solving Analogies has three simple steps:

1. Build a bridge between the stem words.

2. Plug in the answer choices.

3. Adjust your bridge, if you need to.

Here's an Analogy stem. We've left out the answer choices because you need to focus first on the stem.

KAPLAN RULES

To solve an analogy:

1. Build a bridge between the stem words.
2. Plug in the answer choices.
3. Adjust your bridge, if you need to.

> **EXAMPLE**
>
> LILY:FLOWER::

1. Build a Bridge

The best bridge here is "a LILY is a type of FLOWER."

2. Plug in the Answer Choices

Here is the complete question.

> **EXAMPLE**
>
> LILY:FLOWER::
> (A) rose:thorn
> (B) cocoon: butterfly
> (C) brick:building
> (D) maple:tree
> (E) sky:airplane

Take the bridge you have built and plug in answer choices (A) through (E). If only one pair fits, it's the answer.

HINT—Be sure to try all 5 choices.

Here's how plugging in the answer choices works:
- (A) A rose is a type of thorn – no.
- (B) A cocoon is a type of butterfly – no.
- (C) A brick is a type of building – no.
- (D) A maple is a type of tree – yes.
- (E) A sky is a type of airplane – no.

We've got four no's and only one yes, so the answer is (D).

3. Adjust Your Bridge if You Need To

If no answer choice seems to fit, your bridge is too specific and you should go back and adjust it. If more than one answer choice fits, your bridge is not specific enough. Look at this example.

EXAMPLE

SNAKE:SLITHER::
(A) egg:hatch
(B) wolf:howl
(C) rabbit:hop
(D) turtle:snap
(E) tarantula:bite

With a simple bridge, such as "a SNAKE SLITHERs," you'd have a hard time finding the answer. All the answer choices make sense: an egg hatches, a wolf howls, a rabbit hops, a turtle snaps, a tarantula bites. Don't worry. Go back to step one and build another bridge — this time making it more specific. Think about what SLITHER means.

New bridge: SLITHERing is how a SNAKE gets around.
(A) hatching is how an egg gets around? – no.
(B) howling is how a wolf gets around? – no.
(C) hopping is how a rabbit gets around? – yes.
(D) snapping is how a turtle gets around? – no.
(E) biting is how a tarantula gets around? – no.
Four no's and one yes — the answer is (C).

HINT—If no answer fits, or too many fit,
build a new bridge and plug in again.

<aside>

WHAT MAKES A STRONG BRIDGE?

You might be lured into thinking the words TRUMPET and JAZZ have a strong bridge. They don't.

You can play lots of things on trumpets other than jazz: fanfares, taps, whatever. You can also play jazz on things other than trumpets.

TRUMPET and INSTRUMENT do have a strong bridge. A trumpet is a type of instrument. This is always true — it's a strong, definite relationship.

</aside>

9 Famous Bridges

Bridge on the River Kwai

Golden Gate Bridge

George Washington Bridge

Bridge Over Troubled Water

Bridges of Madison County

Jeff Bridges

Lloyd Bridges

Tappan Zee Bridge

Bridget Fonda

WHAT PART OF SPEECH IS A STEM WORD?

Occasionally with an Analogy you might have to take a quick peek at the answer choices before you can build a bridge for the stem. The part of speech of a stem word may be ambiguous. When you're not sure whether a stem word is a noun, verb, adjective, or adverb, look at the words directly beneath that stem word. The rule is:

HINT — The words in a vertical row are all the same part of speech.

For example, you might see this:

VERB:NOUN::
(A) verb:noun
(B) verb:noun
(C) verb:noun
(D) verb:noun
(E) verb:noun

or this:

ADJECTIVE:NOUN::
(A) adjective:noun
(B) adjective:noun
(C) adjective:noun
(D) adjective:noun
(E) adjective:noun

but you'll *never* see this on an SAT Analogy:

NOUN:NOUN::
(A) verb:noun
(B) noun:noun
(C) verb:verb
(D) verb:noun
(E) verb:noun

To establish the part of speech of a stem word, you don't usually have to look at more than choice (A).

How would you think through the following example?

EXAMPLE

PINE:DESIRE::
- (A) laugh:sorrow
- (B) drink:thirst
- (C) watch:interest
- (D) listen:awe
- (E) starve:hunger

PINE can be a noun, but that's not likely here. You can't build a bridge between a tree with needle-like leaves and DESIRE. Try another part of speech. A glance at the answer choices below PINE (laugh, drink, watch, listen, and starve) tells you PINE is being used as a verb.

What about DESIRE? It could be a noun or a verb, but the answer choices beneath it (sorrow, thirst, interest, awe, and hunger) tell you it's used as a noun.

You've probably heard of someone pining away from unrequited love. As a verb, PINE means "to yearn or suffer from longing." A good bridge would be: to PINE is to suffer from extreme DESIRE. Plugging in the answer choices, you get:

(A) to laugh is to suffer from extreme sorrow? – no.

(B) to drink is to suffer from extreme thirst? – no.

(C) to watch is to suffer from extreme interest? – no.

(D) to listen is to suffer from extreme awe? – no.

(E) to starve is to suffer from extreme hunger? – yes.

Once again, four no's and one yes; the answer is (E).

TEST YOUR ANALOGY SMARTS

Try out what you've learned on these Analogies. Turn the page to see if you got the right answers.

1. SWEEP:BROOM::
   - (A) cut:scissors
   - (B) soil:cloth
   - (C) dry:bucket
   - (D) thread:needle
   - (E) wash:dish

RULE OF THUMB

Try not to spend more than 40 seconds on each Analogy. Then you won't need to rush through Critical Reading, which comes next on the test.

2. MAP:ATLAS::
   (A) lock:key
   (B) road:highway
   (C) recipe:cookbook
   (D) concept:encyclopedia
   (E) theory:hypothesis

3. HUNGRY:FAMINE::
   (A) thirsty:rainfall
   (B) sick:plague
   (C) sated:dinner
   (D) dry:flood
   (E) sore:injury

NINE CLASSIC BRIDGES

It's easier to build bridges when you know the types of bridges that have appeared on the SAT in the past. While no one can give you a list of the words that will appear on SAT Analogies, you can learn what types of relationships to expect. The classic bridges below appear over and over again on the SAT. Don't memorize these bridges, or lists of words that fit these bridges. Instead, learn which types of bridges can lead you to the right answer on SAT Analogies and which cannot.

> HINT — *Become familiar with the types of bridges that connect stem words on the SAT. They can lead you to the right answer.*

Classic bridges may take different forms, depending on what parts of speech are used. But the underlying concepts are what matter. Here are examples of nine classic types:

Bridge Type #1: DESCRIPTION
In many Analogies, one stem word is a person, place, or thing, and the other word is a characteristic of that person, place, or thing. Look at these examples:

PAUPER:POOR—A PAUPER is always POOR.

GENIUS:INTELLIGENT—A GENIUS is always INTELLIGENT.

TRAGEDY:SAD—A TRAGEDY is always SAD.

DO IT YOURSELF

One way to see the inner workings of Analogies is to put some together yourself. Make sure you include five answer choices. This exercise will give you a good feel for the structure of SAT Analogies and may help you spot and avoid bad answer choices.

This classic bridge can also describe a person, place, or thing by what it is NOT.

PAUPER:WEALTHY—A PAUPER is never WEALTHY.

GENIUS:STUPID—A GENIUS is never STUPID.

TRAGEDY:HAPPY—A TRAGEDY is never HAPPY.

TRY IT YOURSELF

Here are more types of classic bridges. Fill in each blank with a stem word that will complete the bridge. There is more than one way to fill in each blank. The important thing is to get the right idea. See pp. 34 - 35 for suggested answers.

Bridge Type #2: CHARACTERISTIC ACTIONS

an INSOMNIAC can't ——.

a GLUTTON likes to ——.

a PROCRASTINATOR tends to ——.

Bridge Type #3: LACK

something MURKY lacks ——.

a PESSIMIST lacks ——.

a PAUPER lacks ——.

Bridge Type #4: CATEGORIES

MEASLES is a type of ——.

a MOTORCYCLE is a type of ——.

a POLKA is a type of ——.

Bridge Type #5: SIZE/DEGREE

to SPEAK very quietly is to ——.

to LIKE strongly is to ——.

to BRUSH is to —— lightly.

Bridge Type #6: CAUSING/STOPPING

a REMEDY stops or cures an ——.

an OBSTACLE prevents ——.

something INCENDIARY causes ——.

Bridge Type #7: PLACES
a JUDGE works in a ——.
a PLAY is performed on a ——.
BREAD is made in a ——.

Bridge Type #8: FUNCTION
GILLS are used for ——.
a PAINT BRUSH is used to ——.
a HELICOPTER is used for ——.

Bridge Type #9: PART/WHOLE
an ARMY is made up of ——.
a CROWD is made up of many ——.
an arrangement of FLOWERS is a ——.

SUGGESTED ANSWERS TO BRIDGE TYPES

Your answers may vary from our suggested answers. As long as you've got the basic idea, that's okay.

CHARACTERISTIC ACTIONS
an INSOMNIAC can't SLEEP.
a GLUTTON likes to EAT.
a PROCRASTINATOR tends to DELAY.

LACK
something MURKY lacks CLARITY.
a PESSIMIST lacks OPTIMISM.
a PAUPER lacks MONEY.

CATEGORIES
MEASLES is a type of ILLNESS.
a MOTORCYCLE is a type of VEHICLE.
a POLKA is a type of DANCE.

SIZE/DEGREE
to SPEAK very quietly is to WHISPER.
to LIKE strongly is to LOVE (or ADORE).
to BRUSH is to TOUCH lightly.

CAUSING/STOPPING

a REMEDY stops or cures an ILLNESS.

an OBSTACLE prevents PROGRESS (or MOVEMENT).

something INCENDIARY causes FIRE.

PLACES

a JUDGE works in a COURTROOM.

a PLAY is performed on a STAGE (or in a THEATER).

BREAD is made in a BAKERY.

FUNCTION

GILLS are used for BREATHING.

a PAINT BRUSH is used to PAINT.

a HELICOPTER is used for FLYING.

PART/WHOLE

an ARMY is made up of SOLDIERS.

a CROWD is made up of many PEOPLE.

an arrangement of FLOWERS is a BOUQUET.

HOW TO FILL VOCABULARY GAPS

Sometimes on an SAT Analogy, you simply don't know one of the stem words. When this happens, the basic three-step process won't do much good. You can't even do Step One. You can't build a bridge using a word you don't know. You need another plan.

The best backup strategy is not to focus on the stem pair. Instead, try looking at the answer pairs and eliminate those that simply can't be right. If you can knock out even one, guessing from the remaining choices is to your advantage. You may be surprised at how far this strategy can take you.

Before you guess, take these three steps to eliminate some answer choices. (And remember, even if you can eliminate only one answer choice, guessing comes out in your favor.)

1. Eliminate answer choices with weak bridges.

2. Eliminate any two answer choices that share the same bridge.

3. Eliminate answer choices with bridges that couldn't work with the stem pair no matter what that unknown word means.

Here's how you do it:

KAPLAN RULES

The following relationships are not SAT-type bridges. If you encounter one, it's wrong.

- Synonyms. (Example: predict:foretell)

- Opposites. (Example: wealthy:impoverished)

- Members of the same category. (Example: dog:cat)

1. Eliminate Answer Choices with Weak Bridges

You learned earlier that a strong, definite relationship always exists between the pair of stem words. The answer pairs, however, don't always have a good bridge — and any choice without a good bridge can't be right. In other words, you can eliminate certain answer choices without looking at the stem at all. Try this exercise:

Here is a list of 6 answer pairs without any stem pairs — answers without questions. Try to make a bridge for each pair. If no strong bridge is possible, mark the pair with an X. The answers are on page 37.

dog:house

aquatic:water

nocturnal:animal

infantile:toy

steak:potatoes

raisin:grape

In many cases, this method alone will allow you to eliminate one, two, or even three answer choices.

2. Eliminate Answer Choices with Identical Bridges

There's another way of eliminating some wrong choices that's so obvious you might not think of it. If two choices have the same bridge, it follows that neither one can be more right than the other. And since they can't both be right, they must both be wrong. For example, look at the following question:

EXAMPLE

LEGERDEMAIN:MAGICIAN::
(A) baggage:immigrant
(B) justice:pragmatist
(C) sluggishness:racer
(D) diplomacy:diplomat
(E) indifference:fanatic

What if you don't know what LEGERDEMAIN means? (C) seems like a possible answer because this pair of words has a strong bridge: "sluggishness is the opposite of what you'd expect from a racer." But choice (E) has a very similar bridge: "indifference is the opposite of what you'd expect from a fanatic."

Since a question can't have two right answers, and both (C) and (E) have the same bridge, both must be wrong. The correct answer is (D).

3. Eliminate Answer Choices with Bridges that Can't Fit the Stem

What do you do with answer pairs that can't be eliminated by either of the first two methods? The next step is to find bridges for the remaining answers, and then to plug in the stem word pair. It's true that you don't even know what one of the stem words means. But in some cases you'll see that the stem word pair can't fit the answer bridge no matter what that unknown word means. Here's an example.

EXAMPLE

GENUFLECT:KNEE::
(A) pierce:ear
(B) hold:hand
(C) nod:neck
(D) stub:toe
(E) pick:tooth

You may not know what GENUFLECT means. Since you can't work directly with this stem, take a look at the answer choices instead.

Answer pair (A) has a strong bridge: To pierce an ear is to put a hole in it. Now try plugging GENUFLECT and KNEE into this same bridge: To genuflect a knee is to put a hole in it. Hmmm. Can you really imagine that there exists a verb in the English language that means "to put a hole in a knee?" No way. The concept doesn't even make sense. So GENU-FLECT:KNEE and pierce:ear can't possibly have the same bridge; and (A) can't be the right answer.

The same technique can be used to eliminate choice (E). Picking your teeth is a way of cleaning between them. Is there a comparable way of cleaning between your knees? Not likely.

So you've been able to eliminate two of the answer choices — without knowing what GENUFLECT means. Sometimes, of course, this technique demands a bit more intuition. Without knowing for sure, you might just have a feeling that there wouldn't be a word for a very large telephone or for a group of hammers. If you're guessing anyway, go with these hunches.

Putting It Together

Now apply all three answer-eliminating techniques to one question. (Pretend that you don't know the word SCIMITAR even if you do.)

EXAMPLE

SCIMITAR:SWORD::
(A) diamond:ring
(B) greyhound:dog
(C) saddle:horse
(D) lance:shield
(E) forest:tree

DON'T FALL FOR SAME SUBJECT TRAPS

Same Subject Traps are wrong answer choices that lure you in by giving you words that remind you of stem words.

The same subject doesn't make it right.

Remember, you're looking for an answer choice that has the same relationship as the stem, not an answer choice that reminds you of the stem.

Choice (A): A diamond may adorn a ring, but plenty of rings don't have diamonds, and plenty of diamonds don't have rings. Choice (A) has a weak bridge. Eliminate.

Choice (B): A greyhound is a kind of dog. Could a SCIMITAR be a kind of SWORD? It sounds possible.

Choice (C): A saddle is used for riding a horse. A scimitar is used for riding a sword? That can't make sense. Eliminate.

Choice (D): A lance and a shield are both part of the traditional gear of a knight, but that's all we can say to connect them. Again, a weak bridge. Eliminate.

Choice (E): A forest is a group of trees. Could a SCIMITAR be a group of swords? Maybe.

Without knowing a stem word, you've gotten down to two answer choices — (B) and (E). Is there more likely to be a word for a kind of sword or for a group of swords? Take your best guess.

(B) is, in fact, the answer.

A DOUBLE VOCABULARY GAP

What if you don't know either of the stem words? You can still eliminate weak bridges and identical bridges. For example:

> **EXAMPLE**
>
> MANUMISSION:THRALL::
> (A) submission:employee
> (B) prediction:artist
> (C) promotion:rank
> (D) tip:waiter
> (E) parole:prisoner

Promotion is the act of raising a soldier in rank. A tip is a type of gratuity or reward given to a waiter. Parole is the act of freeing a prisoner. These are all good bridges, and none of them repeat, so (C), (D), and (E) are all possible answers. But submission is not a characteristic of every employee, and there's no particular connection between prediction and artist. So eliminate (A) and (B).

To make your final decision, of course, you still have to guess. But now that you've eliminated answer choices, guessing works in your favor. The answer here happens to be (E): MANUMISSION is the act of freeing a THRALL or slave.

HINT—When all else fails, make an educated guess.

ANALOGY PRACTICE SET

1. COPPER:METAL::
   (A) grain:sand
   (B) helium:gas
   (C) stem:flower
   (D) tree:trunk
   (E) stone:clay

2. BROOM:DIRT::
   (A) brush:bristles
   (B) fork:plate
   (C) rake:leaves
   (D) mirror:face
   (E) scissors:blades

3. COWARD:BRAVERY::
   (A) eccentric:conformity
   (B) hero:fortitude
   (C) prophet:vision
   (D) sage:wisdom
   (E) comedian:humor

4. REVERE:ADMIRE::
   (A) cherish:conceive
   (B) release:reject
   (C) guess:solve
   (D) propose:change
   (E) despise:disdain

5. PERPLEXING:CONFUSION::
   (A) appalling:dismay
   (B) static:change
   (C) unpleasant:chaos
   (D) dignified:pride
   (E) grave:regret

6. AMUSING:MIRTH::
   (A) ailing:health
   (B) painful:sympathy
   (C) optimistic:objectivity
   (D) protective:insecurity
   (E) terrifying:fear

RULE OF THUMB

Not all bridges are classic bridges, but there is always a strong and definite relationship between the stem words.

7. FOOD:MENU::
   (A) accounting:inventory
   (B) index:foreword
   (C) silverware:spoon
   (D) merchandise:catalog
   (E) films:credits

8. IMPERCEPTIBLE:DETECT::
   (A) fundamental:begin
   (B) inconceivable:imagine
   (C) rugged:seize
   (D) costly:overcharge
   (E) immense:notice

9. PERSEVERE:DOGGED::
   (A) comply:obedient
   (B) inspire:pompous
   (C) hesitate:reckless
   (D) speak:laconic
   (E) retard:expeditious

10. ENTHRALLING:TEDIUM::
   (A) witty:frivolity
   (B) insipid:appetite
   (C) glaring:illumination
   (D) wearisome:redundancy
   (E) trite:originality

Explanations for Analogy Practice Set

1. (B) – Copper is a kind of metal.
2. (C) – A broom is used to clear away dirt.
3. (A) – A coward does not display bravery.
4. (E) – To revere is to admire very much.
5. (A) – Something that is perplexing causes confusion.
6. (E) – Something that is amusing causes mirth.
7. (D) – A menu is a list of available food.
8. (B) – If something is imperceptible, you cannot detect it.
9. (A) – A dogged person is one who perseveres.
10. (E) – Something that is enthralling lacks tedium.

F·A·S·T P·R·E·P

✍ CHAPTER CHECKLIST ✍

Once you've mastered a concept, check it off:

MASTERING SENTENCE COMPLETIONS

❑ THE FORMAT
❑ KAPLAN'S 4-STEP METHOD
❑ PICKING UP ON CLUES
❑ TACKLING HARD QUESTIONS

💡 PANICPLAN 💡

If you have a month or less to prep for the SAT, here's the best way to spend your time:

1: Learn the Kaplan 4-Step Method for Sentence Completions (pp. 44 - 47).

2: Do the practice set on p. 53 - 54. If you miss an answer, read and do practice questions on pp. 47 - 53.

CHAPTER 6

SENTENCE COMPLETIONS

Of all the verbal question types, Sentence Completions are probably the most student-friendly. Unlike Analogies, they give you some context in which to think about vocabulary words, and unlike Critical Reading, they only require you to pay attention to a single sentence at a time.

Statistic: The 19 Sentence Completions count for about one-fourth of your verbal score.

THE FORMAT

There are 19 Sentence Completions in all on the SAT. You'll probably see one set of nine and one set of ten. They appear in both 30-minute Verbal Sections. The instructions for Sentence Completions look something like this:

> Select the lettered word or set of words that best completes the sentence.

EXAMPLE

Today's small, portable computers contrast markedly with the earliest electronic computers, which were ——.
(A) effective
(B) invented
(C) useful
(D) destructive
(E) enormous

In the example, the new computers, which are small and portable, are contrasted with old computers. You can infer that the old computers must be the opposite of small and portable, so (E) **enormous** is right.

MASTERING COMPLETIONS

You can see the direction some sentences are headed in from a mile away. Consider these examples:

"I still want to be your friend..."

"Despite your impressive qualifications ..."

"If I ever get my hands on you, you little ..."

You could probably finish off these sentences on your own with pretty much the same language that the speaker would use. That's because the tone and structure of a sentence often clue you in to the meaning of the sentence.

On SAT Sentence Completions, you need to fill in missing pieces. Do this by using the sentence's clue words (e.g. despite, although) and structural clues (construction and punctuation) to determine where the sentence is headed.

KAPLAN'S 4-STEP METHOD

Here's the basic method for Sentence Completions:

1. Read the Sentence Carefully

Think about the sentence before looking at the answer choices. Figure out what the sentence means, taking special note of clue words.

> *HINT — Clue words like "and," "but," "such as," and "although" tell you where a sentence is heading.*

2. Anticipate the Answer

Predict the word that goes in the blanks. Do this before looking at the answer choices.

> *HINT — You don't have to make an exact prediction. A rough idea of the kind of word you'll need will do. It's often enough simply to predict whether the missing word is positive or negative.*

3. Compare Your Prediction With Each Answer Choice, and Pick the Best Match

> *HINT — Scan every answer choice before deciding.*

4. Read the Sentence With Your Answer Choice in the Blank or Blanks

> *HINT — Only one choice will make sense.*

If you've gone through the 4 steps and more than one choice seems possible, don't get stuck on the sentence. If you can eliminate at least one answer as wrong, guess and move on. If a question really stumps you, skip it and come back when you're done with the section.

Here's how the 4-step approach works on some examples.

EXAMPLE

Alligators, who bask in the sun for hours, appear to be —— creatures, yet they are quite capable of sudden movement.

(A) active

(B) violent

(C) stern

(D) content

(E) sluggish

---

1. Read the Sentence Carefully, Looking for Clue Words

"Yet" is a major clue. It tells you that the sentence switches direction mid-stream. The word in the blank must be the opposite of "sudden."

2. Predict the Word That Goes in the Blank

You can guess that alligators seem like "lazy"or "idle" creatures.

3. Compare Your Prediction with Each Answer Choice, and Pick the Best Match

(A) **active** has nothing to do with being lazy or idle.

Neither does (B) **violent**.

Neither does (C) **stern**.

Neither does (D) **content**.

But (E) **sluggish** means inactive or slow-moving, so pick (E).

4. Check Your Answer by Plugging It Into the Sentence

Let's check: "Alligators, who bask in the sun for hours, appear to be **sluggish** creatures, yet they are quite capable of sudden movement." Sounds okay. Finally, scan the other choices to make sure this is the best choice. None of the other choices works in the sentence, so (E)'s correct.

> *HINT — Don't read the sentence five times, plugging in every answer choice. That method takes too much time and makes you vulnerable to traps. Think about the question before you look for the answer.*

EXAMPLE

The king's —— decisions as a diplomat and administrator led to his legendary reputation as a just and —— ruler.

(A) quick..capricious

(B) equitable..wise

(C) immoral..perceptive

(D) generous..witty

(E) clever..uneducated

---

1. Read the Sentence Carefully, Looking for Clue Words

A big clue here is the phrase "led to." You know that the kind of decisions the king made led to his reputation as a just and —— ruler. So whatever goes in both blanks must be consistent with "just."

KAPLAN RULES

Timing Tip: Spend no more than 40 seconds per Sentence Completion question.

GET CHARGED

Look for word charges, the positive or negative connotations that a word may have, to help you make your prediction about what to put in the blanks.

See page 23 in the Vocabulary chapter for more on word charges.

2. Predict the Word that Goes in the Blank

Notice that both blanks must be similar in meaning. Because of his —— decisions, the king is viewed a certain way, as a just and —— ruler. So if the king's decisions were good, he'd be remembered as a good ruler, and if his decisions were bad, he'd be remembered as a bad ruler. "Just," which means "fair," is a positive-sounding word; you can predict that both blanks will be similar in meaning, and that both will be positive words. Write a "+" in the blanks or over the columns of answer choices to remind you.

3. Compare Your Prediction With Each Answer Choice, and Pick the Best Match

One way to do this is to determine which answers are positive and which are negative.

- In (A), **quick** and **capricious** aren't similar. (**Capricious** means "erratic or fickle.")

- In (B), **equitable** means fair. **Equitable** and **wise** are similar and they're both positive. When you plug them in, they make sense, so (B)'s right.

- In (C), **immoral** and **perceptive** aren't similar at all. **Perceptive** is positive but **immoral** isn't.

- In (D), **generous** and **witty** are both positive qualities, but they aren't really similar and they don't make sense in the sentence.

- In (E), **clever** and **uneducated** aren't similar. **Clever** is positive but **uneducated** isn't.

4. Check Your Answer by Plugging It Into the Sentence

"The king's equitable decisions as a diplomat and administrator led to his legendary reputation as a just and wise ruler." (B) makes sense in the sentence. Finally, a scan of the other choices reveals that none works as well. So (B)'s our answer.

EXAMPLE

Charlie Parker was —— artist, inspiring a generation of modern jazz musicians with his brilliant improvisations and experiments in bebop style.

(A) an arbitrary

(B) a benign

(C) a seminal

(D) an emphatic

(E) a candid

1. Read the Sentence Carefully, Looking for Clues
The big clue is: whatever goes in the blank must fit with the phrase "inspiring a generation."

2. Predict the Word That Goes in the Blank
The sentence tells you Parker was brilliant and inspiring, so you can predict that he was an "original" artist.

3. Compare Your Prediction to Each Answer Choice and Pick the Best Match

(A) **arbitrary** is too negative — you need a positive word.

(B) **benign** means "mild or gentle" — again, not what you want.

(C) **seminal** most closely matches your prediction — it means "original and innovative."

(D) **emphatic** might sound reasonable at first, but it means "expressive or forceful," which is not the same as "major or important."

Finally, (E) **candid** means "frank or open," which doesn't adequately describe how Parker influenced a generation.

(C) **seminal** is the answer. Notice that you could have found this answer by elimination, without actually knowing what the word means.

4. Check Your Answer By Plugging It Into the Sentence
Charlie Parker was a **seminal**, or creative, artist inspiring a generation with his brilliant improvisations. Sounds fine.

PICKING UP ON CLUES

To do well on Sentence Completions, you need to see how a sentence fits together. Clue words help you do that. The more clues you get, the clearer the sentence becomes, and the better you can predict what goes in the blanks.

What do we mean by clue words? Take a look at this example:

> **EXAMPLE**
>
> Though some have derided it as ——, the search for extraterrestrial intelligence has actually become a respectable scientific endeavor.

Here, **though** is an important clue. **Though** contrasts the way some have derided, belittled, or ridiculed the search for extraterrestrial intelligence, with the fact that that search has become respectable. Another clue is **actually**. **Actually** completes the contrast — **though** some see the search one way, it has **actually** become respectable.

GET A CLUE

Clue words help you get to the right answer. Look for the following types of words:

Contrasts:
- but
- however
- although

Continuations
- ; (a semicolon)
- also
- and
- because
- due to
- notably

You know that whatever goes in the blank must complete the contrast implied by the word **though**. So for the blank, you need something that describes the opposite of "a respectable scientific endeavor." A word like "useless" or "trivial" would be a good prediction for the blank.

Try using clue words to predict the answers to the questions below. First, look at the sentences without the answer choices and:

- Circle clue words.
- Think of a word or phrase that might go in each blank.
- Write your prediction below each sentence.

1. One striking aspect of Caribbean music is its —— of many African musical ——, such as call-and-response singing and polyrhythms.

   _____   _____

2. Although Cézanne was inspired by the Impressionists, he —— their emphasis on the effects of light and —— an independent approach to painting that emphasized form.

   _____   _____

3. They —— until there was no recourse but to —— a desperate, last-minute solution to the problem.

   _____   _____

4. Her normally —— complexion lost its usual glow when she heard the news of her brother's accident.

   _____

Here are the same questions with their answer choices. Now find the right answer to each question, referring to the predictions you just made. Turn the page for the answers.

1. One striking aspect of Caribbean music is its —— of many African musical ——, such as call-and-response singing and polyrhythms.
   (A) recruitment..groups
   (B) proficiency..events
   (C) expectation..ideas
   (D) absorption..forms
   (E) condescension..priorities

2. Although Cézanne was inspired by the Impressionists, he —— their emphasis on the effects of light and —— an independent approach to painting that emphasized form.
   (A) accepted..developed
   (B) rejected..evolved
   (C) encouraged..submerged
   (D) dismissed..aborted
   (E) nurtured..founded

3. They —— until there was no recourse but to —— a desperate, last-minute solution to the problem.
   (A) compromised..try
   (B) delayed..envision
   (C) procrastinated..implement
   (D) debated..maintain
   (E) filibustered..reject

4. Her normally —— complexion lost its usual glow when she heard the news of her brother's accident.
   (A) wan
   (B) pallid
   (C) sallow
   (D) ashen
   (E) sanguine

TACKLING HARD QUESTIONS

The last few Sentence Completions in a set are usually difficult. If you're getting stuck, there are a few special techniques to pull you through.

1. Avoid tricky wrong answers.

2. Take apart tough sentences.

3. Work around tough vocabulary.

1. AVOIDING TRICKY WRONG ANSWERS

Towards the end of a set, watch out for tricky answer choices. Avoid:

- opposites of the correct answer

- words that sound right because they're hard

- two-blankers where one word fits but the other doesn't

HINT — Questions go from easiest to hardest — the higher the question number, the harder the question.

PICKING UP ON CLUES ANSWERS

1. (D) – Clue: "aspect."

The only choice that could logically complete a description of Caribbean music is (D): Caribbean music is characterized by its **absorption** of many African musical **forms**.

2. (B) – Clue: "Although."

"Although" indicates that Cézanne must have somehow differed from the Impressionists. So he must have (B) **rejected** or (D) **dismissed** their emphasis on the effects of light. For the second blank, there's no reason to say that Cezanne **aborted** an independent approach to painting. Only (B) works for both blanks.

3. (C) – Clues: "until, desperate."

For the first blank, you can predict that they must have waited until only a "desperate solution" was possible. (C) and (D) fit this prediction. (C) **implement**, or carry out, makes more sense in the second blank.

4. (E) – Clue: "usual glow."

If her complexion had a "usual glow." it must have been normally rosy. The only choice that means rosy is (E) **sanguine.**

SENTENCE COMPLETIONS

TWO-BLANKERS

Two-blank sentences can be easier than one-blankers.

• Try the easier blank first.

• Eliminate all choices that won't work for that blank.

The following example would be question number 7 out of a 10-problem set.

> **EXAMPLE**
>
> Granted that Joyce is extremely ——, it is still difficult to imagine her as a professional comedian.
> (A) dull
> (B) garrulous
> (C) effusive
> (D) conservative
> (E) witty

• A sentence like this may show up towards the end of a set
Read this sentence carefully or you may get tricked.

If you read too quickly, you might think, "If Joyce is hard to imagine as a comedian, she's probably extremely dull or conservative. So I'll pick either (A) or (D)." But the sentence is saying something else.

• Pick up the clues
The key is the clue word **granted.** It's another way of saying "although." So the sentence means "Sure Joyce is funny, but she's no professional comedian." Therefore, the word in the blank must resemble "funny." That means (E) **witty** is correct.

• Don't pick an answer just because it sounds hard
Garrulous means "talkative" and **effusive** means "overly expressive." You might be tempted to pick one of these simply because they sound impressive. But they're put there to trick you. Don't choose them without good reason.

Now try a two-blank sentence:

The following example is another question 7 out of a 10-problem set.

> **EXAMPLE**
>
> When the state government discovered that thermal pollution was killing valuable fish, legislation was passed to —— the dumping of hot liquid wastes into rivers and to —— the fish population.
> (A) discourage..decimate
> (B) regulate..quantify
> (C) facilitate..appease
> (D) discontinue..devastate
> (E) prohibit..protect

Look at All the Choices

- Check out the first blank first. Legislation was not passed to facilitate dumping, so that eliminates choice (C). The other four are all possible.

- Now check the second blanks. The legislature wouldn't pass a law to **decimate,** or **quantify** or **devastate** the fish population, so (A), (B), and (D) are wrong. Only choice (E), **prohibit..protect,** fits for both blanks. The legislature might well pass a law to **prohibit** dumping hot liquids and to **protect** fish.

HINT — Don't jump at an answer choice because one blank fits. Check both blanks.

2. TAKING APART TOUGH SENTENCES

Try the following example, question 7 of a 9-problem set.

EXAMPLE

Although this small and selective publishing house is famous for its —— standards, several of its recent novels have a mainly popular appeal.

(A) proletarian

(B) naturalistic

(C) discriminating

(D) imitative

(E) precarious

> **WEIRD WORDS DON'T WORK**
>
> Rule out even one or two weird-sounding choices, and then you can profit by making an educated guess.

What if you were stumped, and had no idea which word to pick? Try this strategy.

HINT —Listen to the part of the sentence around the blank.
Rule out funny-sounding answer choices.

The process might go like this:

Proletarian standards? Hmmm…sounds funny.

Naturalistic standards? Not great.

Discriminating standards? That's got a familiar ring.

Imitative standards? Weird-sounding.

Precarious standards? Nope.

(C) sounds best and, as it turns out, is correct. Although the small publishing house has **discriminating,** or picky, standards, several of its recent novels appeal to a general audience.

Now try a complex sentence with two blanks. Remember our rules:
• Try the easier blank first.
• Save time by eliminating all choices that won't work for one blank.
The following example is question number 5 out of a 9-problem set.

> **EXAMPLE**
>
> These latest employment statistics from the present administration are so loosely documented, carelessly explained, and potentially misleading that even the most loyal Senators will —— the —— of the Presidential appointees who produced them.
> (A) perceive..intelligence
> (B) understand..tenacity
> (C) recognize..incompetence
> (D) praise..rigor
> (E) denounce..loyalty

It's not so easy to see what goes in the first blank, so try the second blank. You need a word to describe Presidential appointees who produced the "loosely documented," "carelessly explained," and "misleading" statistics. So it's got to be negative. The only second-word answer choice that's definitely negative is (C) **incompetence,** or inability to perform a task. Now try **recognize** in the first blank. It fits, too. (C) must be correct.

Kaplan Rules

If you find a word you don't understand, look in the sentence for its definition.

3. WORKING AROUND TOUGH VOCABULARY

The following example is question number 2 out of a 9-problem set.

> **EXAMPLE**
>
> Despite her —— of public speaking experience, the student council member was surprisingly cogent, and expressed the concerns of her classmates persuasively.
> (A) hope
> (B) depth
> (C) method
> (D) lack
> (E) union

If you don't know what cogent means, work around it.

HINT—Look in the sentence for the definition of a hard word.

From the sentence, especially the clue word "and," you know that cogent goes with "expressed the concerns of her classmates persuasively." So you don't have to worry about what "cogent" means. All you need to know is that the student council member was persuasive despite a —— of speaking experience. Only **lack** (D) fits. Despite her **lack** of public speaking experience, the student council member expressed the concerns of her classmates persuasively. By the way, "cogent" means "convincing, believable," roughly the same as "expressing concern persuasively."

Try this Sentence Completion problem. This time the tough vocabulary is in the answer choices. This example is question 6 out of 9 questions.

EXAMPLE

Advances in technology occur at such a fast pace that dictionaries have difficulty incorporating the —— that emerge as names for new inventions.
(A) colloquialisms
(B) euphemisms
(C) compensations
(D) neologisms
(E) clichés

Again, look at the sentence. Whatever goes in the blank has to describe "names for new inventions." If you don't know what **colloquialisms** or **euphemisms** are, don't give up. Rule out as many choices as you can, and guess among the remaining ones.

You can eliminate (C) and (E) right off the bat. They don't describe names for new inventions. Now you can make an educated guess. Again, educated guessing will help your score more than guessing blindly or skipping the question.

Or, if you studied your word roots, you might know that neo- means new, so **neologisms** might be the best choice for names of new inventions. In fact, it's the right answer. **Neologisms** are newly-coined words.

> HINT— *To help yourself earn extra points, study the Root List at the end of this book.*

If All Else Fails

If you're really stumped, don't be afraid to guess. Eliminate all answer choices that seem wrong and guess from the remaining choices.

SENTENCE COMPLETIONS PRACTICE SET

1. In the years following World War II, almost all Canadian Inuits —— their previously nomadic lifestyle; they now live in fixed settlements.
   (A) abandoned
   (B) continued
   (C) fashioned
   (D) preserved
   (E) rebuilt

2. A newborn infant's —— skills are not fully ——, for it cannot discern images more than ten inches from its face.
   (A) perceptual..stimulated
   (B) visual..developed
   (C) descriptive..ripened
   (D) olfactory..shared
   (E) average..familiar

3. Some geysers erupt regularly while others do so ——.
   (A) consistently
   (B) copiously
   (C) perennially
   (D) sporadically
   (E) violently

4. Because of the lead actor's —— performance, the play received poor reviews from influential theater critics, and was canceled only one week after it opened.
   (A) erudite
   (B) corporeal
   (C) overwrought
   (D) fractious
   (E) resplendent

5. Sociologists have found that, paradoxically, many children of unorthodox, creative parents grow up to be rather tame ——.
   (A) idealists
   (B) conformists
   (C) individualists
   (D) alarmists
   (E) elitists

6. In Han mortuary art, the —— and the —— are combined; one tomb may contain eerie supernatural figures placed next to ordinary likenesses of government administrators at work.
   (A) fantastic..mundane
   (B) inventive..remorseful
   (C) illusory..derivative
   (D) enlightened..conservative
   (E) unique..historical

EXPLANATIONS

Sentence Completions Practice Set

1. (A) – "Nomadic" means "wandering, transient." If Inuit people now live in fixed settlements, we can predict that they rejected, or **abandoned,** "their previously nomadic lifestyle."

2. (B) – If a newborn infant "cannot discern (or perceive) images more than ten inches from its face," then the infant's ability to see things has not fully evolved. In other words, its visual skills are not fully developed. (D) **olfactory** means "relating to sense of smell."

3. (D) – The clue words "while others" indicate contrast. If some geysers "erupt regularly," we can predict that others do so irregularly. The best choice is (D) — **sporadically** means "infrequently or irregularly."

4. (C) – If the play "received poor reviews" and was canceled because of something about the lead actor's performance, that performance must have been quite bad. (C) **overwrought,** overdone or excessively agitated, is one of two negative words in the answer choices, and the only one that could logically describe a performance.

5. (B) – "Paradoxically" or "contrary to what one would expect," children of creative and unorthodox parents grow up to be something other than creative and unorthodox. We need a word that contrasts with "creative and unorthodox" and goes along with tame. (B) is the best choice — **conformists** are people who follow established norms and customs without challenging anything or anyone.

6. (A) – If "one tomb contains eerie supernatural figures" and "ordinary likenesses of government administrators," it's likely that Han mortuary art combines the unearthly or bizarre with the ordinary or mundane. The best answer is (A) — In Han art, the **fantastic** (eerie supernatural figures) and the **mundane** (administrators) are combined.

HIGHLIGHTS

- The 4-step method
- Use clue words
- How to avoid tricky wrong answers
- How to take apart tough sentences
- How to work around tough vocabulary

F·A·S·T P·R·E·P

✍ CHAPTER CHECKLIST ✍
Once you've mastered a concept, check it off:

DOING YOUR BEST ON CRITICAL READING
❏ QUICK TIPS FOR READING A PASSAGE
❏ KAPLAN'S 5-STEP METHOD FOR ANSWERING QUESTIONS
❏ HOW TO DO PAIRED PASSAGES
❏ WHAT TO DO WHEN TIME IS RUNNING OUT

HOW TO DO SPECIFIC QUESTION TYPES
❏ HOW TO ANSWER BIG PICTURE QUESTIONS
❏ HOW TO ANSWER LITTLE PICTURE QUESTIONS
❏ HOW TO DO VOCABULARY QUESTIONS
❏ HOW TO FIND THE RIGHT ANSWERS

🧠 PANICPLAN 🧠
If you have a month or less to prep for the SAT, here's the best way to spend your time:

1: Since Critical Reading makes up half of the Verbal section of the SAT, it's important that you read the whole chapter.

2: Pay special attention to the practice test on p. 61 - 63.

CHAPTER 7

CRITICAL READING: THE BASICS

Improving your Critical Reading score means building the skills you have and applying them to the SAT. You don't need outside knowledge to answer the Critical Reading questions. And you don't need an amazing vocabulary, since unfamiliar words will be defined for you.

Critical Reading passages and questions are very predictable, since the testmakers use a formula to write them. You'll be given four reading passages, 400-850 words each, drawn from the arts, humanities, social sciences, sciences, and fiction. One of these is a "paired passage" consisting of two related excerpts. You'll be asked about the overall tone and content of a passage, the details, and what the passage suggests. You'll also be asked to compare and contrast the related passages.

THE FORMAT

Critical Reading instructions tell you to: "Answer questions based on what is stated or implied in the accompanying passage or passages." Actual SAT instructions may be worded differently, but the idea's the same. As with other question types, you should get familiar enough with the Critical Reading format that you don't waste time reading the directions again on Test Day.

Each reading passage begins with a brief introduction. Related questions follow the passage.

HINT— Don't skip the brief introductions. They'll help you focus your reading.

Critical Reading questions have a specific order: the first few questions ask about the beginning of the passage, the last few about the end.

Questions following "paired passages" are also ordered: the first few questions relate to the first passage, the next few to the second passage, and

---

IF YOU CAN READ THIS, YOU CAN DO WELL ON SAT VERBAL

If you bought a new VCR, as soon as you unpacked it you'd read the instruction manual to figure out how to hook it up and get it working.

You probably wouldn't sit down and read the whole book, though. You'd skip the pages that contain step-by-step instructions on how to record programs from the TV until you'd gotten the VCR connected and plugged in.

If the manual said, "connect the xygupts to terminal c," you'd probably figure out how to do that, even though you don't know the word xygupts.

In setting up your VCR, you'd have demonstrated that you know how to read with a purpose; know how and when to deal with details; and can figure out the meaning of unfamiliar words from context.

HOW NOT TO READ

DON'T wait for important information to jump out and hit you in the face. Search for important points. As you read, ask yourself, "What's this all about? What's the point of this?"

DON'T read the passage thoroughly. It's a waste of your time. Skim the passage to get the drift.

DON'T skim so quickly that you miss the passage's main point. Read quickly but don't race.

DON'T get caught up in details.

ASK YOURSELF

- What's this passage about?
- What's the point of this?
- Why did someone write this?
- What's the author trying to say?
- What are the 2 or 3 most important things in this passage?

the final questions ask about the passages as a pair.

Critical Reading questions are not ordered by difficulty. Unlike the other kinds of questions on the SAT, the location of a Critical Reading question tells you nothing about its potential difficulty. So don't get bogged down on a hard Critical Reading question. The next one might be a lot easier.

HOW TO READ A PASSAGE

Some students find Critical Reading passages dull or intimidating. Remember that each passage is written for a purpose — the author wants to make a point, describe a situation, or convince you of his or her ideas. As you're reading, ask yourself, "What's the point of this? What's this all about?" This is active reading, and it's key to staying focused on the page.

Active reading doesn't mean reading the passage word-for-word. It means reading lightly, but with a focus. This is what we mean by skimming.

> *HINT — The questions will help you fill in the details by directing you back to important information in the passage.*

Getting hung up on details is a major Critical Reading pitfall. You need to grasp the outline, but you don't need to get all the fine features.

> *HINT — The less time you spend on reading the passages, the more time you'll have to answer the questions — and that's where you score points. To increase your reading speed and skimming skills, turn to the skimming exercises in Chapter 8, p.73 - 75.*

TEST YOUR CRITICAL READING SMARTS

Test your reading skills on the following sample passage, keeping our tips in mind. Remember that active reading will make this difficult passage — and every passage — more doable.

EXAMPLE

In this essay, the author writes about her childhood on a Caribbean island that was an English colony for many years.

When I saw England for the first time, I was a child in school sitting at a desk. The England I was looking at was laid out on a map gently, beautifully, delicately, a very special jewel; it lay on a bed of sky blue, its yel-
Line low form mysterious, because though it looked like a leg of mutton*, it
(5) could not really look like anything so familiar as a leg of mutton because it was England. England was a special jewel all right, and only special people got to wear it. The people who got to wear England were English people. They wore it well and they wore it everywhere: in jungles, in deserts, on plains, in places where they were not welcome, in places
(10) they should not have been. When my teacher had pinned this map up on the blackboard, she said, "This is England" — and she said it with authority, seriousness, and adoration, and we all sat up. We understood then — we were meant to understand then — that England was to be our source of myth and the source from which we got our sense of reali-
(15) ty, our sense of what was meaningful, our sense of what was meaning-less — and much about our own lives and much about the very idea of us headed that last list.

At the time I was a child sitting at my desk seeing England for the first time, I was already very familiar with the greatness of it. Each morn-
(20) ing before I left for school, I ate a breakfast of half a grapefruit, a bowl of oat porridge, bread and butter and a slice of cheese, and a cup of cocoa. The can of cocoa was often left on the table in front of me. It had written on it the name of the company, the year the company was established, and the words "Made in England." Those words, "Made in England,"
(25) were written on the box the oats came in too. The shoes I wore were made in England; so were my socks and cotton undergarments and the satin ribbons I wore tied at the end of two plaits of my hair. My father, who might have sat next to me at breakfast, was a carpenter and cabinet maker. The shoes he wore to work would have been made in England, as
(30) were his khaki shirt and trousers, his underpants and undershirt, his socks and brown felt hat. Felt was not the proper material from which a hat that was expected to provide shade from the hot sun should be made, but my father must have seen and admired a picture of an Englishman wearing such a hat in England. As we sat at breakfast a car
(35) might go by. The car, a Hillman or a Zephyr, was made in England. The very conception of the meal itself, breakfast, and its substantial quality and quantity was an idea from England; we somehow knew that in Eng-land they began the day with this meal called breakfast and a proper breakfast was a big breakfast.
(40) At the time I saw this map — seeing England for the first time — I did not say to myself, "Ah, so that's what it looks like," because there was no longing in me to put a shape to those three words that ran through every part of my life, no matter how small; for me to have had such a

CRITICAL READING IS CRITICAL

The 38 to 40 Critical Reading questions count for about *half* your Verbal score.

longing would have meant that I lived in a certain atmosphere, an atmo-
(45) sphere in which those three words were felt as a burden. But I did not
live in such an atmosphere. My father's brown felt hat would develop a
hole in its crown, the lining would separate from the hat itself, and six
weeks before he thought that he could not be seen wearing it — he was
a very vain man — he would order another hat from England. And my
(50) mother taught me to eat my food in the English way: the knife in the
right hand, the fork in the left, my elbows held still close to my side.
When I had finally mastered it, I overheard her saying to a friend, "Did
you see how nicely she can eat?" But I knew then that I enjoyed my food
more when I ate it with my bare hands, and I continued to do so when
(55) she wasn't looking. And when my teacher showed us the map, she
asked us to study it carefully, because no test we would ever take would
be complete without this statement: "Draw a map of England."

I did not know then that the statement "Draw a map of England"
was something far worse than a declaration of war. I did not know then
(60) that this statement was part of a process that would result in my erasure,
not my physical erasure, but my erasure all the same. I did not know
then that this statement was meant to make me feel in awe and small
whenever I heard the word "England": awe at its existence, small
because I was not from it. I did not know very much of anything then —
(65) certainly not what a blessing it was that I was unable to draw a map of
England correctly.

*the flesh of a sheep

It's important to learn how to read the passage quickly and efficiently.
Remember, though, that reading the passage won't earn you points — it's
the questions that count.

THE 5-STEP METHOD FOR CRITICAL READING QUESTIONS

Here's a proven approach to Critical Reading questions:
- Read the question stem.
- Locate the material you need.
- Come up with an idea of the right answer.
- Scan the answer choices.
- Select your answer.

1. Read the Question Stem
This is the place to really read carefully. Take a second to make sure you
understand what the question is asking.

KAPLAN RULES

To approach Critical Reading:
- Read the question stem.
- Locate the material you need.
- Come up with an idea of the right answer.
- Scan the answer choices.
- Select your answer.

2. Locate the Material You Need

If you are given a line reference, read the material surrounding the line mentioned. It will clarify exactly what the question is asking.

If you're not given a line reference, scan the text to find the place where the question applies, and quickly reread those few sentences. Keep the main point of the passage in mind.

3. Come Up With an Idea of the Right Answer

Don't spend time making up a precise answer. You need only a general sense of what you're after, so you can recognize the correct answer quickly when you read the choices.

4. Scan the Answer Choices

Scan the choices, looking for one that fits your idea of the right answer. If you don't find an ideal answer, quickly eliminate wrong choices by checking back to the passage. Rule out choices that are too extreme or go against common sense. And get rid of answers that sound reasonable, but don't make sense in the context of the passage.

5. Select Your Answer

You've eliminated the obvious wrong answers. One of the few remaining should fit your ideal. If you're left with more than one contender, consider the passage's main idea, and make an educated guess.

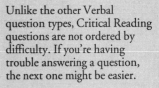

HAVING TROUBLE?

Unlike the other Verbal question types, Critical Reading questions are not ordered by difficulty. If you're having trouble answering a question, the next one might be easier.

NOW TRY THE QUESTIONS

1. According to the author, England could not really look like a leg of mutton (line 5) because
   (A) maps generally don't give an accurate impression of what a place looks like
   (B) England was too grand and exotic a place for such a mundane image
   (C) England was an island not very different in appearance from her own island
   (D) the usual metaphor used to describe England was a precious jewel
   (E) mutton was one of the few foods familiar to her that did not come from England

2. The author's reference to felt as "not the proper material" (line 31) for her father's hat chiefly serves to emphasize her point about the
   (A) extremity of the local weather
   (B) arrogance of island laborers
   (C) informality of dress on the island
   (D) weakness of local industries
   (E) predominance of English culture

3. The word "conception" as used in line 36 means
   (A) beginning
   (B) image
   (C) origination
   (D) notion
   (E) plan

4. The word "substantial" in line 36 means
   (A) important
   (B) abundant
   (C) firm
   (D) down-to-earth
   (E) materialistic

5. In the third paragraph, the author implies that any longing to put a shape to the words "made in England" would have indicated
   (A) a resentment of England's predominance
   (B) an unhealthy desire to become English
   (C) an inability to understand England's authority
   (D) an excessive curiosity about England
   (E) an unfamiliarity with English customs

6. The author cites the anecdotes about her father and mother in lines 46-55 primarily to convey their
   (A) love for their children
   (B) belief in strict discipline
   (C) distaste for anything foreign
   (D) reverence for England
   (E) overemphasis on formal manners

7. The word "erasure" (line 60) as used by the author most nearly means
   (A) total annihilation
   (B) physical disappearance
   (C) sense of insignificance
   (D) enforced censorship
   (E) loss of freedom

8. The main purpose of the passage is to
   (A) advocate a change in the way a subject is taught in school
   (B) convey the personality of certain figures from the author's childhood
   (C) describe an overwhelming influence on the author's early life
   (D) analyze the importance of a sense of place to early education
   (E) relate a single formative episode in the author's life

9. For the author, the requirement to "Draw a map of England" (lines 58-66) represented an attempt to
(A) force students to put their studies to practical use
(B) glorify one culture at the expense of another
(C) promote an understanding of world affairs
(D) encourage students to value their own heritage
(E) impart outmoded and inappropriate knowledge

10. At the end of the passage, the author suggests that her inability "to draw a map of England correctly" indicated a
(A) heartfelt desire to see the country in person rather than through maps
(B) serious failure of the education she received
(C) conscious rejection of the prestige of a foreign power
(D) harmful preoccupation with local affairs and customs
(E) beneficial ignorance of her own supposed inferiority

APPLYING THE 5-STEP METHOD

Try the five-step method on question 1 from the sample reading passage on page 59 - 60.

1. Read the Question Stem
In this case, the question is straightforward: Why couldn't England really look like a leg of mutton? (Notice that "mutton" is defined for you at the end of the passage — you aren't expected to know the meaning of unfamiliar terms.)

2. Locate the Material You Need
You're given a clue: the answer lies somewhere near line 5. But don't read just that line — read the line or two before and after as well. By doing so, you learn that England was mysterious and special, so it couldn't look like something as familiar (to the author) as a leg of mutton.

3. Come Up With an Idea of the Right Answer
After reading those couple of lines, you'd expect the answer to be something like, "England was too special to look like a familiar leg of mutton."

4. Scan the Answer Choices
Choice (B) comes close to the ideal — it should have popped out. But if you weren't sure, you could have quickly eliminated the other choices. Thinking of the main idea would have helped you eliminate (A) and (C). England was precious — like a jewel — but the author doesn't imply that England was usually compared to a jewel (D). And you never learn where mutton comes from (E).

WHAT'S MUTTON?

When a word is too obscure for the SAT, they'll define it at the bottom of the reading passage.

ANSWER KEY TO CRITICAL READING SMARTS

1. (B)
2. (E)
3. (D)
4. (B)
5. (B)
6. (D)
7. (C)
8. (C)
9. (B)
10. (E)

5. Select Your Answer

Choice (B) is the only one that works here. By reading the material surrounding the line reference and putting an answer into your own words, you should have been able to choose (B) with confidence.

PRACTICE: Now try the 5-step method on the remaining questions for the passage on page 59 - 60.

HINT— From the questions, you can "fill in" the information you don't get in a quick reading. It's a way of working backwards, to reconstruct the passage.

BIG PICTURE, LITTLE PICTURE, AND VOCABULARY-IN-CONTEXT

Most SAT Critical Reading questions fall into three basic types. "Big Picture" questions test your overall understanding of the passage's biggest points. "Little Picture" questions ask about localized bits of information. Vocabulary-in-Context questions ask for the meaning of a single word.

In the passage on pages 59 - 60, question 8 is an example of a Big Picture question. Number 2 is an example of a Little Picture question. Number 3 is a Vocabulary-in-Context question.

HINT—Remember to skip around if you need to. You can tackle whichever passage you like in any order you like within the same section. But once you've read through the passage, try all the questions that go with it.

THE BIG PICTURE

Big Picture questions test your overall understanding of a passage. They might ask:

• the main point or purpose of a passage.

• the author's attitude or tone.

• the logic underlying the author's argument.

• how ideas relate to each other.

One way to see the Big Picture is to read actively. As you read, ask yourself, "What's this all about? What's the point of this?"

HINT—Still stumped after reading the passage? Do the Little Picture questions first. They can help you fill in the Big Picture.

Turn back to the passage you tried on pages 59 - 60. What did you get out of the first reading? Something like, "England was a profound influence on the author's early life, but not a completely positive influence"? That would have been enough.

Now look at question 8. It's a Big Picture question, asking for the main point of the passage. Use the 5-step method to find your answer.

1. Read the Question Stem
Simple enough: what's the main point of the passage?

2. Locate the Material You Need
In this case, you're asked about the overall point. You should have gotten a sense of that from reading the passage.

3. Get an Idea of the Right Answer
Again, you just need a rough statement. Here, something like this would do: "The purpose is to describe how England was a huge influence, but maybe not a completely positive one, in the author's young life."

4. Scan the Answer Choices
(C) should have popped out. But (D) might have looked good too if you focused on the words "sense of place." So put those two aside as contenders. How a subject was taught in school (A), figures in the author's childhood (B), and a single formative episode (E) are too narrow.

5. Select Your Answer
You've crossed off the poor choices, and you're down to two possibilities. Which matches your ideal? (C) comes closer. Look closely at (D) and you'll see that it's too general. Go with the best choice.

THE LITTLE PICTURE

More than two-thirds of Critical Reading questions ask about Little Pictures. Little Picture questions usually give you a line reference or refer you to a particular paragraph — a strong clue to where in the passage you'll find your answer.

Little Picture questions might:

• test whether you understand significant information that's stated in the passage.

• ask you to make inferences or draw conclusions based on a part of the passage.

• ask you to relate parts of the passage to one another.

Question 2 is a Little Picture question. You're asked about the felt hat of the author's father — what does this point emphasize? Applying Kaplan's Step 2, locate the material you'll need. You're given a clue — a line reference — to help you here. Reread that, and the lines before and after it as well.

HINT—Don't pick farfetched inferences. SAT inferences tend to be strongly implied in the passage.

So why did the father wear a felt hat, which was probably quite hot in the tropical sun? Because it was English. That's what correct choice (E) says. Rereading that bit of the passage should have led you right to that answer. (A) comes close, but doesn't fit the main point of the passage. Even with Little Picture questions, grasping the main point of the passage can help you find the correct answer.

HINT— Beware of answer choices that provide a reasonable answer to the stem, but don't make sense in the context of the passage.

VOCABULARY-IN-CONTEXT

> ### A STRATEGY FOR VOCABULARY-IN-CONTEXT QUESTIONS
>
> Once you find the tested word in the passage, you can treat a Vocabulary-in-Context question like a Sentence Completion.
>
> Pretend the word is a blank in the sentence. Read a line or two around the "blank," if you need to.
>
> Then predict a word for the "blank." Check the answer choices for a word that comes close to your prediction.

Vocabulary-in-Context questions ask about an even smaller part of the passage than other Little Picture questions do — they ask about the usage of a single word. These questions do not test your ability to define hard words like "archipelago" and "garrulous." They do test your ability to infer the meaning of a word from context.

In fact, the words tested in these questions will probably be familiar to you — they are usually fairly common words with more than one definition. Many of the answer choices will be definitions of the tested word, but only one will work in context. Vocabulary-in-Context questions always have a line reference, and you should always use it!

HINT— CONTEXT is the most important part of Vocabulary-in-CONTEXT questions.

Sometimes one of the answer choices will jump out at you. It'll be the most common meaning of the word in question — but it's rarely right! We call this the "obvious" choice. For example, say "curious" is the word being tested. The obvious choice is "inquisitive." But "curious" also means "odd," and that's more likely to be the answer. Using context to find the answer will help prevent you from falling for this trap. You can use these choices to your advantage though: if you get stuck on a Vocabulary-in-Context question, you can eliminate the "obvious" choice and guess.

HINT— If a question has an "obvious" choice, steer clear of it.

VOCABULARY-IN-CONTEXT PRACTICE

1. Embodied and given life in the social realities of her own period, Jane Austen's satire still has currency in ours.

   In the lines above, "currency" most nearly means
   (A) usualness
   (B) stylishness
   (C) prevalence
   (D) funds
   (E) relevance

2. A perpetual doubting and a perpetual questioning of the truth of what we have learned is not the temper of science.

   In the lines above, "temper" most nearly means
   (A) disposition
   (B) nature
   (C) anger
   (D) mood
   (E) mixture

3. Captain Wentworth had no fortune. He had been lucky in his profession, but, spending freely what had come freely, had realized nothing.

   Which most nearly captures the meaning of the word "realized" in the sentence above?
   (A) understood
   (B) accomplished
   (C) learned
   (D) accumulated
   (E) fulfilled

4. Anyone with more than a superficial knowledge of Shakespeare's plays must necessarily entertain some doubt concerning their true authorship.

   In the lines above, "entertain" most nearly means
   (A) amuse
   (B) harbor
   (C) occupy
   (D) cherish
   (E) engage

5. Many people who invested in the booming art market of the 1980s were disappointed; few of the works appreciated in value.

In the lines above, "appreciated" most nearly means
(A) admired
(B) applauded
(C) spiraled
(D) increased
(E) acknowledged

6. Charles de Gaulle's independence of mind can be seen by the fact that he negotiated with Algerian nationalists, although he was pressed by his advisors, French colonists, and the army itself to continue the war.

Which most nearly captures the meaning of the word "pressed" in the sentence above?
(A) squeezed
(B) urged
(C) troubled
(D) required
(E) compelled

7. Today some would say that those struggles are all over —that all the horizons have been explored —that all the battles have been won — that there is no longer an American frontier. But I trust that no one in this vast assemblage will agree with those sentiments.

In the lines above, "sentiments" most nearly means
(A) beliefs
(B) results
(C) loyalties
(D) challenges
(E) emotions

8. The convicts made their escape by scaling the prison walls and stealing away under the cover of darkness.

Which most nearly captures the meaning of the word "stealing" in the line above?
(A) seizing
(B) taking
(C) slipping
(D) grabbing
(E) abducting

PAIRED PASSAGES — A (NOT-SO) SPECIAL CASE

Don't let the paired passages worry you — they're not twice as hard as the single reading selections. In fact, students often find the paired passages the most interesting on the test. With paired passages, focus as you read on the relationship between the two passages. Just as with single passages, the questions following paired passages can help fill in the picture.

Questions following paired passages are ordered: the first few questions relate to the first passage, the next few to the second passage, and the final questions ask about the passages as a pair.

How to Do Paired Passages

1. Skim the first passage, looking for the drift (as you would with a single passage).

2. Do the questions that relate to the first passage.

3. Skim the second passage, looking for the drift and thinking about how the second passage relates to the first.

4. Do the questions that relate to the second passage.

5. Now you're ready to do the questions that ask about the relationship between the two passages.

Alternating skimming passages and answering questions is especially important if you're short of time. You'll be able to answer at least some of the questions before time runs out. By the time you've looked at both passages and answered the questions about each passage, you'll have a firm sense of the relationship between the pair. That will help you to answer the last group of questions.

Active reading can help you answer these questions too. Remember to ask yourself, "What are these passages about? What is each author's point? What is similar about the two passages? What is different?"

WHAT TO DO IF YOU RUN OUT OF TIME

It's always best to skim the passage before you hit the questions. But if you only have a few minutes left, here's how to score points even while time is running out.

You can answer Vocabulary-in-Context questions and many Little Picture questions without reading the passage. If the question has a line reference, locate the material you need to find your answer and follow the 5-step method as usual. You won't have the overall picture to guide you, but you might be able to reach the correct answer just by understanding the "Little Picture."

ANSWERS
1. (E)
2. (B)
3. (D)
4. (B)
5. (D)
6. (B)
7. (A)
8. (C)

HIGHLIGHTS
• How to read the passage
• How to use the 5-step method for answering questions
• Big Picture and Little Picture questions
• Vocabulary-in-context
• Paired passages

F·A·S·T P·R·E·P

✍ Chapter Checklist ✍

Once you've mastered a concept, check it off:

BUILDING READING SKILLS

❏ How to skim
❏ How to paraphrase
❏ How to make an inference

💡 PanicPlan 💡

If you have a month or less to prep for the SAT, here's the best way to spend your time:

1: Read the section on skimming, pp. 71 - 73.

2: Hold off on the rest of the chapter until you've covered all the basics in this book.

3: If you have time to come back, work on the paraphrasing and inference sections.

CHAPTER 8

CRITICAL READING SKILLS:

SKIMMING, PARAPHRASING, MAKING INFERENCES

In Chapter 7 you learned the basics of Critical Reading—what it looks like, what to expect, how to read the passages, how to tackle the questions. This chapter will help you improve the Critical Reading skills tested on the SAT: skimming, paraphrasing, and drawing inferences. You already have these skills.

- Skimming means reading quickly and lightly. You do this when you look information up in a phone book, or glance at a newspaper article only long enough to get the gist of the story.

- When you restate something in your own words, that's paraphrasing. You do it all the time in daily life — when you give a phone message, or re-tell a story.

- When you deduce information from a statement or situation, you're making inferences. You do it every day. If your best friend doesn't talk to you for a week, you'd probably infer that your friend was mad at you, even if your friend didn't actually say so.

SKIMMING

HINT—Don't read each word separately. Move your eyes lightly over the page, grouping words.

READ THIS QUICKLY

Joe stood at the edge of town, a cigarette in his left hand, a bottle of bourbon in his right. He'd had tough ones before, but this was gonna be the end of him. He looked back towards the light of the city below him. "If only I could get Martinez to talk," he thought to himself. In a flash, Joe was back in the Mustang racing towards town...

What was this little story about? Chances are, even with a quick read, you took away some information that helped you piece it together. That's because you've already developed your reading skills (you're reading this, aren't you?).

Your challenge on the SAT is to apply these skills in a peculiar context and not to be intimidated by the passages they throw at you.

Skimming is a specific reading style where you read quickly and in less detail than usual. These two characteristics are what make skimming the best way to read SAT passages. You want to read quickly because time is limited, and you want to read lightly because the questions direct you to the details you need. Spending a lot of time with the passage before you see the questions just doesn't make sense. So skimming works well—as long as you read with three things in mind:

- the content of the passage;

- the organization of the passage;

- the author's purpose or point of view.

If you have a general idea of these three things when you're done skimming, then you're ready for the questions.

In order to be an effective skimmer, you need to practice. Treat your practice sessions as an opportunity to learn — in time, you'll notice improvement.

- Practice frequently, in short sessions.

- Use these methods every time you read.

WHAT DO WE MEAN BY SKIMMING?

Skimming is still reading. It means reading quickly, looking only for the main ideas and the organization of the passage.

HOW TO SKIM

To improve your reading speed, get your eyes to move quickly and lightly along each line of type. Think about the way you usually read. Do you dwell on each word, as if you were plodding through a field of mud? Or do your eyes move quickly over the page, as if you were walking on hard, dry ground?

The way your eyes habitually move across each line of type and return to the beginning of the next line is your tracking style. That's what you'll work on here. The object is to make it light and swift, rather than heavy and deliberate.

Improving your "tracking style" will help you perform your best when under pressure.

SKIMMING TIPS

Don't Sub-Vocalize

Sub-vocalizing is "sounding out" words as you read. Even if you don't move your lips, you're probably sub-vocalizing if you read one word at a time. Sub-vocalizing costs you time — because you can't read faster than you speak. If you group words, you won't sub-vocalize.

Keep Asking Yourself Where the Author's Going
Stay alert for the author's signals. Each SAT passage takes you on a journey, and every passage contains phrases or paragraph breaks that signal the next phase of this journey. As you skim, notice where each passage changes course.

Keep Your "Footsteps" Light
Don't read a passage slowly and deliberately. On the other hand, don't race as fast as you can. The idea is to increase your reading rate slightly while remaining comfortable.

SKIMMING EXERCISES

Now try a few exercises to see how skimming works. Read the following paragraph word by word.

> The prohibitive prices of some exhibits, as well as the continued depression of the local economy, prevented the 1939 World's Fair from being a great financial success. In a cultural sense, however, the Fair was enormously successful, and a landmark event of the era. As one historian noted, the Fair became "a cultural document of American values and aspirations at a crucial crossroads." After a decade of hardship, many Americans were ready to embrace a vision of social harmony, prosperity, and a bright future.

Now read the same paragraph, concentrating phrase by phrase.

> The prohibitive prices/ of some exhibits, /as well as/ the continued depression/ of the local economy, /prevented/ the 1939 World's Fair/ from being/ a great financial success. /In a /cultural sense,/ however,/ the Fair/ was enormously successful,/ and a landmark event/ of the era./ As one historian noted,/ the Fair became / "a cultural document/ of American values and aspirations/ at a crucial crossroads." /After a decade /of hardship,/ many Americans/ were ready to embrace/ a vision of social harmony,/ prosperity,/ and a bright future.

OKAY TO SLASH?

Don't put slash marks in your test booklet on the real SAT. You're allowed to, but it's a waste of time.

The point is to make "mental" slash marks so that you get in the habit of moving briskly through the passage.

Here's another paragraph. Put in the slash marks yourself, phrase by phrase.

The theme of the 1939 World's Fair was "Building the World of Tomorrow." Indeed, the modern and the futuristic were everywhere apparent. The main symbols of the Fair were the Trylon and the Perisphere, a huge pyramid and orb which were lit up at night in a dazzling display. The most popular exhibit, sponsored by General Motors, was the Futurama, which claimed to provide visitors with a glimpse of automotive America in 1960. Patrons were carried by individual moving chairs on a simulated cross-country voyage, along a superhighway which would allow drivers to reach speeds up to 100 miles an hour.

No two readers will mark up this paragraph the same way, because each person sees phrases differently. That's okay. What's important is to begin working phrase-by-phrase, instead of word-by-word.

Now try another method. Read the following paragraphs, letting your eyes move down the page, and coming to rest at only two places per line:

The Catcher in the Rye, published in 1951, is the only novel written by J.D. Salinger in a career that lasted less than twenty years. It is the story of Holden Caulfield, a sensitive, rebellious New York City teen-ager taking his first hesitant steps into adulthood. Holden flees the confines of his snobbish Eastern prep school, searching for innocence and truth, but finds only "phoniness." Filled with humor and pathos, The Catcher in the Rye won wide critical acclaim at the time of its publication. In the four decades since then, however, it has become a true phenomenon, selling hundreds of thousands of copies each year, and Holden Caulfield has gained the status of a cultural icon. What accounts for this book's remarkable hold on generation after generation of American youth?

Holden Caulfield is the narrator of The Catcher in the Rye, and his narration is a stylistic tour de force, revealing Salinger's masterful ear for the linguistic idioms and rhythms of adolescent speech. Slang evolves continuously, of course, and yesterday's "in" expressions are usually passé by tomorrow. But Holden's characteristic means of expression — the vernacular of a teen-age social misfit, desperately trying to find his niche — transcends the particulars of time and place. Like another 1950s icon, James Dean in "Rebel Without a Cause," Holden Caulfield has "outlived" his era and become an enduring symbol of sensitive youth, threatened by an indifferent society.

See how your eye takes in whole phrases, though you haven't read every word? That's another skimming method.

Remember, skim the passage before you turn to the questions. When you tackle the questions, you'll focus more tightly on parts of the passage. Many questions will direct you back to specific lines or paragraphs, so you won't be desperately searching for relevant information.

PARAPHRASING

HINT—A good paraphrase accurately restates the meaning of the original, without adding or losing important points.

What happens when your best friend misses a day of school? You probably tell her or him what went on that night on the phone, or the next day before class. You'd be paraphrasing — condensing a day's worth of events into a few minutes, highlighting the most important things. Critical Reading questions often ask you to do a similar thing. They ask what a passage, or part of it, says. The right answer accurately paraphrases the meaning of the passage or excerpt, that is, it restates the meaning without losing any important points. Let's see how this works. Here are a few sentences from a Critical Reading passage:

> **EXAMPLE**
>
> No doubt because it painted a less than flattering picture of American life in America for Asian immigrants, East Goes West was not well received by contemporary literary critics. According to them, Kang's book displayed a curious lack of insight regarding the American effort to accommodate those who had come over from Korea. The facet of the novel reviewers did find praiseworthy was Han's perseverance and sustained optimism in the face of adversity.
>
> The passage indicates that the response of critics to East Goes West was one of
> (A) irony regarding the difference between Han's expectations and reality
> (B) admiration of the courage and creativity Kang showed in breaking from literary tradition
> (C) confusion about the motivation of the protagonist
> (D) qualified disapproval of Kang's perception of his adopted homeland
> (E) anger that Kang had so viciously attacked American society

There's a lot going on in the passage, but don't let it confuse you. Follow our advice:

Kaplan's Paraphrasing Method
1. Read the question stem. That's the partial sentence leading into the answer choices.
2. Read the lines you're referred to, searching for the relevant phrases. (If

WHY SKIM?

You gain points by answering the questions, not by reading the passages. Read quickly for the main idea and the structure, so you'll know where to look for the answers to the questions. The place to really concentrate is on the questions.

a question gives you a line reference, be sure to read a line or two before and after the keyed line.)

3. Predict a good paraphrase for what's being asked.

4. Find a similar answer choice.

Now Apply Kaplan's Method to the Reading Question Above

1 - 2. After reading the stem and relevant lines of the passage (in this case, we found them for you), the key phrases should have popped out: "not well received," "a curious lack of insight," and "the facet reviewers did find praiseworthy."

3. Predicted paraphrase: The critics were displeased with Kang's view of the immigrant's experience, but approved of the hero's persistence.

4. Look for the answer choice that means the same as your paraphrase.

Choice (D) comes closest. Qualified means "modified" or "limited," so qualified disapproval captures both the negative and the positive reaction the reviewers had.

Notice that Choice (E) is too negative, and choice (B) is too positive. Choices (A) and (C) don't reflect what the extract says. So (D) is the answer.

PRACTICE PARAPHRASING

The exercise below will help you recognize a good paraphrase quickly. Follow the method you've just learned. Notice as you go if your paraphrase includes too much or too little information, or if it has the wrong focus. If so, adjust it.

Each excerpt below is followed by a space where you can write your own paraphrase. Compare your paraphrase with the answer choices and pick the best approximation. Answers on p. 81.

1. He was not in love with Margaret, and he believed, though one could never be sure, that she was not in love with him — that her preference was for the handsome young clergyman who read Browning with her every Tuesday afternoon. But he was aware also that she would marry him if he asked her; he knew that the hearts of four formidable parents were set on the match; and in his past experience his mother's heart had invariably triumphed over his less intrepid resolves.

   The protagonist believes that Margaret will marry him because (give the reason in your own words):
   _____
   _____

   Now find the best paraphrase:
   (A) she wouldn't have the resolve to refuse him
   (B) they are in love with each other
   (C) they both feel parental pressure
   (D) she knows the clergyman won't marry her
   (E) his mother will talk her into accepting him

2. Only with effort can the camera be forced to lie: basically it is an honest medium: so the photographer is much more likely to approach nature in a spirit of inquiry, of communion, instead of with the saucy swagger of self-dubbed "artists."

   The distinction made in the passage between a photographer and an "artist" can best be summarized as which of the following (summarize the distinction in your own words):
   _____
   _____

   Now find the best paraphrase:
   (A) The photographer's job is to record the world, and the artist's is to embellish it.
   (B) The photographer's work is realistic, while the artist's is impressionistic.
   (C) The artist finds his inspiration in the urban environment, the photographer in nature.
   (D) The photographer has a more open and unassuming attitude toward the natural world than the artist does.
   (E) Photographers are more pretentious than artists are.

3. The following excerpt is from a speech given by Frederick Douglass.
"...What to the American slave is your Fourth of July? I answer, a day that reveals more to him than all other days of the year, the gross injustice and cruelty to which he is the constant victim. To him your celebration is a sham; your boasted liberty an unholy license; your national greatness, swelling vanity..."

According to Douglass, for slaves, the Fourth of July (complete the sentence in your own words):

_____

_____

Now find the best paraphrase:
(A) highlights the hypocrisy of stated American ideals
(B) reveals the injustice of not being invited to participate
(C) is a reminder of the greatness of their homeland
(D) shows the depravity of the celebrants
(E) is a completely meaningless day

INFERENCES

Inferences are conclusions you reach that are hinted at, but not directly stated in the reading passage. When you infer, you're "reading between the lines." In Critical Reading:

• If you're given a line reference, be sure to read a line or two around it.

• Always look for evidence in the passage to support an inference.

Many SAT questions test your power to make accurate inferences.

EXAMPLE

My father was a justice of the peace, and I supposed that he possessed the power of life and death over all men and could hang anybody that offended him. This distinction was enough for me as a general thing; but the desire to become a steamboat man kept intruding, nevertheless. I first wanted to be a cabin boy, so that I could come out with a white apron on and shake a tablecloth over the side, where all my old comrades could see me. Later I thought I would rather be the deck hand who stood on the end of the stage plank with a coil of rope in his hand, because he was particularly conspicuous.

The author makes the statement that "I supposed he possessed the power of life and death over all men and could hang anybody that offended him" primarily to suggest the
(A) power held by a justice of the peace in a frontier town
(B) naive view that he held of his father's importance
(C) respect which the townspeople had for his father
(D) possibility of miscarriages of justice on the American frontier
(E) harsh environment in which he was brought up

The answer is implied here. The author doesn't say "my view of my father's importance at the time was naive." But the idea is implicit in the excerpt.

As the author explains it, he supposed at the time that his father was all powerful and that he could kill almost anyone. On a first reading, that probably struck you as odd. You also probably wondered why the son was proud of it. But read the passage carefully and you'll realize the tone is ironic. The author is making fun of his youthful ideas. So the correct answer has to be (B).

Don't Go Too Far With Inferences

SAT inferences tend to be straightforward and consistent with the overall idea of the passage. They are not extreme, complex, or subtle. In fact, they're incredibly predictable. You can use this to your advantage.

Choices (A) and (E) above go too far.

• Is it realistic that the author's father could hang anyone he wanted? Even if he could, would the author be proud of it? Very unlikely.

• Do the boy's early assumptions about his father's power indicate anything about the environment he grew up in? Not a thing.

Look at another question about the same excerpt:

EXAMPLE

The author decides that he would rather become a deck hand than a cabin boy because
(A) the job offers higher wages
(B) he believes that the work is easier
(C) he wants to avoid seeing his older friends
(D) deck hands often go on to become pilots
(E) the job is more visible to passers-by

The author never says, "I decided to become a deck hand because the job was more visible to casual bystanders."

He does say he wanted to become a cabin boy so his old comrades could see him. And he adds the deck hand job would make him conspicuous. Between the lines, the correct answer (E) is strongly implied.

INFERENCE PRACTICE

To sharpen your ability to deal with all kinds of inferences, do the following exercise. Answers on page 81.

1. The graduating classes were the nobility of the school. Like travelers with exotic destinations on their minds, the graduates were remarkably forgetful. They came to school without their books, or tablets, or even pencils. Volunteers fell over themselves to secure replacements for the missing equipment. Even the teachers were respectful of the now quiet and aging seniors, and tended to speak to them, if not as equals, as beings only slightly lower than themselves.

    In the lines above, the author most likely mentions the eagerness of the "volunteers" in order to
    (A) indicate the ambition of younger school members
    (B) explain a double standard in teachers' attitudes
    (C) underline the respect with which seniors were treated
    (D) emphasize how careless seniors were with their equipment
    (E) point out a shortage in school supplies

2. Without knowing exactly what he'd done, Marc realized that he'd really done it now, and he felt the silence incriminating him. "Now wait just a minute. Hold on there," he said, producing a laugh from somewhere. Marc was the statesman of the class. People joked about how much money he was going to make coming out of law school. But he was groping for his words now, his eyes flickering over the countertop as if the words he was looking for were visible there.

    In the lines above, Marc's reputation as "the statesman of the class" is most likely mentioned in order to indicate that
    (A) he is noted for his diplomacy
    (B) many people resent his success
    (C) he is generally an articulate speaker
    (D) he is a popular student on campus
    (E) his ambitions are not realistic

3. Everyone seems to agree that there is something wrong with the way science is being taught these days. But no one is at all clear about what went wrong or what is to be done about it. The term "scientific illiteracy" has become almost a cliché in educational circles. Graduate schools blame the colleges, colleges blame the high schools, the high schools blame the elementary schools, which, in turn, blame the family. I suggest that the scientific community is partly, perhaps largely, to blame.

> In the lines above, the phrase "almost a cliché in educational circles" is used to indicate
> (A) the lack of unity between different sectors of education
> (B) the widespread concern about the way science is being taught
> (C) the inability of many scientists to communicate effectively
> (D) the ignorance displayed by the scientific community about literature
> (E) the extent of agreement over specific educational reforms

ANSWER KEY

Paraphrasing

1. (C) Their parents want them to get married.

2. (D) A photographer is more open to nature and less pretentious than an "artist" is.

3. (A) is a sham because the holiday celebrates freedom and they are not free.

Inferences

1. (C)

2. (C)

3. (B)

HIGHLIGHTS
• How to Skim
• How to Paraphrase
• How to Make Inferences

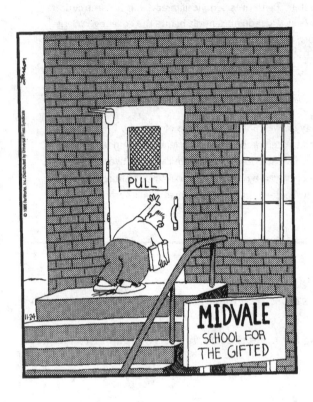

CHAPTER 9

INTRODUCING SAT MATH

Mathematics is many things. It is linear algebra and complex analysis. It is topology and trigonometry. It is number theory and multivariable calculus. Mathematics is a huge and daunting field, which requires years of study to master. But SAT Math is different. To ace the SAT, you need only a small body of mathematical knowledge covering basic concepts in arithmetic, algebra, and geometry. These concepts have been distilled into 75 principles that appear as an appendix to this book.

A solid grasp of these principles will get you a good SAT score. Understanding the ways in which these principles are tested—the twists and turns that the testmakers throw into many SAT problems—can get you a great score.

This chapter explains:
- The SAT Math sections
- The SAT Math question types
- How to approach SAT Math problems
- Picking Numbers
- Backsolving

Then, in chapters 10 through 15 you'll learn:
- When to use your calculator
- Specific strategies for solving Regular Math questions, Quantitative Comparisons (QCs), and Grid-ins
- How to avoid math traps the testmakers have set
- How to make educated guesses on difficult math problems

SAT MATH: THE WARNING SIGNS

- When smoke starts coming out of your calculator, you're overusing it.
- If you are counting on your fingers and starting to remove your socks, you're off the track.
- If your answer depends on calculating the weight of the moon, in kilograms, you've read something wrong.
- "One potato, two potato" is not a useful guessing technique.

HOW SAT MATH IS SET UP

There are three scored Math sections on the new SAT:

- one 30-minute section with 25 Regular Math questions
- one 30-minute section with a set of 15 QCs and a set of 10 Grid-ins
- one 15-minute section with 10 Regular Math questions

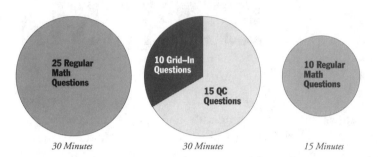

25 Regular Math Questions	10 Grid-In Questions / 15 QC Questions	10 Regular Math Questions
30 Minutes	*30 Minutes*	*15 Minutes*

Difficulty Level

All sets of SAT Math questions start off easy and gradually increase in difficulty.

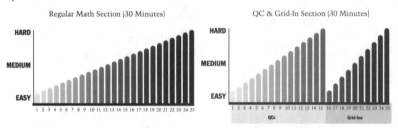

Regular Math Section (30 Minutes)   QC & Grid-In Section (30 Minutes)

The 10 Regular Math Questions also get more difficult.

Always be aware of the difficulty level as you go through a question set. Easy problems call for different strategies. The harder the questions, the more traps you will encounter. If you know you're dealing with a hard question (even though it may look easy) you'll be prepared.

DON'T READ THE DIRECTIONS ON TEST DAY— KNOW WHAT TO EXPECT

You'll save a lot of time on the SAT Math by knowing the directions. They take a fair amount of time to plow through and they are the same for every test. With just a little prior experience, you'll know what to do with each question type and you'll skip the directions and go straight to the first question.

At the start of each Math section you will find the following information:

Time—30 Minutes 25 Questions	Solve each of the following problems, decide which is the best answer choice, and darken the corresponding oval on the answer sheet. Use available space in the test booklet for scratchwork.*

Notes:

(1) Calculator use is permitted.

(2) All numbers used are real numbers.

(3) Figures are provided for some problems. All figures are drawn to scale and lie in a plane UNLESS otherwise indicated.

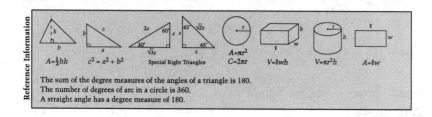

$A=\frac{1}{2}bh$ $c^2 = a^2 + b^2$ Special Right Triangles $A=\pi r^2$ $V=lwh$ $V=\pi r^2 h$ $A=lw$
$C=2\pi r$

The sum of the degree measures of the angles of a triangle is 180.
The number of degrees of arc in a circle is 360.
A straight angle has a degree measure of 180.

Note (2) means you won't have to deal with imaginary numbers, like i (the square root of -1).

Note (3) tells you diagrams are drawn to scale, which means you can use these diagrams to estimate measurements. However, if the diagrams are labeled "Figure not drawn to scale," you can't do this.

Saying the figures "lie in a plane" simply means you are dealing with flat figures, like rectangles or circles, unless the question says otherwise.

The math information you're given includes many basic geometry formulas. By test day you should know all these formulas by heart. But if you forget one at the last minute, you'll find them in the directions.

The QCs and Grid-ins have slightly different instructions which we'll discuss in detail in Chapter 12 and Chapter 11.

HOW TO APPROACH SAT MATH

To maximize your Math score, you need to learn to use your time efficiently. Then you won't get bogged down on a single hard question and miss other problems you could have solved if you'd had more time.

The key to working systematically is: Think about the question before you look for the answer. A few seconds spent up front looking for traps, thinking about your approach, and deciding whether to tackle the problem now or come back to it later will pay off in SAT points. On easy problems, you may know what to do right away. But on hard problems, the few extra seconds is time well spent.

> ### RULE OF THUMB
>
> If you always mess up the same type of problem, circle it, skip it, and come back to it if you have time.

Now apply it to the problem below:

EXAMPLE

12. At a certain diner, Joe orders 3 donuts and a cup of coffee and is charged $2.25. Stella ordered 2 donuts and a cup of coffee and is charged $1.70. What is the price of two donuts?

(A) $0.55
(B) $0.60
(C) $1.10
(D) $1.30
(E) $1.80

IRRELEVANT COMMENT

Joe's gonna get pretty fat if he keeps eating all those donuts. Warning: This is not a good breakfast for test day.

Read Through the Question

This means the *whole* question. If you try to start solving the problem before reading it all the way through, you may end up doing unnecessary work.

• Decide whether the question is easy, medium, or hard. All SAT Math questions are arranged in order of difficulty. Within a set, the first questions are easy, the middle ones moderately difficult, and the last ones are hard. Problem #12 above is a moderately difficult word problem.

> HINT—On difficult questions, watch out for Math Traps. Hard questions are often misleadingly worded to trip up careless readers. (For more on Math Traps, See Chapter 14, p. 173.)

• Make sure you know what's being asked. Problem #12 looks straightforward but read through it carefully and you'll see a slight twist. You're asked to find the cost of two donuts, not one. Many people will find the price of a single donut and forget to double it.

Decide Whether to Do the Problem, or Skip It for Now

• If you have no idea what to do, skip the problem and circle it in your test booklet. Spend your time on the problems you can solve.

• If you think you can solve it, but it will take a lot of time, circle the question number in your test booklet and make a note to come back to it later if you have time.

• If you can eliminate one or more answer choices, do so and make an educated guess. Mark that you guessed in your test booklet, and try solving later if time permits. (For details on educated guessing, see Chapter 15, p. 199).

WHAT TO DO WHEN YOU SKIP A QUESTION

Circle it in your test booklet and make sure you skip it on your answer grid.

If You Do Tackle the Problem, Look for the Fastest Approach

•Look for hidden information. On an easy question all the information you need to solve the problem may be given up front, in the stem, or in a diagram. But in a harder question, you may need to look for hidden information that will help you solve the problem. Since questions are arranged in order of difficulty, you should be a little wary of #12. If you get the answer too easily, you may have missed something. In this case, you're asked to find the price of two donuts, not one. For more on Hidden Instructions see Chapter 14.

• Look for shortcuts. Sometimes the obvious way of doing a problem is the long way. If the method you choose involves lots of calculating, look for another route. There's usually a shortcut you can use that won't involve you in tons of arithmetic.

In problem 12, for example, the cost of donuts and coffee could be translated into two distinct equations using the variables d and c. You could find c in terms of d, then plug this into the other equation. But if you think carefully, you'll see there's a quicker way: the difference in price between 3 donuts and a cup of coffee and two donuts and a cup of coffee is the price of one donut. So one donut costs $2.25 – $1.70 = $0.55. (Remember, you have to find the price of two donuts. Twice $0.55 is $1.10.)

• Use a variety of strategies. Chapter 13, Classic Problem-Solving Techniques, reviews many strategies for specific problem types that will help you get to the answer faster. You can also use special Kaplan approaches, such as Backsolving and Picking Numbers. (For more on this, see pages 88 - 92 in this chapter.)

If You Get Stuck, Make an Educated Guess

If you're not sure what to do, or if you've tried solving a problem but got stuck, cut your losses. Eliminate any answer choices you can, and make an educated guess.

> *HINT— When you skip a question, make a note in your test booklet to come back to it later, if you have time.*

Let's say it's taking too long to solve the donut problem. Can you eliminate any answer choices? The price of two donuts and a cup of coffee is $1.70. That means the cost of two donuts alone can't be $1.80, which eliminates choice (E). Now you can choose between the remaining choices, and your odds of guessing correctly have improved. (See Chapter 15, Math Guessing.)

If you practice using this approach to the Math problems on the SAT, you will save time and avoid mistakes on test day.

WHEN YOU'RE STUCK

The great thing about Math, even if you hate it, is that there are usually a lot of different ways to get to the right answer. On the SAT, there are two methods in particular that are really useful when you don't see the straightforward way to solve the problem: Picking Numbers and Backsolving. These strategies can take longer than traditional methods, but they're worth trying if you have enough time.

PICKING NUMBERS—THE 5-STEP METHOD

SAT problems that involve variables can be tricky and time consuming. One way around them is to simply pick numbers to stand in for the variables. Picking numbers on percents and odd/even problems is particularly helpful. Picking numbers may also be a good strategy on certain other problems covering ratios, rates, factors, multiples and remainders, and even some algebra problems.

The Key: If you're having trouble with a question that has variables in the answer choices, try Picking Numbers.

Here's How It Works

1. Pick a number for the variable.
2. Plug the number into the question.
3. Solve the problem.
4. Substitute your number for the variable in all the answer choices.
5. Figure out the answer choices. If two or more answer choices yield the same result, try another number or guess. The correct answer choice matches the value you solved for.

USING THE 5-STEP METHOD FOR PERCENTS

HINT — Where you're not asked to find specific quantities, try Picking Numbers.

EXAMPLE

At the Frosty Ice Cream store, the number of cones sold fell by 20 percent in November. If sales fell by a further 25 percent in December, what was the percent decrease in the number of cones sold in the whole two-month period?

(A) 10%
(B) 20%
(C) 35%
(D) 40%
(E) 45%

1. Pick a Number for the Variable

Since it's easy to find percents of 100, let the original number of cones sold be 100.

2. Plug Your Number Into the Question

- The number of cones sold in November fell by 20%.
  20% of 100 = 20.

- The number of cones sold in November = 100 - 20 = 80.

- The number of cones sold in December is 25% less than this amount.
  25% of 80 = $\frac{1}{4}$ of 80 = 20.

- So the number of cones sold in December is 80 - 20 = 60.

3. Solve for the Value the Question Asks For

You're asked to find the percent decrease, that is the percentage difference between the original number of cones sold (100) and the cones sold in December (60).

- First find the drop in the number of cones: 100 - 60 = 40 cones.

- Then find the percent decrease. If sales fell by 40 cones, the percent decrease in sales was $\frac{40}{100} \times 100\% = 40\%$.

- This is answer choice (D) and steps 4 and 5 are unnecessary.

PICKING NUMBERS FOR ODD/EVEN

Picking Numbers is the best strategy to use when dealing with odd/even questions.

> ### EXAMPLE
>
> If a is even and b is odd, which of the following must be even?
>
> (A) $a + b$
>
> (B) $\dfrac{ab}{2}$
>
> (C) $a^2 + b^2$
>
> (D) $(a + b)^2$
>
> (E) ab^2

1. Pick an even number for a and an odd number for b, say $a = 2$ and $b = 3$.

2. Now plug these into the answer choices and see which gives an even result.

- Choice (A) $a + b = 2 + 3 = 5$. Discard.

- Choice (B) $\dfrac{ab}{2} = \dfrac{6}{2} = 3$. Discard.

- Choice (C) $a^2 + b^2 = 4 + 9 = 13$. Discard.

- Choice (D) $(a + b)^2 = 5^2 = 25$. Discard.

- Choice (E) $ab^2 = 2 \times 9 = 18$. This must be the correct answer.

HINT — In questions with two variables, pick a different number for each. Avoid picking 0 and 1, as these often give several "possibly correct" answers.

KAPLAN RULES

Remember the answer is always in front of you on multiple choice questions. Your job is to find it.

BACKSOLVING

On some Math questions, when you can't figure out the question you can try working backwards from the answer choices. Plug the choices back into the question till you find the one that works.

Backsolving Works Best:

- when the question is a complex word problem and the answer choices are numbers;

- when the alternative is setting up multiple algebraic equations.

Don't Backsolve:

- if the answer choices include variables;

- on algebra questions or word problems that have ugly answer choices (radicals, fractions, etc.). Plugging them in takes too much time.

HOW BACKSOLVING WORKS

When the Question Is Complex and the Answer Choices Are Simple

> **EXAMPLE**
>
> An office has 27 employees. If there are 7 more women than men in the office, how many employees are women?
>
> (A) 8
> (B) 10
> (C) 14
> (D) 17
> (E) 20

HINT—Sometimes backsolving is faster than setting up an equation.

The five answer choices represent the possible number of women in the office, so try them in the question stem. The choice that gives a total of 27 employees, with 7 more women than men, will be the correct answer.

Plugging in choice (C) gives you 14 women in the office. Since there are 7 more women than men, there are 7 men in the office. But $14 + 7 < 27$. The sum is too small, so the number of women must be greater than 14. Eliminate answer choices (A), (B), and (C).

Either (D) or (E) will be correct. Plugging in (D) gives you 17 women in the office and $17 - 7$, or 10 men. $17 + 10 = 27$ employees total. Answer choice (D) is correct.

> **SPEED TIP**
>
> To speed things up, start with the middle-range number. Since answer choices are always listed in increasing or decreasing order, that means starting with choice (C). If (C) is too large, move to the smaller choices. If it's too small, move to the bigger ones.

Algebra Problems Where You Need to Solve Multiple Equations

EXAMPLE

If $a + b + c = 110$, $a = 4b$, and $3a = 2c$, then $b =$
(A) 6
(B) 8
(C) 9
(D) 10
(E) 14

You're looking for b, so plug in the answer choices for b in the question and see what happens.

Plug in the answer choices for b. The choice that gives us 110 for the sum $a + b + c$ must be correct.

Start with the mid-range number, 9, choice (C).

• If $b = 9$, then $a = 4 \times 9 = 36$.

• $2c = 3a = 3 \times 36 = 108$.

• $c = 54$.

• $a + b + c = 36 + 9 + 54 = 99$.

Since this is a smaller sum than 110, the correct value for b must be greater. Therefore, eliminate answer choices (A), (B), and (C).

Now plug in (D) to see if it works. If it doesn't, (E) must be correct.

Short of time? Try guessing between (D) and (E). But guess intelligently. Since (C) wasn't far wrong, you want a number just slightly bigger. That's choice (D).

HIGHLIGHTS

• Approaching SAT Math
• Picking Numbers
• Backsolving

F·A·S·T P·R·E·P

✍ CHAPTER CHECKLIST ✍

Once you've mastered a concept, check it off:

SUCCEEDING WITH A CALCULATOR

❑ WHAT TO BRING
❑ WHEN TO REACH FOR YOUR CALCULATOR
❑ TWO MOST COMMON CALCULATOR TRAPS

💀 PanicPlan 💀

If you have a month or less to prep for the SAT, here's the best way to spend your time:
Skim pp. 98 - 100.

CHAPTER 10

CALCULATORS AND THE NEW SAT

Y ou are allowed to use a calculator on the new SAT. That's a mixed blessing. The good news is you can now do computation faster. The bad news is you may be tempted to waste time using a calculator on questions that shouldn't involve lengthy computation.

Remember, you never *need* a calculator to solve an SAT problem. If you ever find yourself doing extensive calculation on the SAT — elaborate long division or long drawn-out multiplication — stop and look again because you probably missed a shortcut.

SHOULD I BRING A CALCULATOR?

You definitely want to bring your calculator on test day. The fact is, there are some problems where using the calculator will really come in handy. By using your calculator on particular problem types and by zeroing in on the parts of problems that need calculation, you can increase your score and save yourself time on the SAT.

WHAT KIND OF CALCULATOR SHOULD I BRING?

The best calculator to bring is one you're comfortable with. The most important thing is not how fancy your calculator is, but how good you are at using it. Remember, you won't be doing logs, trig functions, or preprogrammed formulas on the SAT. Most of the time you'll be multiplying and dividing.

> ### THE MORE YOU KNOW ABOUT THE SAT...
>
> ...The less you'll use your calculator.
>
> Studies have shown that students who regularly use calculators score better on the SAT than those who don't.
>
> But using a calculator too much could actually hurt your score. In fact, the better you are at the SAT, the less you'll need your calculator.

You can use the following calculators on the SAT:
- a 4-function calculator (that adds, subtracts, multiplies, divides);
- a scientific calculator (that also does radicals, exponents, etc.);
- a graphing calculator (that displays the graph of an equation in a coordinate plane).

But the following are not allowed:
- a calculator that prints out your calculations;
- a hand-held mini-computer or a laptop computer;
- any calculator with a typewriter keypad.

WHEN SHOULD I USE A CALCULATOR?

Calculators help the most on Grid-ins and the least on QCs.

The reason for this is that QCs are designed to be done very quickly, and never involve much computation—if you think you need a calculator on them, then you're missing something. Both Grid-ins and Regular Math will sometimes involve computation—never as the most important part of the question, but often as a final step.

Since Grid-ins don't give you answer choices to choose from, it's especially important to be sure of your work. Calculators can help you avoid careless errors.

Remember, a calculator can be useful when used selectively. Not all parts of a problem are necessarily easier on a calculator. Consider this problem:

> **EXAMPLE**
>
> If four grams of cadmium yellow pigment can make 3 kilograms of cadmium yellow oil paint, how many kilograms of paint could be produced from 86 grams of pigment?

This word problem has two steps. Step one is to set up the following proportion:

$$\frac{4\,\text{gms}}{3\,\text{kgs}} = \frac{86\,\text{gms}}{x\,\text{kgs}}$$

A little algebraic engineering tells you that:

$$x\,\text{kgs} = \frac{3\,\text{kgs} \times 86\,\text{gms}}{4\,\text{gms}}$$

Here's where you whip out that calculator. This problem has now been reduced down to pure calculation: $(3 \times 86) \div 4 = 64.5$.

KAPLAN RULES

The best calculator in the world won't help if the batteries are dead or if you forget to put them in. Make sure you have fresh batteries in your machine on test day.

Your calculator will also be especially useful for picking numbers and backsolving.

When You Pick Numbers

When you plug in real numbers to replace variables in complex equations, your calculator can speed things up. (See Picking Numbers, Chapter 9, pp. 88 - 90.)

When You Backsolve

When you plug multiple-choice answers into a problem, to see which answer is right, your calculator can speed up the process. (See Backsolving, Chapter 9, pp. 90 - 92.)

WHEN SHOULDN'T I USE A CALCULATOR?

Don't be fooled. On most SAT problems you may be tempted to use your calculator, but many questions will be easier without a calculator. That's particularly true on QCs.

Consider this problem:

EXAMPLE

Column A	Column B
$\dfrac{5}{8} + \dfrac{9}{14}$	$\dfrac{4}{9} + \dfrac{10}{21}$

Sure, you could grab your calculator and divide out those fractions. Relatively quickly you could calculate the new values and compare the columns.

But why bother?

If you just compare these terms to $\frac{1}{2}$ you'll be out of this problem much faster. After all, $\frac{5}{8}$ and $\frac{9}{14}$ from column A are both greater than $\frac{1}{2}$, and $\frac{4}{9}$ and $\frac{10}{21}$ (from column B) are both less than $\frac{1}{2}$. Column A must be greater.

Using your calculator would slow you down.

Be careful on non-QC questions, too. Consider this:

EXAMPLE

If $x^2 \times 8^2 = 49 \times 64 \times 81$, $x^2 =$

(A) 49^2
(B) 56^2
(C) 63^2
(D) 72^2
(E) 81^2

Now if you punch in $49 \times 64 \times 81$ you'll get 254,016. But that won't be too helpful. Look at the answer choices! Instead realize that:

$$(x^2) \times 8^2 = (49 \times 81) \times 64.$$

8^2 is the same thing as 64, so get rid of the 64's on both sides. You get:

$$x^2 = 49 \times 81.$$

So that's $x^2 = 7^2 \times 9^2$

or $x^2 = 7 \times 7 \times 9 \times 9$

which is 63×63 or 63^2.

No calculator required.

COMMON MISTAKE #1:
CALCULATING BEFORE YOU THINK

On the Grid-in problem below, how should you use your calculator?

EXAMPLE

The sum of all the integers from 1 to 44, inclusive, is subtracted from the sum of all the integers from 7 to 50, inclusive. What is the result?

The Wrong Approach
- Grab calculator.
- Punch in all the numbers.
- Put down answer and hope you didn't hit any wrong buttons.

**CALCULATOR ABUSE:
THE WARNING SIGNS**

- Punching in numbers before you've read the question.
- Hand cramps from punching in too many numbers.
- Repeatedly spelling "Hello" or "Shell Oil" on your calculator rather than answering the question.

The wrong approach is to punch in all the numbers from 1 to 44, find their sum, then do the same for numbers 7 through 50, and subtract the first sum from the second. Doing that means punching 252 keys. The odds are you'll slip up somewhere, hit the wrong key, and get the wrong answer. Even if you don't, punching in all those numbers takes too much time.

The Kaplan Approach
- Think first.
- Decide on the best way to solve it.
- Only then, use your calculator.

The right approach is to *think first*. The amount of computation involved in solving this directly tells you that there *must* be an easier way. You'll see this if you realize that both sums are of the same number of consecutive integers. Each integer in the first sum has a corresponding integer 6 greater than it in the second sum, like so:

1	7
+2	+8
+3	+9
.	.
.	.
.	.
+42	+48
+43	+49
+44	+50
=	=

There are 44 pairs of integers which are 6 apart.

So the total difference between the two sums will be the difference between each pair of integers times the number of pairs.

Now take out your calculator, punch "6 times 44 =," and get the correct answer of 264, with little or no time wasted.

WARNING — If you're punching buttons for long stretches at a time, you're approaching the problem the wrong way.

RULE OF THUMB

Different calculators do chain calculations different ways. Make sure you know how your calculator does chains so you don't miscalculate.

COMMON MISTAKE #2: FORGETTING THE ORDER OF OPERATIONS

Watch out. Even when you use your calculator, you can't just enter numbers in the order they appear on the page — you've got to follow the order of operations. This is a very simple error but it can cost you lots of points.

The order of operations, or PEMDAS, means you do whatever is in Parentheses first, then deal with Exponents, then Multiplication and Division, and finally Addition and Subtraction.

For example, say you want to find the value of the expression

$$\frac{x^2+1}{x+3} \quad \text{when } x = 7$$

HIGHLIGHTS

• Bring your calculator to the SAT
• Practice using it before test day
• Think before you calculate

If you just punched in "$7 \times 7 + 1 \div 7 + 3 =$" you would get the wrong answer.

The correct way to work it out is

$$(7^2 + 1) \div (7 + 3) = (7 \times 7 + 1) \div (7 + 3) = (49 + 1) \div 10 = 50 \div 10 = 5$$

Combining a calculator with an understanding of when and how to use it can help you boost your score.

Midway through the exam,
Allen pulls out a bigger brain.

F·A·S·T P·R·E·P

 CHAPTER CHECKLIST

Once you've mastered a concept, check it off:

GRID-INS

❏ THE FORMAT
❏ WHAT THE ANSWER GRID LOOKS LIKE
❏ KAPLAN'S GRID-IN INSTRUCTIONS

PANICPLAN

If you have a month or less to prep for the SAT, here's the best way to spend your time:

1: Read this entire chapter. It's pretty short and the gridding tips that we discuss can help prevent you from making careless mistakes that cost you points.

2: Do the gridding drills at the end of the chapter.

CHAPTER 11

GRID-INS: A NEW FORMAT

In high school math class, you usually don't get five answer choices to choose from on a test. And you don't lose a quarter of a point for a wrong answer. Instead, you are given a problem and you're asked to find the answer.

The new Grid-in section on the SAT is a lot like the math tests you're already used to taking. Unlike other questions on the SAT, Grid-ins have no multiple choice answers and there's no penalty for wrong answers. You have to figure out your own answer and fill it in on a special grid. Note that some Grid-ins have only one correct answer, while others have several, or even a range of correct answers.

THE FORMAT

You'll get 10 Grid-ins, following the QCs, in one of the Math Sections. To get an idea of what the instructions will look like on test day, turn the page.

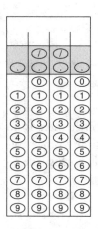

For each question, you'll see a grid with four boxes and a column of ovals beneath each. First write your numerical answer in the boxes, one digit, decimal point, or fraction sign per box. Then fill in the corresponding ovals below.

WARNING:

• *Fill in no more than one oval per column.*

• *Make the oval you grid match your number above.*

GRID-INS HAVE NO HEART

The fact that there's an entire chapter devoted to showing you how to do Grid-ins should tell you something: it's real easy to mess them up.

The SAT is scored by computer. If you write the correct answer in the boxes at the top of the grid but forget to grid in the bubbles, you don't get the points.

If you forget to convert a mixed number to a fraction or decimal equivalent, you won't get credit for your answer. The golden rule: be careful.

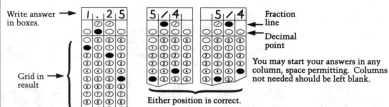

For each of the questions below (16-25), solve the problem and indicate your answer by darkening the ovals in the special grid. For example:

Answer: 1.25 or $\frac{5}{4}$ or 5/4

Write answer in boxes.

Grid in result

Either position is correct.

Fraction line

Decimal point

You may start your answers in any column, space permitting. Columns not needed should be left blank.

- It is recommended, though not required, that you write your answer in the boxes at the top of the columns. However, you will receive credit only for darkening the ovals correctly.

- Grid only one answer to a question, even though some problems have more than one correct answer.

- Darken no more than one oval in a column.

- No answers are negative.

- Mixed numbers cannot be gridded. For example: the number $1\frac{1}{4}$ must be gridded as 1.25 or 5/4.

(If [grid image] is gridded, it will be interpreted as $\frac{11}{4}$ not $1\frac{1}{4}$.)

- <u>Decimal Accuracy:</u> Decimal answers must be entered as accurately as possible. For example, if you obtain an answer such as 0.1666. . ., you should record the result as .166 or .167. **Less accurate values such as .16 or .17 are not acceptable.**

Acceptable ways to grid $\frac{1}{6}$ = .1666. . .

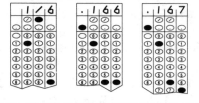

FILLING IN THE GRID

The grid cannot accommodate
- negative answers
- answers with variables
- answers greater than 9999
- answers with commas
- mixed numbers.

Recommendation: Start your answer in the first column box.
Do that even if your answer has only one or two figures. If you always start with the first column, your answers will always fit. Since there is no oval for zero in the first column, grid an answer of 0 in any other column. (Technically, you can start in any column, but follow this rule to avoid mistakes.)

In a fractional answer, grid (/) in the correct column.
The sign (/) separates the numerator from the denominator. It appears only in columns two and three.

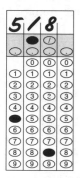

Example: If you get an answer of 5/8. Grid (/) in column two.

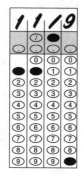

Example: If you get an answer of 11/9. Grid (/) in column three.

Warning: A fractional answer with four digits won't fit.

Change mixed numbers to decimals or fractions before you grid.

If you try to grid a mixed number, it will be read as a fraction, and be counted wrong. For example, $4\frac{1}{2}$ will be read as the fraction $\frac{41}{2}$, which is $20\frac{1}{2}$.

So first change mixed numbers to fractions or decimals, then grid in. In this case:

- change $4\frac{1}{2}$ to $\frac{9}{2}$ and grid in as shown below;

- or change $4\frac{1}{2}$ to 4.5 and grid in the decimal.

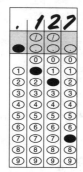

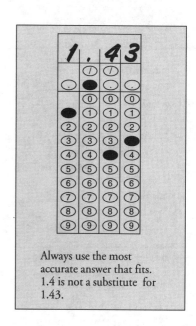

Always use the most accurate answer that fits. 1.4 is not a substitute for 1.43.

Watch where you put your decimal points.

- For a decimal less than 1, such as .127, enter the decimal point in the first box as shown in the figure above.

- Only put a zero before the decimal point if it's part of the answer—don't just put one there to make your answer *look* more accurate.

- Never grid a decimal point in the last column.

With long or repeating decimals, grid the first three digits only and plug in the decimal point where it belongs.

- Say three answers are .45454545, 82.452312, and 1.428743. Grid .454, 82.4, and 1.42 respectively.

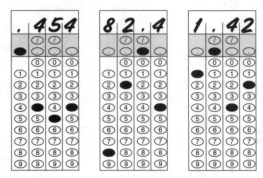

- You could round 1.428743 up to the nearest hundredth (1.43), but it's not required, so don't bother since you could make a mistake.
- Shorter, less accurate answers — such as 1.4 — are wrong.

On Grid-ins with more than one right answer, choose one, and enter it. Say you're asked for a two-digit integer that is a multiple of 2, 3, and 5. You might answer 30, 60, or 90. Whichever you grid would be right.

Some Grid-ins have a range of possible answers.

Suppose you're asked to grid a value of m—given that $1 - 2m < m$ and $5m - 2 < m$. Solving for m in the first inequality, you find that $\frac{1}{3} < m$. Solving for m in the second inequality, you find that $m < \frac{1}{2}$. So $\frac{1}{3} < m < \frac{1}{2}$. Grid in any value between $\frac{1}{3}$ and $\frac{1}{2}$. (Gridding in $\frac{1}{3}$ or $\frac{1}{2}$ would be wrong.) When the answer is a range of values, it's often easier to work with decimals: $.333 < m < .5$. Then you can quickly grid .4 (or .35 or .45, etc.) as your answer.

Write your answers in the number boxes.
You will make fewer mistakes if you write your answers in the number boxes.

You may think that gridding directly will save time, but writing first, then gridding, ensures accuracy, which means more points.

PRACTICE GRIDDING

With just a little practice, you can master the gridding-in process. Complete the Grid-ins below, following our instructions. After you finish, check your work with the grid on the next page.

126     $\dfrac{3}{8}$ 85.9   2,143 $5\dfrac{1}{2}$

0   .141414 $\dfrac{14}{5}$ $1\dfrac{2}{3}$ 8.175

GRIDDING ANSWERS

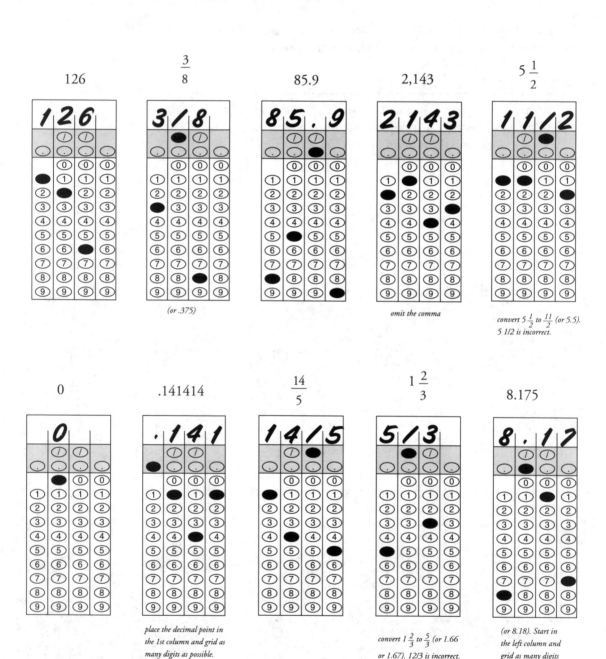

126

$\dfrac{3}{8}$

(or .375)

85.9

omit the comma

2,143

$5\dfrac{1}{2}$

convert $5\dfrac{1}{2}$ to $\dfrac{11}{2}$ (or 5.5).
5 1/2 is incorrect.

0

.141414

place the decimal point in
the 1st column and grid as
many digits as possible.

$\dfrac{14}{5}$

$1\dfrac{2}{3}$

convert $1\dfrac{2}{3}$ to $\dfrac{5}{3}$ (or 1.66
or 1.67). 12/3 is incorrect.

8.175

(or 8.18). Start in
the left column and
grid as many digits
as possible.

436 CASES OF POCKET CALCULATORS WITH 24 UNITS PER CASE, AT $3.69 PER UNIT, CARRY THE SEVEN..... PLUS NINE.... THAT COMES TO....UH.....WAIT.......... DANG! LET ME START OVER....
Adfast POCKET CALCULATORS
PIRARO © CHRONICLE FEATURES 1987

F·A·S·T P·R·E·P

✐ Chapter Checklist ✐

Once you've mastered a concept, check it off:

KAPLAN'S 6 STRATEGIES FOR QCs

❑ How to compare piece by piece
❑ How to make one column look like the other
❑ How to do the same thing to both columns
❑ The picking numbers strategy
❑ When to redraw the diagram
❑ QC traps

PanicPlan

If you have a month or less to prep for the SAT, here's the best way to spend your time:

1: Skim pp. 111 - 113.

2: Learn the two rules for choice (D) on page 112.

3: Do the practice problems on pp. 123 - 124. If you miss an answer, review the strategy before continuing.

CHAPTER 12

QUANTITATIVE COMPARISONS

In Quantitative Comparisons, instead of solving for a particular value, you need to compare two quantities. At first, QCs may appear really difficult because of their unfamiliar format. However, once you become used to them, they can be quicker and easier than the other types of math questions.

THE FORMAT

Where They Appear
The 15 QCs appear in the Math section that also contains the 10 Grid-in questions. They are arranged in order of increasing difficulty.

The Questions
In each question, you'll see two mathematical expressions. They are boxed, one in Column A, the other in Column B. Your job is to compare them.

Some questions include additional information about one or both quantities. This information is centered, unboxed, and essential to making the comparison.

> *HINT — To score high on QCs, learn what the answer choices stand for.*

The Directions
The directions you'll see will look something like those on the next page. Get familiar with them now.

THE ANSWER CHOICES

If you remember anything from this chapter, it should be a thorough understanding of the four answer choices.

You won't have time to keep referring back to the directions. You've got to know them cold.

A if Column A is greater

B if Column B is greater

C if the columns are equal

D if more information is needed to determine the relationship

E will not be scored

D-DAY

As soon as you find that more than one relationship is possible, you know the answer is (D). Don't waste your time looking for other possibilities.

DIRECTIONS FOR QUANTITATIVE COMPARISON QUESTIONS

Compare the boxed quantity in Column A with the boxed quantity in Column B. Select answer choice

  A if Column A is greater;
  B if Column B is greater;
  C if the columns are equal; or
  D if more information is needed to determine the relationship.
An E response will be treated as an omission.

Notes:

1. Some questions include information about one or both quantities. That information is centered and unboxed.
2. A symbol that appears in both Column A and Column B stands for the same thing in both columns.
3. All numbers used are real numbers.

EXAMPLES

	Column A	Column B	Answers
E1	3×4	$3 + 4$	● Ⓑ Ⓒ Ⓓ Ⓔ
E2	x	160	Ⓐ Ⓑ ● Ⓓ Ⓔ
E3	$x + 1$	$y - 1$	Ⓐ Ⓑ Ⓒ ● Ⓔ

(E2: angles $x°$ and $20°$)

(x and y are positive)

Warning! Never pick choice (E) as the answer to a QC.

TWO RULES FOR ANSWER CHOICE (D)

Choices (A), (B), and (C) all represent definite relationships between the quantities in Column A and Column B. But choice (D) represents a relationship that cannot be determined. Here are two things to remember about choice (D) that will help you decide when to pick it:

1. Choice (D) is never correct if both columns contain only numbers. The relationship between numbers is unchanging, but choice (D) means more than one relationship is possible.

2. Choice (D) is correct if you can demonstrate two different relationships between the columns. Suppose you ran across the following QC:

Column A	Column B
$2x$	$3x$

If x is a positive number, Column B is greater than Column A. If $x = 0$, the columns are equal. If x equals any negative number, Column B is less than Column A. Since more than one relationship is possible, the answer is (D). In fact, as soon as you find a second possibility, stop work and pick choice (D).

RULE OF THUMB

Usually there's a simpler way to solve a QC than using your calculator.

COMPARE, DON'T CALCULATE: KAPLAN'S 6 STRATEGIES

Here are 6 Kaplan strategies that will enable you to make quick comparisons. In the rest of this chapter you'll learn how they work and you'll try them on practice problems.

Strategy #1 — Compare piece by piece.
This works on QCs that compare two sums or two products.

Strategy #2 — Make one column look like the other.
This is a great approach when the columns look so different that you can't compare them directly.

Strategy #3 — Do the same thing to both columns.
Change both columns by adding, subtracting, multiplying, or dividing by the same amount on both sides in order to make the comparison more apparent.

Strategy #4 — Pick numbers.
Use this to get a handle on abstract algebra QCs.

Strategy #5 — Redraw the diagram.
Redrawing a diagram can clarify the relationships between measurements.

Strategy #6 — Avoid QC traps.
Stay alert for questions designed to fool you by leading you to the obvious, wrong answer.

Now learn how these strategies work.

STRATEGY 1: COMPARE PIECE BY PIECE

EXAMPLE

Column A Column B

$$w > x > 0 > y > z$$

w + y x + z

In the problem above, there are four variables—w, x, y, and z. Compare the value of each "piece" in each column. If every "piece" in one column is greater than a corresponding "piece" in the other column and the only operation involved is addition, the column with the greater individual values will have the greater total value.

From the given information we know that $w > x$ and $y > z$. Therefore, the first term in Column A, w, is greater than the first term in Column B, x. Similarly, the second term in Column A, y, is greater than the second term in Column B, z. Since each piece in Column A is greater than the corresponding piece in Column B, Column A must be greater; the answer is (A).

STRATEGY 2: MAKE ONE COLUMN LOOK LIKE THE OTHER

When the quantities in Columns A and B are expressed differently, you can often make the comparison easier by changing one column to look like the other. For example, if one column is a percent, and the other a fraction, try converting the percent to a fraction.

EXAMPLE

Column A	Column B
$x(x-1)$	$x^2 - x$

Here Column A has parentheses, and Column B doesn't. So make Column A look more like Column B: get rid of those parentheses. You end up with $x^2 - x$ in both columns, which means they are equal and the answer is (C).

Try another example, this time involving geometry.

EXAMPLE

Column A	Column B

The diameter of circle O is d and the area is a.

$$\frac{\pi d^2}{2} \qquad\qquad a$$

Make Column B look more like Column A by rewriting a, the area of the circle, in terms of the diameter, d. The area of any circle equals πr^2, where r is the radius.

Since the radius is half the diameter, we can plug in $\frac{d}{2}$ for r in the area formula to get $\pi(\frac{d}{2})^2$ in Column B. Simplifying we get $\frac{\pi d^2}{4}$. Since both columns contain π, we can simply compare $\frac{d^2}{2}$ with $\frac{d^2}{4}$. $\frac{d^2}{4}$ is half as much as $\frac{d^2}{2}$, and since d^2 must be positive, Column A is greater. Choice (A).

KAPLAN RULES

Lengths and areas are always greater than zero.

STRATEGY 3: DO THE SAME THING TO BOTH COLUMNS

Some QC questions become much clearer if you change not just the appearances, but the values of both columns. Treat them like two sides of an inequality, with the sign temporarily hidden.

You can add or subtract the same amount from both columns, and multiply or divide by the same positive amount without altering the relationship.

You can also square both columns if you're sure they're both positive. But watch out. Multiplying or dividing an inequality by a negative number reverses the direction of the inequality sign. Since it alters the relationship between the columns, avoid multiplying or dividing by a negative number.

> *HINT — Don't multiply or divide both QC columns by a negative number.*

In the QC below, what could you do to both columns?

EXAMPLE

Column A	Column B
$4a + 3 = 7b$	
$20a + 10$	$35b - 5$

All the terms in the two columns are multiples of 5, so divide both columns by 5 to simplify. You're left with $4a + 2$ in Column A and $7b - 1$ in Column B. This resembles the equation given in the centered information. In fact, if you add 1 to both columns, you have $4a + 3$ in Column A and $7b$ in Column B. The centered equation tells us they are equal. Thus choice (C) is correct.

RULE OF THUMB

There are a number of traps to watch out for in QCs. QC traps may appear anywhere in the QC section, but they occur most often near the end because QCs are arranged in order of difficulty.

For more on traps, see the Top Ten Math Traps chapter (p. 173).

In the next QC, what could you do to both columns?

EXAMPLE

Column A   Column B

$$y > 0$$

$1+ \dfrac{y}{(y+1)}$ $1+ \dfrac{1}{(1+y)}$

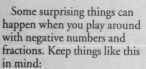

KAPLAN RULES

Some surprising things can happen when you play around with negative numbers and fractions. Keep things like this in mind:

When you square a positive fraction less than 1, the result is smaller than the original fraction.

When you square a negative number, the result is a positive number.

When you square 0 and 1, they stay the same.

Solution: First subtract 1 from both sides. That gives you $\dfrac{y}{(1 + y)}$ in Column A, and $\dfrac{1}{(1+y)}$ in Column B. Then multiply both sides by $(1 + y)$, which must be positive since y is positive. You're left comparing y with 1.

You know y is greater than 0, but it could be a fraction less than 1, so it could be greater or less than 1. Since you can't say for sure which column is greater, the answer is (D).

STRATEGY 4: PICK NUMBERS

If a QC involves variables, try picking numbers to make the relationship clearer. Here's what you do:

- Pick numbers that are easy to work with.
- Plug in the numbers and calculate the values. Note the relationship between the columns.
- Pick another number for each variable and calculate the values again.

EXAMPLE

Column A	Column B

$$r > s > t > w > 0$$

Column A	Column B
$\dfrac{r}{t}$	$\dfrac{s}{w}$

Try $r = 4$, $s = 3$, $t = 2$, and $w = 1$. Then Column A = $\dfrac{r}{t} = \dfrac{4}{2} = 2$. And Column B = $\dfrac{s}{w} = \dfrac{3}{1} = 3$. So in this case Column B is greater than Column A.

Always Pick More Than One Number and Calculate Again

In the example above, we first found Column B was bigger. But that doesn't mean Column B is always bigger and that the answer is (B). It does mean the answer is not (A) or (C). But the answer could still be (D) — not enough information to decide.

If time is short, guess between (B) and (D). But whenever you can, pick another set of numbers and calculate again.

As best you can, make a special effort to find a second set of numbers that will alter the relationship. Here for example, try making r a lot larger. Pick $r = 30$ and keep the other variables as they were. Now Column A = $\dfrac{30}{2}$ = 15. This time, Column A is greater than Column B, so answer choice (D) is correct.

> HINT— *If the relationship between Columns A and B changes when you pick other numbers, (D) must be the answer.*

Pick Different Kinds of Numbers

Don't assume all variables represent positive integers. Unless you're told otherwise, variables can represent zero, negative numbers, or fractions. Since different kinds of numbers behave differently, always pick a different kind of number the second time around. In the example above, we plugged

in a small positive number the first time and a larger number the second.

In the next three examples, we pick different numbers and get different results. Since we can't find constant relationships between Columns A and B, in all these cases the answer is (D).

DON'T OVER (D) IT

Choice (D) doesn't mean *you* can't determine which is greater — it means no one can.

If you frequently find (D) is your answer, double check your work.

EXAMPLES

Column A	Column B
w	−w

If $w = 5$, Column A = 5 and Column B = −5, so Column A is greater.
If $w = −5$, Column A = −5 and Column B = 5, so Column B is greater.

Column A	Column B
	$x \neq 0$
x	$\frac{1}{x}$

If $x = 3$, Column A = 3 and Column B = $\frac{1}{3}$, so Column A is greater.

If $x = \frac{1}{3}$, Column A = $\frac{1}{3}$ and Column B = $\frac{1}{\frac{1}{3}}$ = 3, so Column B is greater.

KAPLAN RULES

Remember:

Not all numbers are positive.

Not all numbers are integers.

Column A	Column B
x	x^2

If $x = \frac{1}{2}$, Column A = $\frac{1}{2}$ and Column B = $\frac{1}{4}$, so Column A is greater.

If $x = 2$, Column A = 2 and Column B = 4, so Column B is greater.

STRATEGY 5: REDRAW THE DIAGRAM

• Redraw a diagram if the one that's given misleads you.

• Redraw scale diagrams to exaggerate crucial differences.

Some geometry diagrams may be misleading. Two angles or lengths may look equal as drawn in the diagram, but the given information tells you that there is a slight difference in their measures. The best strategy is to redraw the diagram so that their relationship can be clearly seen.

EXAMPLE

Column A   Column B

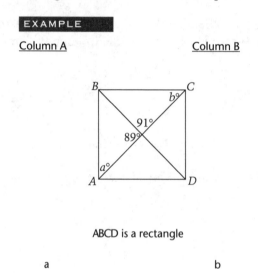

ABCD is a rectangle

a   b

Redraw this diagram to exaggerate the difference between the 89-degree angle and the 91-degree angle. In other words, make the larger angle much larger, and the smaller angle much smaller. The new rectangle that results is much wider than it is tall.

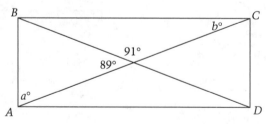

In the new diagram, where the crucial difference jumps out, a is clearly greater than b.

STRATEGY 6. AVOID QC TRAPS

To avoid QC traps, always be alert. Don't assume anything. Be especially cautious near the end of the question set.

Don't Be Tricked by Misleading Information

EXAMPLE

Column A   Column B

John is taller than Bob.

John's weight in pounds   Bob's weight in pounds

The testmakers hope you think, "If John is taller, he must weigh more." But there's no guaranteed relationship between height and weight, so you don't have enough information. The answer is (D). Fortunately, problems like this are easy to spot if you stay alert.

Don't Assume

A common QC mistake is to assume that variables represent positive integers. As we saw in using the Picking Numbers strategy, fractions or negative numbers often show another relationship between the columns.

EXAMPLE

Column A   Column B

When 1 is added to the square of x the result is 37.

x   6

It is easy to assume that x must be 6, since the square of x is 36. That would make choice (C) correct. However, it is possible that $x = -6$. Since x could be either 6 or -6, the answer is (D).

HINT — Be aware of negative numbers!

Don't Forget to Consider Other Possibilities

Column A		Column B
	R	
	S	
	T	
	—	
	1W	

In the addition problem above, R, S, and T are different digits that are multiples of 3, and W is a digit.

W	8

Since you're told that *R*, *S*, and *T* are digits and different multiples of 3, most people will think of 3, 6, and 9, which add up to 18. That makes *W* equal to 8, and Columns A and B equal. But that's too obvious for a QC at the end of the section.

There's another possibility. 0 is also a multiple of 3. So the three digits could be 0, 3, and 9, or 0, 6, and 9, which give totals of 12 and 15, respectively. That means *W* could be 8, 2, or 5. Since the columns could be equal, or Column B could be greater, answer choice (D) must be correct.

Don't Fall for Look-Alikes

EXAMPLE

Column A	Column B
$\sqrt{5} + \sqrt{5}$	$\sqrt{10}$

At first glance, forgetting the rules of radicals, you might think these quantities are equal and that the answer is (C). But use some common sense to see this isn't the case. Each $\sqrt{5}$ in Column A is bigger than $\sqrt{4}$, so Column A is more than 4. The $\sqrt{10}$ in Column B is less than another familiar number, $\sqrt{16}$, so Column B is less than 4. The answer is (A).

Now use Kaplan's 6 strategies to solve nine typical QC questions. Then check your work against our solutions.

TEST YOUR QC SMARTS

Column A	Column B

1. $x^2 + 2x - 2$ $x^2 + 2x - 1$

$$x = 2y$$
$$y > 0$$

2. 4^{2y} 2^x

$$\frac{x}{y} = \frac{z}{4}$$

x, y, and z are positive

3. $6x$ $2yz$

---

q, r, and s are positive integers
$$qrs > 12$$

4. $\dfrac{qr}{5}$ $\dfrac{3}{s}$

$$x > 1$$
$$y > 0$$

5. y^x $y^{(x+1)}$

$$7p + 3 = r$$
$$3p + 7 = s$$

6. r s

In triangle XYZ, the measure of angle X equals the measure of angle Y.

7. The degree measure of angle Z   The degree measure of angle X plus the degree measure of angle Y

$$h > 1$$

8. The number of minutes in h hours $\dfrac{60}{h}$

123

Column A	Column B

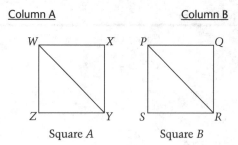

Square *A*   Square *B*

Note: Figures not drawn to scale.

9. $\dfrac{\text{Perimeter of square } A}{\text{Perimeter of square } B}$ $\dfrac{\text{Length of } WY}{\text{Length of } PR}$

ANSWER KEY

1. (B)

Comparing the respective pieces of the two columns, the only difference is the third piece: -2 in Column A and -1 in Column B. We don't know the value of x, but whatever it is, x^2 in Column A must have the same value as x^2 in Column B, and $2x$ in Column A must have the same value as $2x$ in Column B. Since any quantity minus 2 must be less than that quantity minus 1, Column B is greater than Column A.

2. (A)

Replacing the x exponent in Column B with the equivalent value given in the problem, we're comparing 4^{2y} to 2^{2y}. Since y is greater than zero, raising 4 to the $2y$ power will result in a greater value than raising 2 to the $2y$ power.

3. (B)

Do the same thing to both columns until they resemble the centered information. When we divide both columns by $6y$ we get $\frac{6x}{6y}$, or $\frac{x}{y}$ in Column A, and $\frac{2yz}{6y}$, or $\frac{z}{3}$ in Column B. Since $\frac{x}{y} = \frac{z}{4}$, and $\frac{z}{3} > \frac{z}{4}$ (because z is positive), $\frac{z}{3} > \frac{x}{y}$.

4. (D)

Do the same thing to both columns to make them look like the centered information. When we multiply both columns by $5s$ we get qrs in Column A and 15 in Column B. Since qrs could be any integer greater than 12, it could be greater than, equal to, or less than 15.

5. (D)

Try $x = y = 2$. Then Column A = $y^x = 2^2 = 4$. Column B = $y^{x+1} = 2^3 = 8$, making Column B greater. But if $x = 2$ and $y = \frac{1}{2}$, Column A = $(\frac{1}{2})^2 = \frac{1}{4}$ and Column B = $(\frac{1}{2})^3 = \frac{1}{8}$. In this case, Column A is greater than Column B, so the answer is (D).

6. (D)

Pick a value for p, and see what effect this has on r and s. If $p = 1$, $r = (7 \times 1) + 3 = 10$, and $s = (3 \times 1) + 7 = 10$, and the two columns are equal. But if $p = 0$, $r = (7 \times 0) + 3 = 3$, and $s = (3 \times 0) + 7 = 7$, and Column A is smaller than Column B. Since there are at least two different possible relationships, the answer is choice (D).

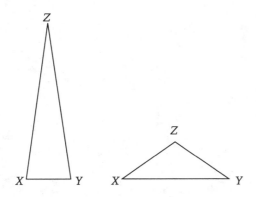

7. (D)

Since angle X = angle Y, this is an isosceles triangle. We can draw two diagrams with X and Y as the base angles of an isosceles triangle. In one diagram, make the triangle tall and narrow, so that angle X and angle Y are very large, and angle Z is very small. In this case, column B is greater. In the second diagram, make the triangle short and wide, so that angle Z is much larger than angle X and angle Y. In this case, Column A is greater. Since more than one relationship between the columns is possible, the correct answer is choice (D).

8. (A)

The "obvious" answer here is choice (C), because there are 60 minutes in an hour, and 60 appears in Column B. But the number of minutes in h hours would equal 60 times h, not 60 divided by h. Since h is greater than 1, the number in Column B will be less than the actual number of minutes in h hours, so Column A is greater. (A) is correct.

9. (C)

We don't know the exact relationship between Square *A* and Square *B*, but it doesn't matter. The problem is actually just comparing the ratios of corresponding parts of two squares. Whatever the relationship between them is for one specific length in both squares, the same relationship will exist between them for any other corresponding length. If a side of one square is twice the length of a side of the second square, the diagonal will also be twice as long. The ratio of the perimeters of the two squares is the same as the ratio of the sides. Therefore, the columns are equal. (C) is correct.

F·A·S·T P·R·E·P

☞ CHAPTER CHECKLIST ☜

Once you've mastered a concept, check it off:

PROBLEM-SOLVING TECHNIQUES

- ❑ REMAINDERS
- ❑ AVERAGES
- ❑ RATIOS
- ❑ RATES
- ❑ PERCENTS
- ❑ COMBINATIONS
- ❑ EQUATIONS
- ❑ SYMBOLISM
- ❑ SPECIAL TRIANGLES
- ❑ MULTIPLE FIGURES

😱 PanicPlan 😱

If you have a month or less to prep for the SAT, here's the best way to spend your time:

1: In each of the ten sections, try the sample problems.

2: Review any section where you have trouble.

CHAPTER 13

CLASSIC PROBLEM-SOLVING TECHNIQUES

The testmakers are not paid to be creative. In fact, there are certain types of problems that they like to use again and again on the SAT. This chapter gives you ten of their favorite question types, along with Kaplan's classic techniques for solving these kinds of problems.

REMAINDERS

Remainder questions can be easier than they look. You might think you have to solve for a certain value, but often you don't.

> **EXAMPLE**
>
> When n is divided by 7, the remainder is 4. What is the remainder when 2n is divided by 7?
> (A) 0
> (B) 1
> (C) 2
> (D) 3
> (E) 4

The question above doesn't depend on knowing the value of *n*. In fact, *n* has an infinite number of possible values.

HINT — Pick a number for n.

Which number should you pick? Since the remainder when *n* is divided by 7 is 4, pick any multiple of 7 and add 4. The easiest multiple to work with is 7. So, 7 + 4 = 11. Use 11 for *n*.

Plug 11 into the question and see what happens:

---

7 THINGS MORE DIFFICULT THAN SAT MATH

1. Open heart surgery
2. Dunking on Michael Jordan
3. Finding Sinatra on MTV
4. Getting Dead Tickets
5. Beating curfew without getting caught
6. Reading Moby Dick without falling asleep
7. Getting a date for the prom

• What is the remainder when $2n$ is divided by 7?

-the remainder when 2(11) is divided by 7?

-the remainder when 22 is divided by 7?

$$\frac{22}{7} = 3 \text{ remainder } 1$$

The remainder is 1 when $n = 11$. So the answer is (B). The remainder will also be 1 when $n = 18, 25,$ or 46.

QC Remainders

EXAMPLE

Column A	Column B

When p is divided by 5 the remainder is 3.
When q is divided by 5 the remainder is 4.

p	q

The centered information tells you that p can be any of the integers 3, 8, 13, 18, 23,...; and that q can be any of the integers 4, 9, 14, 19, 24,....

So how do p and q compare? You can't tell. p could be small and q big, or the other way around. The answer is (D), not enough information to decide.

PRACTICE PROBLEMS: REMAINDERS

REGULAR MATH

1. When z is divided by 8, the remainder is 5. What is the remainder when 4z is divided by 8?

   (A) 1
   (B) 3
   (C) 4
   (D) 5
   (E) 7

QC

Column A	Column B

When x is divided by 6 the remainder is 3.
When y is divided by 6 the remainder is 4.

2.   x   y

When m is divided by 5 the remainder is 2.
When n is divided by 5 the remainder is 1.

3. The remainder   The remainder when
   when m + n is   mn is divided by 5
   divided by 5

ANSWER KEY

1. (C)

Let $z = 13$ and plug in $4z = 4(13) = 52$, which leaves a remainder of 4 when divided by 8.

2. (D)

x can be any of the integers 3, 9, 15, 21,..., and y can be any of the integers 4, 10, 16, 22,.... Since x could be greater than or less than y, the correct answer must be choice (D).

3. (A)

m can be any integer that ends in either a 2 or a 7; n can be any integer that ends in either a 1 or a 6. Plugging in will show that in any case, $m + n$ will leave a remainder of 3 when divided by 5, and mn will leave a remainder of 2 when divided by 5, so Column A is greater.

AVERAGES

> **EXAMPLE**
>
> The average weight of 5 dogs in a certain kennel is 32 pounds. If four of the dogs weigh 25, 27, 19, and 35 pounds, what is the weight of the fifth dog?
> (A) 28
> (B) 32
> (C) 49
> (D) 54
> (E) 69

USE YOUR HEAD

Use common sense to learn about the size of the value you're asked to find. If all the terms listed are less than the given average, then the unknown term must be greater than the average to balance it out.

Likewise, if adding a new value, x, to a group of numbers raises the average value of the group, then x must be greater than the average of the original numbers.

Instead of giving you a list of values to plug into the average formula, SAT average questions often put a slight spin on the problem. They tell you the average of a group of terms and ask you to find the value of the missing term.

HINT— Work with the sum.

Let x = the weight of the fifth dog. Plug this into the average formula:

$$32 = \frac{25 + 27 + 19 + 35 + x}{5}$$

$$32 \times 5 = 25 + 27 + 19 + 35 + x$$

So the average weight of the dogs, times the number of dogs, equals the total weight of the dogs, or mathematically:

Average $\times$ Number of Terms = Sum of Terms

Remember this manipulation of the average formula so that whenever you know the average of a group of terms and the number of terms, you can find the total sum.

Now you can solve for the weight of the fifth dog:

$$32 \times 5 = 25 + 27 + 19 + 35 + x$$
$$160 = 106 + x$$
$$54 = x$$

So the weight of the fifth dog is 54 pounds, choice (D).

CALCULATOR FUN

This is a good time to use your calculator. Enjoy yourself.

PRACTICE PROBLEMS: AVERAGES

1. The average (arithmetic mean) of 6 numbers is 16. If five of the numbers are 15, 37, 16, 9, and 23, what is the sixth number?

   (A) −20

   (B) − 4

   (C)   0

   (D)   6

   (E)   16

2. Bart needs to buy 5 gifts with $80. If two of the gifts cost a total of $35, what is the average (arithmetic mean) amount Bart can spend on each of the remaining three gifts?

   (A) $45

   (B) $17

   (C) $16

   (D) $15

   (E) $10

3. The average (arithmetic mean) of five numbers is 8. If the average of two of these numbers is −6, what is the sum of the other three numbers?

   (A) 28

   (B) 34

   (C) 46

   (D) 52

   (E) 60

ANSWER KEY

1. (B)

Average $\times$ Number of Terms = Sum of Terms;

$16 \times 6 = 15 + 37 + 16 + 9 + 23 + x$

$\quad 96 = 100 + x$

$\quad -4 = x$

2. (D)

Bart has $80 and spent $35 on 2 gifts; therefore he has $45 left to spend on the remaining three. So,

$x = \dfrac{\$45}{3}$

$x = \$15$

3. (D)

Average $\times$ Number of Terms = Sum of Terms;

The sum of all five numbers is

$$8 \times 5 = 40$$

The sum of two of these numbers is

$$(-6) \times 2 = -12$$

So, the difference of these two sums, $40 - (-12) = 52$, is the sum of the other numbers.

RATIOS

EXAMPLE

Out of every 50 chips produced in a certain factory, 20 are defective. What is the ratio of non-defective chips produced to defective chips produced?

(A) 2:5

(B) 3:5

(C) 2:3

(D) 3:2

(E) 5:2

HINT — Identify the parts and the whole in the problem.

Find the parts and the whole in the problem. In this case the total number of chips is the whole, and the number of non-defective chips and the number of defective chips are the parts that make up this whole.

You're given a part-to-whole ratio — the ratio of defective chips to all chips, and asked to find a part-to-part ratio — the ratio of non-defective chips to defective chips.

If 20 chips out of every 50 are defective, the remaining 30 chips must be non-defective. So the part-to-part ratio of non-defective to defective chips is 30/20, or 3/2, which is equivalent to 3:2. Answer choice (D).

If you hadn't identified the part and the whole first it would be easy to get confused and compare a part to the whole, like the ratios in answer choices (A) and (B).

This approach also works for ratio questions where you need to find actual quantities. For example:

> Out of every 5 chips produced in a certain factory, 2 are defective. If 2,200 chips were produced, how many were defective?

Here you need to find a quantity—the number of defective chips.

HINT — If you're looking for the actual quantities in a ratio, set up and solve a proportion.

You're given a part-to-whole ratio (the ratio of defective chips to all chips), and the total number of chips produced. You can find the answer by setting up and solving a proportion:

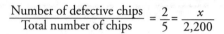
$$\frac{\text{Number of defective chips}}{\text{Total number of chips}} = \frac{2}{5} = \frac{x}{2,200}$$

$x =$ Number of defective chips

$5x = 4,400$

$x = 880$

HINT — Remember that ratios only compare relative size — they don't tell you the actual quantities involved.

KAPLAN RULES

When you look at a ratio, make sure you know if you're dealing with *parts* to *parts* or *parts* to *whole*.

You also need to see if the parts that you're given add up to the whole. For example, the number of male and female students in a classroom must add up to the whole. The number of students with blonde hair and the number of students with brown hair are parts, but do not necessarily add up to the whole.

PRACTICE PROBLEMS: RATIOS

REGULAR MATH

1. The ratio of right-handed pitchers to left-handed pitchers in a certain baseball league is 11 to 7. What fractional part of the pitchers in the league are left-handed?

   (A) $\frac{6}{7}$

   (B) $\frac{6}{11}$

   (C) $\frac{7}{11}$

   (D) $\frac{7}{18}$

   (E) $\frac{11}{18}$

---

2. In a group of 24 people who are either homeowners or renters, the ratio of homeowners to renters is 5:3. How many homeowners are in the group?

   (A) 15
   (B) 14
   (C) 12
   (D)   9
   (E)   8

---

3. Magazine A has a total of 28 pages, 16 of which are advertisements and 12 of which are articles. Magazine B has a total of 35 pages, all of them either advertisements or articles. If the ratio of the number of pages of advertisements to the number of pages of articles is the same for both magazines, then Magazine B has how many more pages of advertisements than Magazine A?

   (A) 2
   (B) 3
   (C) 4
   (D) 5
   (E) 6

ANSWER KEY

1. (D)

The parts are the number of right-handed (11) and the number of left-handed pitchers (7). The whole is the total number of pitchers (right-handed + left-handed) which is 11 + 7, or 18.

So $\dfrac{\text{part}}{\text{whole}} = \dfrac{\text{left-handed}}{\text{total}} = \dfrac{7}{11 + 7} = \dfrac{7}{18}$.

2. (A)

The parts are the number of homeowners (5) and the number of renters (3). The whole is the total (homeowners + renters). So $\dfrac{\text{part}}{\text{whole}} =$

$\dfrac{\text{Homeowners}}{\text{Homeowners + Renters}} = \dfrac{5}{5 + 3} = \dfrac{5}{8}$. Since we are trying to find an actual quantity, set up a proportion.

$$\dfrac{\text{Homeowners}}{\text{Total people}} = \dfrac{5}{8} = \dfrac{x}{24}$$
$$8x = 120$$
$$x = 15$$

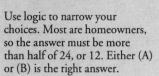

TIME TROUBLE?

Use logic to narrow your choices. Most are homeowners, so the answer must be more than half of 24, or 12. Either (A) or (B) is the right answer.

3. (C)

The $\dfrac{\text{part}}{\text{whole}}$ ratio of advertisements (16) to total pages (28) in Magazine *A*

is $\dfrac{16}{28}$, or $\dfrac{4}{7}$. Magazine *B* has the same ratio, so if there are 35 pages in

Magazine *B*, $\dfrac{4}{7} \times 35$, or 20 pages are advertisements. Therefore, there are

4 more pages of advertisements in Magazine *B* than in Magazine *A*.

RATES

EXAMPLE

If 8 oranges cost a dollars, b oranges would cost how many dollars?

(A) 8ab

(B) $\frac{8a}{b}$

(C) $\frac{8}{ab}$

(D) $\frac{a}{8b}$

(E) $\frac{ab}{8}$

A rate is a ratio that compares quantities that are measured in different units. In the problem above the units are oranges and dollars.

What makes the rate problem above difficult is the presence of variables. It's hard to get a clear picture of the relationship between the units.

HINT — Pick numbers for the variables to make the relationship between the units clearer.

Pick numbers for a and b that are easy to work with in the problem.

Let $a = 16$. Then 8 oranges cost 16 dollars. So the cost per orange at this rate is $\frac{16 \text{ dollars}}{8 \text{ oranges}} = 2$ dollars per orange.

Let $b = 5$. So the cost of 5 oranges at this rate is 5 oranges $\times$ 2 dollars per orange = 10 dollars.

Now plug in $a = 16$ and $b = 5$ into the answer choices to see which one gives you a value of 10.

Choice (A): $8 \times 16 \times 5 = 640$. Eliminate.

Choice (B): $\frac{8 \times 16}{5} = \frac{128}{5}$. Eliminate.

Choice (C): $\frac{8}{16 \times 5} = \frac{1}{10}$. Eliminate.

Choice (D): $\frac{16}{8 \times 5} = \frac{2}{5}$. Eliminate.

Choice (E): $\frac{16 \times 5}{8} = 10$.

Since (E) is the only one that gives the correct value, it is correct.

PRACTICE PROBLEMS: RATES

REGULAR MATH

1. If David paints at the rate of h houses per day, how many houses does he paint in d days, in terms of h and d?

   (A) $\dfrac{h}{d}$

   (B) hd

   (C) $h + \dfrac{d}{2}$

   (D) $h - d$

   (E) $\dfrac{d}{h}$

WARNING

Remember to try all the answer choices when picking numbers. If two or more choices give you the correct value, try another set of numbers on those choices only. (See Chapter 9)

2. Bill has to type a paper that is p pages long, where each page contains w words. If Bill types an average of x words per minute, how many hours will it take him to finish the paper?

   (A) $60wpx$

   (B) $\dfrac{wx}{60p}$

   (C) $\dfrac{60wp}{x}$

   (D) $\dfrac{wpx}{60}$

   (E) $\dfrac{wp}{60x}$

3. If Seymour drove 120 miles in x hours at constant speed, how many miles did he travel in the first twenty minutes of his trip?

   (A) $60x$

   (B) $3x$

   (C) $\dfrac{120}{x}$

   (D) $\dfrac{40}{x}$

   (E) $\dfrac{6}{x}$

ANSWER KEY

1. (B)

Pick numbers for h and d. Let $h = 2$ and $d = 3$; that is, suppose he paints 2 houses per day and he paints for 3 days, so in 3 days he can paint 6 houses. You are multiplying the rate (h) by the number of days (d). The only answer choice that equals 6 when $h = 2$ and $d = 3$ is choice (B).

2. (E)

Pick numbers for p, w, and x that work well in the problem. Let $p = 3$ and let $w = 100$. So there are 3 pages with 100 words per page, or 300 words total. Say he types 5 words a minute, so $x = 5$. So he types 5×60, or 300 words an hour. Therefore, it takes him 1 hour to type the paper. The only answer choice that equals 1 when $p = 3$, $w = 100$, and $x = 5$ is choice (E).

3. (D)

Let $x = 4$. That means that he drove 120 miles in 4 hours, so his speed was $\frac{120 \text{ miles}}{4 \text{ hours}}$, or 30 miles per hour. Since 20 minutes = $\frac{1}{3}$ of an hour, the distance he traveled in the first 20 minutes is $\frac{1}{3}$ hours $\times$ 30 miles per hour = 10 miles. The only answer choice that equals 10 when $x = 4$ is choice (D).

PERCENTS

> **EXAMPLE**
>
> Last year Julie's annual salary was $20,000. This year's raise brings her to an annual salary of $25,000. If she gets the same percent raise every year, what will her salary be next year?
> (A) $27,500
> (B) $30,000
> (C) $31,250
> (D) $32,500
> (E) $35,000

In percent problems, you're usually given two pieces of information and asked to find the third. When you see a percent problem, remember:

• If you are solving for a percent:

$$\text{Percent} = \frac{\text{Part}}{\text{Whole}}$$

• If you need to solve for a part:

$$\text{Percent} \times \text{Whole} = \text{Part}$$

This problem asks for Julie's projected salary for next year—that is, her current salary plus her next raise.

You know last year's salary ($20,000) and you know this year's salary ($25,000), so you can find the difference between the two salaries:

$25,000 - $20,000 = $5,000 = her raise.

Now find the percent of her raise, by using the formula

"$\text{Percent} = \frac{\text{Part}}{\text{Whole}}$."

Since Julie's raise was calculated on last year's salary, divide by $20,000.

> *HINT — Be sure you know which whole to plug in. Here you're looking for a percent of $20,000, not $25,000.*

$$\text{Percent raise} = \frac{\$5,000}{\$20,000} = \frac{1}{4} = 25\%.$$

You know she will get the same percent raise next year, so solve for the part. Use the formula Percent × Whole = Part.

Her raise next year will be $25\% \times \$25,000 = \frac{1}{4} \times 25,000 = \$6,250.$

MIRROR IMAGE

x percent of $y = y$ percent of x

20% of 50 = 50% of 20

$$\frac{1}{5} \times 50 = \frac{1}{2} \times 20$$

$$10 = 10$$

Add that sum to this year's salary and you have her projected salary: $25,000 + $6,250 = $31,250 or answer choice (C).

Make sure that you change the percent to either a fraction or a decimal before beginning calculations.

PRACTICE PROBLEMS: PERCENTS

QC

Column A	Column B
1. 5% of 3% of 45	6.75

GRID-IN

2. Eighty-five percent of the members of a student organization registered to attend a certain field trip. If 16 of the members who registered were unable to attend, resulting in only 65 percent of the members making the trip, how many members are in the organization?

REGULAR MATH

3. If a sweater sells for $48 after a 25 percent markdown, what was its original price?
   (A) $56
   (B) $60
   (C) $64
   (D) $68
   (E) $72

ANSWER KEY

1. (B)

Percent × Whole = Part. 5% of (3% of 45) = .05 × (.03 × 45) = .05 × 1.35= .0675, which is less than 6.75 in Column B.

2. (80)

You need to solve for the Whole, so identify the Part and the Percent. If 85% planned to attend and only 65% did, 20% failed to attend, and you know that 16 students failed to attend.

$$\text{Percent} \times \text{Whole} = \text{Part}$$
$$\frac{20}{100} \times \text{Whole} = 16$$
$$\text{Whole} = 16 \times \frac{100}{20}$$
$$\text{Whole} = 80$$

3. (C)

We want to solve for the original price, the Whole. The percent markdown is 25%, so $48 is 75% of the whole: Percent × Whole = Part

$$75\% \times \text{Original Price} = \$48$$
$$\text{Original Price} = \frac{\$48}{0.75} = \$64.$$

COMBINATIONS

> **EXAMPLE**
>
> If Alice, Betty, and Carlos sit in three adjacent empty seats in a movie house, how many different seating arrangements are possible?
> (A) 3
> (B) 4
> (C) 5
> (D) 6
> (E) 8

Combination problems ask you to find the different possibilities that can occur in a given situation.

HINT — Simply count the number of possibilities by listing them in a quick but systematic way.

To solve this problem, let the first letter of each name stand for that person. First, find all the combinations with Alice in the first seat:

ABC

ACB

Using the same system, try Betty in the first seat, and then Carlos:

BAC

BCA

CAB

CBA

At this point we've exhausted every possibility. So there are six possible arrangements, and that's answer choice (D).

Some problems set up conditions that limit the possibilities somewhat. Some may ask for the number of distinct possibilities, meaning that if the same combination shows up twice in different forms, you should only count it once. Consider the following problem:

EXAMPLE

Set I: {2, 3, 4, 5}
Set II: {1, 2, 3}

If x is a number generated by multiplying a number from Set I by a number from Set II, how many possible values of x are greater than 5?

(A) 3
(B) 4
(C) 5
(D) 6
(E) 7

Again, list the possibilities in a systematic way, pairing off each number in the first set with each number in the second set, so every combination is included:

$2 \times 1 = 2 \quad 4 \times 1 = 4$

$2 \times 2 = 4 \quad 4 \times 2 = 8$

$2 \times 3 = 6 \quad 4 \times 3 = 12$

$3 \times 1 = 3 \quad 5 \times 1 = 5$

$3 \times 2 = 6 \quad 5 \times 2 = 10$

$3 \times 3 = 9 \quad 5 \times 3 = 15$

How many of these values are greater than 5? Going down the list: 6, 6, 9, 8, 12, 10, and 15. Although there are seven answers where x is greater than 5, two of them are the same. So there are six different values of x greater than 5, not seven. The answer is (D).

HINT — Always write down the possibilities as you organize them, so you can count them accurately, and so you don't count the same combination twice.

PRACTICE PROBLEMS: COMBINATIONS

REGULAR MATH

1. A three-digit code is made up of three different digits from the set {2,4,6,8}. If 2 is always the first digit in the code, how many three-digit codes can be formed?

   (A)   16
   (B)   12
   (C)   10
   (D)   8
   (E)   6

QC

Column A   Column B

Five people attend a meeting. Each person shakes hands once with every other person at the meeting.

2. The total number   15
   of handshakes that
   take place

REGULAR MATH

3. Three people stop for lunch at a hot dog stand. If each person orders one item and there are three items to choose from, how many different combinations of food could be purchased? (Assume that order doesn't matter; e.g., a hot dog and two sodas are considered the same as two sodas and a hot dog.)

   (A)   6
   (B)   9
   (C)   10
   (D)   18
   (E)   27

ANSWER KEY

1. (E)
Every code starts with 2, so the last two digits determine the number of possibilities. The last two digits could be: 46, 48, 64, 68, 84, and 86. That makes 6 combinations that fit the conditions.

2. (B)
Be careful not to count each handshake twice. Call the 5 people *A, B, C, D,* and *E.* We can pair them off like this:

A with *B, C, D,* and *E* (4 handshakes)

B with *C, D,* and *E* (3 more — note that we leave out *A,* since the handshake between *A* and *B* is already counted)

C with *D* and *E* (2 more)

D with *E* (1 more)

The total is 4 + 3 + 2 + 1, or 10 handshakes.

3. (C)
To find the number, let's call the three items they can purchase *A, B,* and *C.* The possibilities:

All three order the same thing: *AAA, BBB, CCC*

Two order the same thing: *AAB, AAC, BBA, BBC, CCA, CCB*

All three order something different: *ABC*

So there are 10 different ways the three items could be ordered.

SIMULTANEOUS EQUATIONS

EXAMPLE

If p + 2q = 14 and 3p + q = 12, then p =
(A) −2
(B) −1
(C)   1
(D)   2
(E)   3

In order to get a numerical value for each variable, you need as many different equations as there are variables to solve for. So, if you have 2 variables, you need 2 independent equations.

You could tackle this problem by solving for one variable in terms of the other, and then plugging this expression into the other equation.

But the simultaneous equations that appear on the SAT can usually be handled in an easier way.

HINT — Combine the equations — by adding or subtracting them — to cancel out all but one of the variables.

You can't eliminate p or q by adding or subtracting the equations in their present form.

But if you multiply the second equation by 2:

$2(3p + q) = 2(12)$

$6p + 2q = 24$

Now when you subtract the first equation from the second, the q's will cancel out so you can solve for p:

$$6p + 2q = 24$$
$$-[p + 2q = 14]$$
$$\overline{}$$
$$5p + 0 = 10$$

If $5p = 10$, $p = 2$

REMEMBER

When subtracting one equation from another, be sure to distribute the minus sign to each term. In this example,

$-p - 2q = -14$

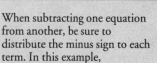

RULE OF THUMB

Simultaneous equations on the SAT are almost always easy to combine.

PRACTICE PROBLEMS: SIMULTANEOUS EQUATIONS

REGULAR MATH

1. If $x + y = 8$ and $y - x = -2$, then $y =$
   (A) -2
   (B) 3
   (C) 5
   (D) 8
   (E) 10

GRID-IN

2. If $4a + 3b = 19$ and $a + 2b = 6$, then $a + b =$

REGULAR MATH

3. If $m - n = 5$ and $2m + 3n = 15$, then $m + n =$
   (A) 1
   (B) 6
   (C) 7
   (D) 10
   (E) 15

ANSWER KEY

1. (B)

When you add the two equations, the x's cancel out and you find that $2y = 6$, so $y = 3$.

2. (5)

Adding the two equations, you find that $5a + 5b = 25$. Dividing by 5 shows that $a + b = 5$.

3. (C)

Multiply the first equation by 2, then subtract the first equation from the second to eliminate the m's and find that $5n = 5$, or $n = 1$. Plugging this value for n into the first equation shows that $m = 6$, so $m + n = 7$, choice (C).

$$
\begin{array}{lll}
2m + 3n = 15 & m - n = 5 & m + n = 6 + 1 = 7 \\
\underline{-2m + 2n = -10} & m - 1 = 5 & \\
\quad\quad 5n = 5 & m = 6 & \\
\quad\quad\ \ n = 1 & &
\end{array}
$$

SYMBOLISM

EXAMPLE

If $a \star b = \sqrt{a + b}$ for all non-negative numbers, what is the value of $10 \star 6$?

(A) 0

(B) 2

(C) 4

(D) 8

(E) 16

You should be quite familiar with the arithmetic symbols $+$, $-$, $\times$, $\div$, and %. Finding the value of $10 + 2$, $18 - 4$, 4×9, or $96 \div 16$ is easy.

However, on the SAT, you may come across bizarre symbols. You may even be asked to find the value of $10 \star 2$, $5 \divideontimes 7$, $10 \divideontimes 6$, or $65 \heartsuit 2$.

The SAT testmakers put strange symbols in questions to confuse or unnerve you. Don't let them. The question stem always tells you what the strange symbol means. Although this type of question may look difficult, it is really an exercise in plugging in.

To solve, just plug in 10 for a and 6 for b into the expression $\sqrt{a + b}$. That equals $\sqrt{10 + 6}$ or $\sqrt{16}$ or 4, choice (C).

How about a more involved symbolism question?

EXAMPLE

If a ▲ means to multiply a by 3 and a ✹ means to divide a by -2, what is the value of $((8 ✹) ▲) ✹$?

(A) -6

(B) 0

(C) 2

(D) 3

(E) 6

HINT — When a symbolism problem includes parentheses, do the operations inside the parentheses first.

First find 8✹. This means to divide 8 by -2, which is -4. Working out to the next set of parentheses, we have $(-4)▲$, which means to multiply -4 by 3, which is -12. Lastly, we find (-12) ✹, which means to divide -12 by -2, which is 6, choice E.

HINT — When two or three questions include the same symbol, expect the last question to be the most difficult, and be extra careful.

PRACTICE PROBLEMS: SYMBOLISM

QC

Column A	Column B

If $x \neq 0$, let $\spadesuit\, x$ be defined by $\spadesuit\, x = x - \dfrac{1}{x}$

1. -3 $\spadesuit -3$

REGULAR MATH

2. If $r \heartsuit s = r(r - s)$ for all integers r and s, then $4 \heartsuit (3 \heartsuit 5)$ equals

(A) -8
(B) -2
(C) 2
(D) 20
(E) 40

Questions 3 – 4 refer to the following definition:

$c \star d = \dfrac{(c - d)}{c}$, where $c \neq 0$.

3. $12 \star 3 =$

(A) -3

(B) $\dfrac{1}{4}$

(C) $\dfrac{2}{3}$

(D) $\dfrac{3}{4}$

(E) 3

---

4. If $9 \star 4 = 15 \star k$, then $k =$

(A) 3

(B) 6

(C) $\dfrac{20}{3}$

(D) $\dfrac{25}{3}$

(E) 9

ANSWER KEY

1. (B)
Plug in −3 for x: $\spadesuit \, x = -3 - \dfrac{1}{-3} = -3 + \dfrac{1}{3} = -2\dfrac{2}{3}$, which is greater than −3 in Column A.

2. (E)
Start in the parentheses and work out: $(3 \heartsuit 5) = 3(3-5) = 3(-2) = -6$; $4 \heartsuit (-6) = 4[4 - (-6)] = 4(10) = 40$.

3. (D)
Plug in 12 for c and 3 for d: $\dfrac{12-3}{12} = \dfrac{9}{12} = \dfrac{3}{4}$.

4. (C)
Plug in on both sides of the equation:
$$\frac{9-4}{9} = \frac{15-k}{15}$$
$$\frac{5}{9} = \frac{15-k}{15}$$
Cross-multiply and solve for k:
$$75 = 135 - 9k$$
$$-60 = -9k$$
$$\frac{-60}{-9} = k$$
$$\frac{20}{3} = k$$

SPECIAL TRIANGLES

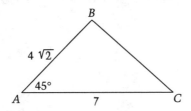

> **THE SPECIALS**
>
> The testmakers often put triangles on the SAT to test your knowledge of *special* triangles.

EXAMPLE

In the triangle above, what is the length of side BC?

(A) 4

(B) 5

(C) 4 √2

(D) 6

(E) 5 √2

HINT — *Look for the special triangles in geometry problems.*

Special triangles contain a lot of information. For instance, if you know the length of one side of a 30-60-90 triangle, you can easily work out the lengths of the others. Special triangles allow you to transfer one piece of information around the whole figure.

The following are the special triangles you should look for on the SAT.

Equilateral Triangles

All interior angles are 60° and all sides are of the same length.

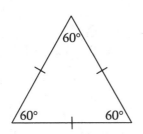

> **SPEED TIP**
>
> Popular right triangles:
>
> 3-4-5
>
> 5-12-13
>
> or multiples of these, like:
>
> 6-8-10 or
>
> 10-24-26

Isosceles Triangles

Two sides are of the same length and the angles facing these sides are equal.

Right Triangles

Contain a 90° angle. The sides are related by the Pythagorean theorem. $a^2 + b^2 = c^2$ where a and b are the legs and c is the hypotenuse.

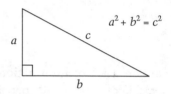

The "Special" Right Triangles

Many triangle problems contain "special" right triangles, whose side lengths always come in predictable ratios. If you recognize them, you won't have to use the Pythagorean theorem to find the value of a missing side length.

The 3-4-5 Right Triangle

(Be on the lookout for multiples of 3-4-5 as well.)

BAD MEMORY?

If you forget the triangle ratios, you can find a description of the isosceles right triangle and 30-60-90 triangle in the information box at the start of every math section on the SAT.

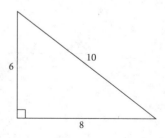

The Isosceles Right Triangle
(Note the side ratio: 1 to 1 to $\sqrt{2}$.)

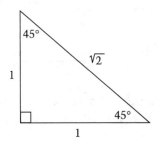

The 30-60-90 Right Triangle
(Note the side ratio: 1 to $\sqrt{3}$ to 2, and which side is opposite which angle.)

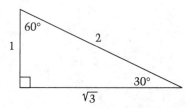

Getting back to our example, you can drop a vertical line from *B* to line *AC*. This divides the triangle into two right triangles.

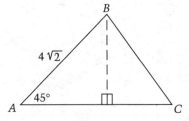

That means you know two of the angles in the triangle on the left; 90° and 45°. So this is an isosceles right triangle, with sides in the ratio of 1 to 1 to $\sqrt{2}$. The hypotenuse here is $4\sqrt{2}$, so both legs have length 4. Filling this in, you have:

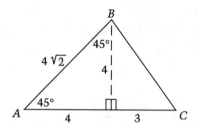

Now you can see that the legs of the smaller triangle on the right must be 4 and 3, making this a 3-4-5 right triangle, and the length of hypotenuse *BC* is 5.

PRACTICE PROBLEMS: SPECIAL TRIANGLES

REGULAR MATH

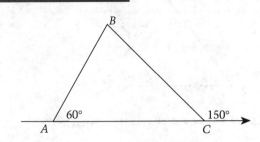

Note: Figure not drawn to scale.

1. In triangle ABC above, if AB = 4, then AC =

(A)   10
(B)   9
(C)   8
(D)   7
(E)   6

QC

Column A   Column B

In the coordinate plane, point R has coordinates (0,0) and point S has coordinates (9,12).

2. The distance from   16
   R to S

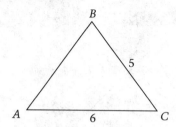

3. If the perimeter of triangle ABC above is 16, what is its area?

(A)   8
(B)   9
(C)   10
(D)   12
(E)   15

ANSWER KEY

1. (C)

Angle *BCA* is supplementary to the angle marked 150°, so angle
BCA = 180° − 150° = 30°. Since the interior angles of a triangle sum to
180°, angle *A* + angle *B* + angle *BCA* = 180°, so angle *B* = 180° − 60° −
30° = 90°. So triangle *ABC* is a 30-60-90 right triangle, and its sides are
in the ratio 1: $\sqrt{3}$: 2. The side opposite the 30°, *AB,* which we know has
length 4, must be half the length of the hypotenuse, *AC.* Therefore *AC* =
8, and that's answer choice (C).

2. (B)

Draw a diagram. Since *RS* isn't parallel to either axis, the way to compute
its length is to create a right triangle with legs that are parallel to the axes,
so their lengths are easy to find. We can then use the Pythagorean
Theorem to find the length of *RS*.

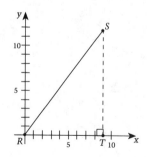

Since *S* has a *y*-coordinate of 12, it's 12 units above the *x*-axis, so the length of *ST* must be 12. And since *T* is the same number of units to the right of the *y*-axis as *S*, given by the *x*-coordinate of 9, the distance from the origin to *T* must be 9. So we have a right triangle with legs of 9 and 12. You should recognize this as a multiple of the 3-4-5 triangle. $9 = 3 \times 3$; $12 = 3 \times 4$; so the hypotenuse *RS* must be 3×5, or 15. That's the value of Column A, so Column B is greater.

3. (D)
To find the area you need to know the base and height. If the perimeter is 16, then $AB + BC + AC = 16$; that is, $AB = 16 - 5 - 6 = 5$. Since $AB = BC$, this is an isosceles triangle. If you drop a line from vertex *B* to *AC*, it will divide the base in half. This divides the triangle up into two smaller right triangles:

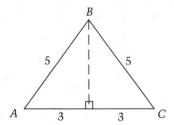

These right triangles each have one leg of 3 and a hypotenuse of 5; therefore they are 3-4-5 right triangles. So the missing leg (which is also the height of triangle *ABC*) must have length 4. We now know that the base of *ABC* is 6 and the height is 4, so the area is $\frac{1}{2} \times 6 \times 4$, or 12, answer choice (D).

BREAKING UP IS EASY

When you see a shape that isn't a triangle, rectangle, or circle try breaking it into familiar figures.

MULTIPLE AND ODDBALL FIGURES

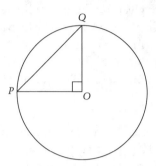

EXAMPLE

In the figure above, if the area of the circle with center O is 9π, what is the area of triangle POQ?

(A) 4.5

(B) 6

(C) 3.5π

(D) 4.5π

(E) 9

In a problem that combines figures, you have to look for the relationship between the figures.

HINT — Look for pieces the figures have in common.

For instance, if two figures share a side, information about that side will probably be the key.

In this case the figures don't share a side, but the triangle's legs are important features of the circle — they are radii. You can see that $PO = OQ$ = the radius of circle O.

The area of the circle is 9π. The area of a circle is πr^2, where r = the radius. So $9\pi = \pi r^2$, $9 = r^2$, and the radius = 3. The area of a triangle is $\frac{1}{2}$ base times height. Therefore, the area of ΔPOQ is $\frac{1}{2}$ (leg$_1$ $\times$ leg$_2$) = $\frac{1}{2}$ (3 $\times$ 3) = $\frac{9}{2}$ = 4.5, answer choice (A).

But what if, instead of a number of familiar shapes, you are given something like this?

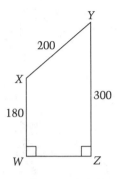

What is the perimeter of quadrilateral WXYZ?

(A)   680
(B)   760
(C)   840
(D)   920
(E)   1000

Try breaking the unfamiliar shape into familiar ones. Once this is done, you can use the same techniques that you would for multiple figures. Perimeter is the sum of the lengths of the sides of a figure, so you need to find the length of *WZ*. Drawing a perpendicular line from point *X* to side *YZ* will divide the figure into a right triangle and a rectangle. Call the point of intersection *A*.

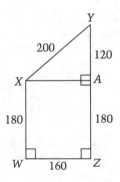

Opposite sides of a rectangle have equal length, so *WZ* = *XA* and *WX* = *ZA*. *WX* is labeled as 180, so *ZA* = 180. Since *YZ* measures 300, *AY* is 300 − 180 = 120. In right triangle *XYA*, hypotenuse *XY* = 200 and leg *AY* = 120; you should recognize this as a multiple of a 3-4-5 right triangle. The hypotenuse is 5 × 40, one leg is 3 × 40, so *XA* must be 4 × 40 or 160. (If you didn't recognize this special right triangle you could

RULE OF THUMB

Multiple figures are almost always made up of either several familiar shapes put together, or one familiar shape with a recognizable piece shaded or cut out of it.

You Can Look It Up
A list of the 75 Math Principles you need to know is included as an appendix in this book. Review it to see what areas you might need to brush up on.

have used the Pythagorean theorem to find the length of *XA*.) Since *WZ* = *XA* = 160, the perimeter of the figure is 180 + 200 + 300 + 160 = 840, answer choice (C).

PRACTICE PROBLEMS:
MULTIPLE AND ODDBALL FIGURES

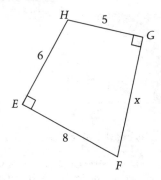

1. What is the value of x in the figure above?

(A) 4
(B) $3\sqrt{3}$
(C) $3\sqrt{5}$
(D) $5\sqrt{3}$
(E) 9

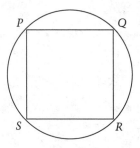

2. In the figure above, square PQRS is inscribed in a circle. If the area of square PQRS is 4, what is the radius of the circle?

(A) 1
(B) $\sqrt{2}$
(C) 2
(D) $2\sqrt{2}$
(E) $4\sqrt{2}$

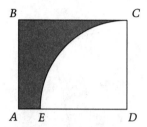

Note: Figure not drawn to scale.

3. In the figure above, the quarter circle with center D has a radius of 4 and rectangle ABCD has a perimeter of 20. What is the perimeter of the shaded region?

(A) $20 - 8\pi$
(B) $10 + 2\pi$
(C) $12 + 2\pi$
(D) $12 + 4\pi$
(E) $4 + 8\pi$

ANSWER KEY

1. (D)
Draw a straight line from point H to point F, to divide the figure into two right triangles.

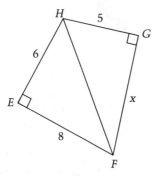

$\triangle EFH$ is a 3-4-5 right triangle with a hypotenuse of length 10. Use the Pythagorean Theorem in $\triangle FGH$ to find x:

$$x^2 + 5^2 = 10^2$$
$$x^2 + 5^2 = 100$$
$$x^2 = 75$$
$$x = \sqrt{75}$$
$$x = \sqrt{25}\sqrt{3}$$
$$x = 5\sqrt{3}$$

2. (B)

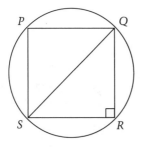

Draw in diagonal QS and you will notice that it is also a diameter of the circle. Since the area of the square is 4 its sides must each be 2. The diagonal of a square is always the length of a side times $\sqrt{2}$.

Think of the diagonal as dividing the square into two isosceles right triangles. Therefore, the diagonal = $2\sqrt{2}$ = the diameter; the radius is half this amount or $\sqrt{2}$.

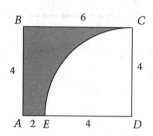

HIGHLIGHTS
Problem-Solving Techniques
• Remainders
• Averages
• Ratios
• Rates
• Percents
• Combinations
• Simultaneous Equations
• Symbolism
• Special triangles
• Multiple and oddball figures

3. (C)

The perimeter of the shaded region is $BC + AB + AE +$ arc EC. The quarter circle has its center at D, and point C lies on the circle, so side DC is a radius of the circle and equals 4. Opposite sides of a rectangle are equal so AB is also 4. The perimeter of the rectangle is 20, and since the two short sides account for 8, the two longer sides must account for 12, making BC and AD each 6. To find AE, subtract the length of ED, another radius of length 4, from the length of AD, which is 6; $AE = 2$. Since arc EC is a quarter circle, the length of the arc EC is $\frac{1}{4}$ of the circumference of a whole circle with radius 4: $\frac{1}{4} \times 2\pi r = \frac{1}{4} \times 8\pi = 2\pi$. So the perimeter of the shaded region is $6 + 4 + 2 + 2\pi = 12 + 2\pi$.

F·A·S·T P·R·E·P

✍ CHAPTER CHECKLIST ✍

Once you've mastered a concept, check it off:

KAPLAN'S TOP TEN SAT MATH TRAPS

- ❏ PERCENT INCREASE/DECREASE
- ❏ WEIGHTED AVERAGES
- ❏ RATIO:RATIO:RATIO
- ❏ EXPRESSIONS THAT LOOK EQUAL — BUT AREN'T
- ❏ UNSPECIFIED ORDER
- ❏ LENGTH:AREA RATIOS
- ❏ NOT ALL NUMBERS ARE POSITIVE INTEGERS
- ❏ HIDDEN INSTRUCTIONS
- ❏ AVERAGE RATES
- ❏ COUNTING NUMBERS

HOW TRAPS WORK AND HOW TO AVOID THEM

- ❏ HOW TO RECOGNIZE THE TEN MOST COMMON TRAPS
- ❏ THE WRONG WAY TO ANSWER THE QUESTIONS
- ❏ STRATEGIES FOR AVOIDING TRAPS
- ❏ HOW TO FIND THE RIGHT ANSWERS

🐭 PANICPLAN 🐭

If you have a month or less to prep for the SAT, here's the best way to spend your time:

1: Skim pp. 176 - 191.

2: Do the first practice set, p. 173 - 175. If you miss an answer, identify the trap that caught you and study that section.

3: Do the second practice set, p. 192 - 195. If you get any answer wrong, identify the trap and study that section. If you get all the answers right, you're strong at avoiding traps.

CHAPTER 14

TOP TEN SAT MATH TRAPS

It's time for us to let you in on a little secret that will allow you to breeze through the entire SAT, get into any college you want, succeed in life, and find eternal happiness.

If you believed a word of the preceding paragraph, you need to pay special attention to this chapter. This chapter presents 10 common SAT traps. Traps lure you into one answer, usually one that's easy to get to. But they conceal the correct answer, which requires some thought. If you're not wary of traps on the SAT, they may trip you up. Learn to recognize common traps and you'll gain more points on test day.

> *HINT—If you see what appears to be an easy problem late in a question set, there is probably a trap.*

WATCH OUT FOR TRAPS

The following ten questions have one thing in common—they all have traps. Take 12 minutes to try to work through all of them. Then check your answers on p. 176.

1. Jackie purchased a new car in 1990. Three years later she sold it to a dealer for 40 percent less than she paid for it in 1990. The dealer then added 20 percent onto the price he paid and resold it to another customer. The price the final customer paid for the car was what percent of the original price Jackie paid in 1990?

   (A) 40%
   (B) 60%
   (C) 72%
   (D) 80%
   (E) 88%

STANLEY'S FAVORITE TRAP

When the hands of your watch show 12:30, how many degrees separate the hour hand from the minute hand?

The obvious answer is 180 degrees. That's a trap. The testmakers hoped that you would jump to the obvious answer, without taking the time to think it through.

Over the years, the SAT has had plenty of problems like this one. Traps catch unwary students who forget to think through the problem before they answer it. How do you prevent yourself from falling for other SAT Math traps? Read this chapter.

2. In a class of 27 students, the average (arithmetic mean) score of the boys on the final exam was 83. If the average score of the 15 girls in the class was 92, what was the average of the whole class?

(A) 86.2
(B) 87.0
(C) 87.5
(D) 88.0
(E) 88.2

3. Mike's coin collection consists of quarters, dimes, and nickels. If the ratio of the number of quarters to the number of dimes is 5 to 2, and the ratio of the number of dimes to the number of nickels is 3 to 4, what is the ratio of the number of quarters to the number of nickels?

(A) 5 to 4
(B) 7 to 5
(C) 10 to 6
(D) 12 to 7
(E) 15 to 8

Column A	Column B
	$p > q > 1$	

4. $p^2 - q^2$ $(p - q)^2$

A, B, and C are points on a line such that point A is 12 units away from point B and point B is 4 units away from point C.

5. Distance from   16
point A to point C

6. The area of a   Twice the area of a
square with a   square with a
perimeter of 14   perimeter of 7

7. If $n \neq 0$, then which of the following must be true?
    I. $n^2 > n$
    II. $2n > n$
    III. $n + 1 > n$

(A) I only
(B) II only
(C) III only
(D) I and III only
(E) I, II, and III

8. At a certain restaurant, the hourly wage for a waiter is 20 percent greater than the hourly wage for a dishwasher, and the hourly wage for a dishwasher is half as much as the hourly wage for a cook's assistant. If a cook's assistant earns $8.50 an hour, how much less than a cook's assistant does a waiter earn each hour?

(A) $2.55
(B) $3.40
(C) $4.25
(D) $5.10
(E) $5.95

9. A car traveled from A to B at an average speed of 40 miles per hour and then immediately traveled back from B to A at an average speed of 60 miles per hour. What was the car's average speed for the round trip, in miles per hour?

(A) 45
(B) 48
(C) 50
(D) 52
(E) 54

10. The tickets for a certain raffle are consecutively numbered. If Louis sold the tickets numbered from 75 to 148 inclusive, how many raffle tickets did he sell?

(A) 71
(B) 72
(C) 73
(D) 74
(E) 75

HOW MATH TRAPS WORK
AND HOW TO AVOID THEM

How did you do? If you got any wrong answers, unless you calculated incorrectly, chances are you got caught in a trap. The same traps occur again and again on the SAT. Learn how they work and how to avoid them. Once you can deal with traps, you'll do much better on the harder math questions.

To see how they work, look again at the ten sample questions. Each contains one of the Top Ten Math Traps.

TRAP 1: PERCENT INCREASE/DECREASE

EXAMPLE

Jackie purchased a new car in 1990. Three years later she sold it to a dealer for 40 percent less than she paid for it in 1990. The dealer then added 20 percent onto the price he paid and resold it to another customer. The price the final customer paid for the car was what percent of the original price Jackie paid in 1990?

(A) 40%
(B) 60%
(C) 72%
(D) 80%
(E) 88%

The increase/decrease percentage problem usually appears at the end of a section and invariably contains a trap. Most students will figure that taking away 40 percent, and then adding 20 percent gives you an overall loss of 20 percent, and pick choice (D), 80 percent, as the correct answer.

The Trap
When a quantity is increased or decreased by a percent more than once, you cannot simply add and subtract the percents to get the answer.
In this kind of percent problem:

- the first percent change is a percent of the starting amount,
- but the second change is a percent of the new amount.

Avoiding the Trap
Percents can only be added and subtracted when they are percents of the same amount.

Finding the Right Answer
We know:

- the 40 percent less that Jackie got for the car is 40 percent of her original price;
- the 20 percent the dealer adds on is 20 percent of what the dealer paid, a much smaller amount;
- adding on 20 percent of that smaller amount is not the same thing as adding back 20 percent of the original price.

So We Can Solve the Problem
- Use 100 for a starting quantity, whether or not it makes sense in the real situation. The problem asks for the relative amount of change. So

TOP TEN TRAP   #1

To get a combined percent increase, don't just add the percents.

you can take any starting number, and compare it with the final result. Because you're dealing with percents, 100 is the easiest number to work with.

HINT—Pick 100 as the starting quantity and see what happens.

• If Jackie paid 100 dollars for the car, what is 40 percent less?

In the case of 100 dollars, each percent equals 1 dollar, so she sold it for 60 dollars.

• If the dealer charges 20 percent more than his purchase price, he's raising the price by 20 percent of 60 dollars, which is 12 dollars (not 20 percent of 100 dollars, which is $20).

• Therefore the dealer sold the car again for 60 + 12, or 72 dollars.

• Finally, what percent of the starting price (100 dollars) is 72 dollars? 72 percent. So the correct answer here is choice (C).

TOP TEN TRAP   #2

Don't just average the averages.

TRAP 2: WEIGHTED AVERAGES

EXAMPLE

In a class of 27 students, the average (arithmetic mean) score of the boys on the final exam was 83. If the average score of the 15 girls in the class was 92, what was the average of the whole class?

(A) 86.2
(B) 87.0
(C) 87.5
(D) 88.0
(E) 88.2

The Wrong Answer
Some students will rush in and simply average 83 and 92 to come up with 87.5 as the class average.

The Trap
You cannot combine averages of different quantities by taking the average of those averages.

In an average problem, if one value occurs more frequently than others it is "weighted" more. Remember that the average formula calls for the sum of all the terms, divided by the total number of terms.

Avoiding the Trap
Work with the sums, not the averages.

Finding the Right Answer
If 15 of the 27 students are girls, the remaining 12 must be boys.

We can't just add 83 to 92 and divide by two. In this class there are more girls than boys, and therefore the girls' test scores are "weighted" more—they contribute more to the class average. So the answer must be either (D) or (E). To find each sum, multiply each average by the number of terms it represents. After you have found the sums of the different terms, find the combined average by plugging them into the average formula.

$$\text{Total class average} = \frac{\text{Sum of girls' scores} + \text{Sum of boys' scores}}{\text{Total number of students}}$$

$$= \frac{(\text{\# of girls} \times \text{girls' average score}) + (\text{\# boys} \times \text{boys' average score})}{\text{Total number of students}}$$

$$= \frac{15(92) + 12(83)}{27} = \frac{1380 + 996}{27} = 88$$

So the class average is 88, answer choice (D).

STUMPED?

Use logic. There are more girls than boys, so the average would be closer to the girls' average—92. The only choices that are closer to 92 than 83 are (D) and (E).

TRAP 3: RATIO:RATIO:RATIO

MONEY

Don't be distracted by money. We only care about the *number* of coins, not their value.

> **EXAMPLE**
>
> Mike's coin collection consists of quarters, dimes, and nickels. If the ratio of the number of quarters to the number of dimes is 5 to 2, and the ratio of the number of dimes to the number of nickels is 3 to 4, what is the ratio of the number of quarters to the number of nickels?
>
> (A) 5 to 4
> (B) 7 to 5
> (C) 10 to 6
> (D 12 to 7
> (E) 15 to 8

The Wrong Answer

If you chose 5 to 4 as the correct answer, you fell for the classic ratio trap.

The Trap

Parts of different ratios don't always refer to the same whole.

In the classic ratio trap, two different ratios each share a common part that is represented by two different numbers. The two ratios do not refer to the same whole, however, so they are not in proportion to each other. To solve this type of problem, restate both ratios so that the numbers representing the common part (in this case "dimes") are the same. Then all the parts will be in proportion and can be compared to each other.

Avoiding the Trap

Make sure parts of ratios refer to the same whole.

Finding the Right Answer

To find the ratio of quarters to nickels, restate both ratios so that the number of dimes is the same in both.

We are given two ratios:

Quarters to Dimes = 5 to 2   Dimes to Nickels = 3 to 4

The number corresponding to dimes in the first ratio is 2.

The number corresponding to dimes in the second ratio is 3.

To restate the ratios, find the least common multiple of 2 and 3.

The least common multiple of 2 and 3 is 6.

TOP TEN TRAP   #3

Don't take one number from one ratio and compare it to another number from another ratio.

Restate the ratios with the number of dimes as 6:

Quarters to Dimes = 15 to 6   Dimes to Nickels = 6 to 8

The ratios are still in their original proportions, but now they're in proportion to each other and they refer to the same whole.

The ratio of quarters to dimes to nickels is 15 to 6 to 8, so the ratio of quarters to nickels is 15 to 8, which is answer choice (E).

TRAP 4: EXPRESSIONS THAT LOOK EQUAL—BUT AREN'T

EXAMPLE

Column A	Column B

$$p > q > 1$$

$p^2 - q^2$ | $(p - q)^2$

The Wrong Answer
If you said the expressions were equal, you'd be wrong.

The Trap
At first glance the expressions look like they're equal—but they're not.

This common SAT trap happens most often in QCs. Problems like this trap students who are too hasty, who answer on the basis of appearance, without considering the mathematical rules involved.

Avoiding the Trap
If two quantities seem obviously equal, double check your answer, using your math knowledge and the techniques discussed in the QC chapter, p. 111.

This is an example of the general rule that whenever an answer to any hard question looks obviously correct, it probably isn't.

Finding the Right Answer
In this case you can use the "make one column look more like the other" technique discussed in the QC chapter.

Get rid of the parentheses in Column B: $(p - q)^2 = (p - q)(p - q)$
Multiply the binomials: $= p^2 + p(-q) + (-q)p + (-q)(-q)$
$= p^2 - 2pq + q^2$

This leaves you comparing

Column A	Column B
$p^2 - q^2$	$p^2 - 2pq + q^2$

Use the do-the-same-thing-to-both-columns technique. Add q^2 and subtract p^2 from both sides to get

Column A	Column B
0	$2q^2 - 2pq$

STUMPED?

Pick numbers.

If $p = 3$ and $q = 2$, then $p^2 - q^2 = 5$ and $(p - q)^2 = 1$.

Column A is bigger, so you know the answer must be either (A) or (D).

Since $p > q$, $q \times q < p \times q$, so $2q^2 < 2pq$. That is, Column B is negative. Since Column A contains 0, Column A is always greater than Column B, and the answer is choice (A).

This trap does not only apply to quadratics. Below are some other quantities that the hasty student might mistake as equal. Go through this list and make sure you can tell why these expressions are not equal except for special cases.

$(x + y)^2$ does NOT equal $x^2 + y^2$

$(2x)^2$ does NOT equal $2x^2$

$x^{20} - x^{18}$ does NOT equal x^2

$x^3 + x^3$ does NOT equal x^6

$\sqrt{x} + \sqrt{x}$ does NOT equal $\sqrt{2x}$

$\sqrt{x} - \sqrt{y}$ does NOT equal $\sqrt{x-y}$

$\dfrac{1}{x} + \dfrac{1}{y}$ does NOT equal $\dfrac{1}{x+y}$

You could prove that any of these quantities need not be equal using the Picking Numbers technique.

TRAP 5: UNSPECIFIED ORDER

TOP TEN TRAP   #5

Don't assume that there's just
one way to draw the diagram.

EXAMPLE

Column A	Column B

A, B, and C are points on a line such that point A is 12 units away
from point B and point B is 4 units away from point C.

| The distance from | 16 |
| point A to point C | |

The Wrong Answer

First you should always draw a diagram to help you visualize the relationship between the points.

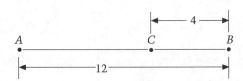

In this diagram, the distance from *A* to *C* is 16, which is the same as
Column B. But choice (C) is not the right answer.

The Trap

Don't assume that there is only one arrangement of the points — in this
case in alphabetical order.

We are not told what the relationship between *A* and *C* is. In fact *C*
could lie to the left of *B*, like so:

Avoiding the Trap

Don't assume points lie in the order they are given or in alphabetical
order — look for alternatives.

Finding the Right Answer

In this case, the distance from *A* to *C* is 8, which is less than Column B.
Since we have two possible relationships between the columns, the answer
must be (D) — you can't be certain from the data given.

<table>
<tr><td>

TOP TEN TRAP #6

The ratio of areas is not the same as the ratio of lengths.

</td></tr>
</table>

TRAP 6: LENGTH:AREA RATIO

EXAMPLE

Column A

The area of a square with a perimeter of 14

Column B

Twice the area of a square with a perimeter of 7

The Wrong Answer

Twice the perimeter doesn't mean twice the area. Choice (C) is wrong.

The Trap

In proportional figures, the ratio of the areas is not the same as the ratio of the lengths.

Avoiding the Trap

Understand that the ratio of the areas of proportional figures is the square of the ratio of corresponding linear measures.

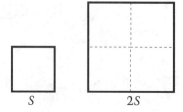

Finding the Right Answer

One way to solve this QC would be to actually compute the respective areas.

A square of perimeter 14 has side length $\frac{14}{4}$ = 3.5. Its area then is $(3.5)^2$ = 12.25. On the other hand, the area of the square in Column B is $(\frac{7}{4})^2$ = $(1.75)^2$ = 3.0625. Even twice that area is still less than the 12.25 in Column A. The answer is (A).

A quicker and cleverer way to dodge this trap is to understand the relationship between the linear ratio and the area ratio of proportional figures. In proportional figures, the area ratio is the *square* of the linear ratio.

In the example above, we are given two squares with sides in a ratio of 14:7 or 2:1.

Using the rule above, we square the linear 2:1 ratio. The areas of the two figures will be in a four-to-one ratio.

The same goes for circles:

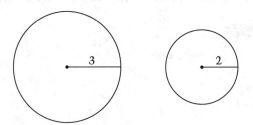

In the figure above, we are given two circles with radii in a 3:2 ratio.
Using the rule above, we square the linear 3:2 ratio.
The areas of the two circles will be in a 9:4 ratio.

TOP TEN TRAP   #7

Not all numbers are positive integers. Don't forget to consider zero, fractions, and negative numbers.

TRAP 7: NOT ALL NUMBERS ARE POSITIVE INTEGERS

EXAMPLE

If n ≠ 0, then which of the following must be true?

I. $n^2 > n$

II. $2n > n$

III. $n + 1 > n$

(A) I only

(B) II only

(C) III only

(D) I and III only

(E) I, II, and III

The Wrong Answer

In the example above, if you considered only positive integers greater than 1 for the value of *n*, you would assume that all three statements are true. However, that is not the case.

The Trap

Not all numbers are positive integers.

Don't forget there are negative numbers and fractions as well. This is important because negative numbers and fractions between 0 and 1 behave very differently from positive integers.

Avoiding the Trap

When picking numbers for variables, consider fractions and negative numbers.

BE AN EQUAL-OPPORTUNITY PICKER

When picking numbers, don't forget to consider fractions, negative numbers, zero, and one. See p. 88 for more details.

Finding the Right Answer

Looking at statement I, you may assume that when you square a number, you end up with a larger number as a result. For example, $4^2 = 16$. $10^2 = 100$. However, when you square a fraction between 0 and 1, the result is quite different: $(\frac{1}{2})^2 = \frac{1}{4}$. $(\frac{1}{10})^2 = \frac{1}{100}$. You get a smaller number.

In statement II, what happens when you multiply a number by 2? $7 \times 2 = 14$. $25 \times 2 = 50$. Multiplying any positive number by 2 doubles that number, so you get a larger result. However, if you multiply a negative number by 2, your result is smaller than the original number. For example, $-3 \times 2 = -6$.

Finally, look at statement III. What happens when you add 1 to any number?

Adding 1 to any number gives you a larger number as a result.

For example, $5 + 1 = 6$; $\frac{1}{2} + 1 = 1\frac{1}{2}$; and $-7 + 1 = -6$. That should be pretty obvious.

Therefore, only statement III must be true. That makes choice (C) correct. If you didn't consider fractions or negative numbers, you would have fallen into the trap and answered the question incorrectly.

HINT— This trap appears most often in QC problems, so watch out.

TRAP 8: HIDDEN INSTRUCTIONS

EXAMPLE

At a certain restaurant, the hourly wage for a waiter is 20 percent greater than the hourly wage for a dishwasher, and the hourly wage for a dishwasher is half as much as the hourly wage for a cook's assistant. If a cook's assistant earns $8.50 an hour, how much less than a cook's assistant does a waiter earn each hour?

(A) $2.55
(B) $3.40
(C) $4.25
(D) $5.10
(E) $5.95

The Wrong Answer

To solve this problem, you must find the hourly wage of the waiter.

The cook's assistant earns $8.50 an hour.
The dishwasher earns half of this: = $4.25 an hour

The waiter earns 20 percent more than this: $4.25 × 1.2 = $5.10.

So the waiter earns $5.10 an hour, and you might reach automatically to fill in answer choice (D). But (D) is the wrong answer.

The Trap

A small step, easily overlooked, can mean the difference between a right and wrong answer.

In this case the word is "less." After spending all this time finding the waiter's hourly wage, in their moment of triumph many students skip right over the vital last step. They overlook that the question asks not what the waiter earns, but how much less than the cook's assistant the waiter earns.

Avoiding the Trap

Make sure you answer the question that's being asked. Watch out for hidden instructions.

Finding the Right Answer

You have figured out that the waiter earns $5.10 an hour.
And the cook's assistant earns $8.50 an hour.
To find out how much less than the cook's assistant the waiter earns, subtract the waiter's hourly wage from the cook's assistant's hourly wage.
The correct answer is (B).

TRAP 9. AVERAGE RATE

EXAMPLE

A car traveled from *A* to *B* at an average speed of 40 miles per hour and then immediately traveled back from *B* to *A* at an average speed of 60 miles per hour. What was the car's average speed for the round trip, in miles per hour?

(A) 45

(B) 48

(C) 50

(D) 52

(E) 54

The Wrong Answer

Do you see which answer choice is too "obvious" to be correct? The temptation is simply to average 40 and 60. The answer is "obviously" (C), 50. But 50 is wrong.

The Trap

To get an average rate, you can't just average the rates.

Why is the average speed not 50 mph? Because the car spent more time traveling at 40 mph than at 60 mph. Each leg of the round trip was the same distance, but the first leg, at the slower speed, took more time.

Avoiding the Trap

You can solve almost any Average Rates problem with this general formula:

$$\text{Average Rate} = \frac{\text{Total Distance}}{\text{Total Time}}$$

Use the given information to figure out the Total Distance and the Total Time. But how can you do that when many problems don't specify the distances?

Finding the Right Answer

In our sample above, we are told that a car went:

"from *A* to *B* at 40 miles per hour and back from *B* to *A* at 60 miles per hour"

In other words it went:

"half the Total Distance at 40 mph and half the Total Distance at 60 mph"

How do you use the formula, Average Rate = $\frac{\text{Total Distance}}{\text{Total Time}}$, if you don't know the Total Distance?

STUMPED?

Use common sense. The car spent more time at 40 mph so the answer will be less than 50 — i.e., weighted more heavily towards 40 (remember weighted averages, trap #2).

If you saw this much but couldn't get the answer, you could guess between (A) and (B). More on guessing in Chapter 15.

HINT — Pick a number! Pick any number you want for the Total Distance.

Divide that Total Distance into Half Distances.

Calculate the time needed to travel each Half Distance at the different rates.

HINT — Pick a number that's easy to work with.

A good number to pick here would be 240 miles for the Total Distance, because you can figure in your head the times for two 120-mile legs at 40 mph and 60 mph:

A to *B*: $\dfrac{120 \text{ miles}}{40 \text{ miles per hour}} = 3$ hours

B to *A*: $\dfrac{120 \text{ miles}}{60 \text{ miles per hour}} = 2$ hours

Total Time = 5 hours

Now plug "Total Distance = 240 miles" and "Total Time = 5 hours" into the general formula:

Average Rate $= \dfrac{\text{Total Distance}}{\text{Total Time}} = \dfrac{240 \text{ miles}}{5 \text{ hours}} = 48$ miles per hour.

Correct answer choice: (B).

TRAP 10: COUNTING NUMBERS

EXAMPLE

The tickets for a certain raffle are consecutively numbered. If Louis sold the tickets numbered from 75 to 148 inclusive, how many raffle tickets did he sell?

(A) 71
(B) 72
(C) 73
(D) 74
(E) 75

> **TOP TEN TRAP** **#10**
>
> Counting integers is tricky. You can't just subtract the first number from the last number; you have to add one.

The Wrong Answer
Many people would subtract 75 from 148 inclusive to get 73 as their answer. But that is not correct.

The Trap
Subtracting the first and last integers in a range will give you the difference of the two numbers. It won't give you the number of integers in that range.

Avoiding the Trap
To count the number of integers in a range, subtract and then add 1.

If you forget the rule, pick two small numbers that are close together, such as 1 and 4. Obviously, there are four integers from 1 to 4, inclusive. But if you had subtracted 1 from 4, you would have gotten 3. In the diagram below, you can see that 3 is actually the distance between the integers, if the integers were on a number line or a ruler.

Finding the Right Answer
In the problem above, subtract 75 from 148.

The result is 73.

Add 1 to this difference to get the number of integers.

That gives you 74 .

The correct answer choice is (D).

The word "inclusive" tells you to include the first and last numbers given. So "the integers from 5 to 15 inclusive" include 5 and 15. Questions always make it clear whether you should include the outer numbers or not, since the correct answer hinges on this point.

MORE PRACTICE

Now that you can recognize the Top Ten Traps, try the following test. This time, try to identify the trap in each problem. Check your answers on p. 195 - 196.

<u>Column A</u>   <u>Column B</u>

A car traveled the first half of a 100-kilometer distance at an average speed of 120 kilometers per hour and it traveled the remaining distance at an average speed of 80 kilometers per hour.

1. The car's average speed,   100
   in kilometers per hour, for
   the 100 kilometers

The ratio of $\frac{1}{4}$ to $\frac{2}{5}$ is equal to the ratio of $\frac{2}{5}$ to x.

2. x $\frac{3}{5}$

---

3. $14 - 6$ $\sqrt{14^2 - 6^2}$

---

4. $\dfrac{a + b}{3}$ $a + b$

John buys 34 books at $6 each, and 17 at $12 each.

5. The average price John $9.00
   pays per book

On a certain highway Town X lies 50 miles away from Town Y, and Town Z lies 80 miles from Town X.

6. The number of minutes a   30
   car traveling at
   an average speed of 60 miles
   per hour takes to travel from
   Town Y to Town Z

---

a, b, and c are positive numbers.
$b < c$

7. $(a + b)^2$ $a^2 + c^2$

---

8. The area of a circle   The sum of the areas of three
   with a diameter of 3   circles each with a diameter of 1

Column A	Column B

Jane invests her savings in a fund that adds 10 percent interest to her savings at the end of every year.

9. The percent by which her money has increased after 3 years

   31 percent

$$x > 1$$

10. $7^{2x} - 7^x$ 7^x

---

11. Pump 1 can drain a 400-gallon water tank in 1.2 hours. Pump 2 can drain the same tank in 1.8 hours. How many minutes longer than pump 1 would it take pump 2 to drain a 100-gallon tank?

    (A) 0.15
    (B) 1.2
    (C) 6
    (D) 9
    (E) 18

---

12. Volumes 12 through 30 of a certain encyclopedia are located on the bottom shelf of a bookcase. If the volumes of the encyclopedia are numbered consecutively, how many volumes of the encyclopedia are on the bottom shelf?

    (A) 17
    (B) 18
    (C) 19
    (D) 29
    (E) 30

---

13. A reservoir is at full capacity at the beginning of summer. By the first day of fall, the level in the reservoir is 30 percent below full capacity. Then during the fall a period of heavy rains raises the level by 30 percent. After the rains, the reservoir is at what percent of its full capacity?

    (A) 100%
    (B) 95%
    (C) 91%
    (D) 85%
    (E) 60%

14. Two classes, one with 50 students, the other with 30, take the same exam. The combined average of both classes is 84.5. If the larger class averages 80, what is the average of the smaller class?

(A) 87.2
(B) 89.0
(C) 92.0
(D) 93.3
(E) 94.5

15. In a pet shop, the ratio of puppies to kittens is 7:6 and the ratio of kittens to guinea pigs is 5:3. What is the ratio of puppies to guinea pigs?

(A) 7:3
(B) 6:5
(C) 13:8
(D) 21:11
(E) 35:18

16. A typist typed the first n pages of a book, where n > 0, at an average rate of 12 pages per hour and typed the remaining n pages at an average rate of 20 pages per hour. What was the typist's average rate, in pages per hour, for the entire book?

(A) $14\frac{2}{3}$

(B) 15

(C) 16

(D) 17

(E) 18

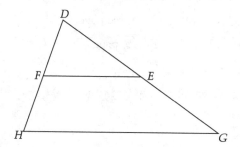

17. In triangle DGH above, DE = EG, EF ||GH, and the area of triangle DGH is 30. What is the area of triangle DEF ?

  (A)   7.5
  (B)   15
  (C)   22.5
  (D)   60
  (E)   It cannot be determined from the information given.

DID YOU FALL FOR THE TRAPS?

How did you do? Did you spot the trap in each problem? Use the answers below to see what your weaknesses are. Each wrong answer represents one trap you need to work on. Go back and reread the section on that trap. Then try the problems again, until you answer right.

1.   (B) Average rates trap (see page 189)

2.   (A) Ratio:ratio:ratio trap (see page 179)

3.   (B) Expressions that look equal — but aren't trap (see page 181)

4.   (D) Not all numbers are positive integers trap (see page 186)

5.   (B) Weighted averages trap (see page 178)

6.   (D) Unspecified order trap (see page 183)

7.   (D) Expressions that look equal — but aren't trap (see page 181)

8.   (A) Length:area ratios trap (see page 184)

9.   (A) Percent increase/decrease trap (see page 176)

10.   (A) Expressions that look equal — but aren't trap (see page 181)

11.   (D) Hidden instructions trap (see page 188)

12.   (C) Counting numbers trap (see page 191)

TOP 10 SAT MATH TRAPS

HIGHLIGHTS

- To get a combined percent increase, don't just add the percents

- Don't just average the averages

- Don't take one number from one ratio and compare it to another number from another ratio

- Don't be fooled by appearances

- Don't assume that there's just one way to draw the diagram

- The ratio of areas is not the same as the ratio of lengths

- Not all numbers are positive integers. Don't forget to consider zero, fractions, and negative numbers

- Make sure you're answering the question that's asked. Hint: underline the last phrase in the question

- Any time it says average rate in the question, be alert: you usually can't just average the rates to get the right answer

- Counting integers is tricky. You can't just subtract the first number from the last number; you have to add one

13. (C) Percent increase/decrease trap (see page 176)

14. (C) Weighted averages trap (see page 178)

15. (E) Ratio:ratio:ratio trap (see page 179)

16. (B) Average rates trap (see page 189)

17. (A) Length:area ratios trap (see page 184)

F·A·S·T P·R·E·P

✍ Chapter Checklist ✍

Once you've mastered a concept, check it off:

GUESSING TECHNIQUES

- ❑ Eliminate unreasonable answer choices
- ❑ Eliminate the obvious on hard questions
- ❑ Eyeball lengths, angles, and areas
- ❑ Eliminate choice (d) on some QCs
- ❑ Find the range of grid-ins and guess

💡 PanicPlan 💡

If you have less than a month to prep for the SAT, here's the best way to spend your time:

Guessing is an important strategy for scoring points, so read this chapter carefully. It's a short chapter, and there are no shortcuts to learning how to guess accurately.

CHAPTER 15

MATH GUESSING

Obviously, the best way to find the answer is to actually solve the problem. But if you're stuck or running out of time, guessing can be a good alternative.

The Regular Math and QC sections, like the Verbal sections, are scored to discourage random guessing. For every question you get right you earn a whole point. For every question you get wrong, you lose a fraction of a point. So if you guess at random on a number of questions, the points you gain from correct guesses are canceled out by the points you lose on incorrect guesses, for no overall gain or loss.

But you can make *educated* guesses. This raises the odds of guessing correctly, so the fractional points you lose no longer cancel out all the whole points you gain. You have just raised your score.

To make an educated guess, eliminate answer choices you know to be wrong, and guess from what's left. Of course, the more answer choices you can eliminate, the better chance you have of guessing the correct answer from what's left over.

Here are five strategies for guessing intelligently on all types of math problems.

1. ELIMINATE UNREASONABLE ANSWER CHOICES

Before you guess, think about the problem, and decide which answers don't make sense. Try the problem on the next page.

GUESSING IS EASY

Quick. Guess the right answer. William H. Harrison's middle name was:
- Hazel
- Hello
- Henry
- Hal
- Herbert

Except for the class clown who said Hazel, most people can safely eliminate two of the five choices. That means you've got a one in three chance of guessing Henry.

If you went into the SAT determined not to guess, you would have passed up this great opportunity to score a point.

Remember, if you can eliminate at least one answer, you should guess.

STUCK?

- Stuck on a QC or Regular Math question? Eliminate at least one answer choice and guess.
- Stuck on a Grid-in? You won't lose points for guessing wrong on Grid-ins. So go ahead and guess.

EXAMPLE

The ratio of men to women in a certain room is 13:11. If there are 429 men in the room, how many women are there?

(A) 143
(B) 363
(C) 433
(D) 507
(E) 792

Solution:

- The ratio of men to women is 13:11, so there are more men than women.
- Since there are 429 men, there must be fewer than 429 women.
- So you can eliminate choices (C), (D), and (E).
- The answer must be either (A) or (B), so guess. The correct answer is (B).

2. ELIMINATE THE OBVIOUS ON HARD QUESTIONS

HINT — Obvious answers are usually wrong on harder questions.

On the hard questions late in a set, obvious answers are usually wrong. So eliminate them when you guess. That doesn't hold true for early, easy questions, where the obvious answer could be right.

Now apply the rule. In the following difficult problem, which obvious answer should you eliminate?

EXAMPLE

A number x is increased by 30% and then the result is decreased by 20%. What is the final result of these changes?

(A) x is increased by 10%
(B) x is increased by 6%
(C) x is increased by 4%
(D) x is decreased by 5%
(E) x is decreased by 10%

NEED MORE HELP?

For more on percent increase/decrease problems, see Classic Traps, pp. 176 - 177.

Solution:

If you picked (A) as the obvious choice to eliminate, you'd be right. Most people would combine the decrease of 20% with the increase of 30%, getting a net increase of 10%. That's the easy, obvious answer, but not the correct answer. If you must guess, avoid (A). The correct answer is (C).

3. EYEBALL LENGTHS, ANGLES, AND AREAS ON GEOMETRY PROBLEMS

Use diagrams that accompany geometry problems to help you eliminate wrong answer choices. First make sure that the diagram is drawn to scale. Diagrams are always drawn to scale unless there's a note like this: "Note: Figure not drawn to scale." If it's not, don't use this strategy. If it is, estimate quantities or eyeball the diagram. Then eliminate answer choices that are way too large or too small.

Length

When a geometry question asks for a length, use the given lengths to estimate the unknown length. Measure off the given length by making a nick in your pencil with your thumbnail. Then hold the pencil against the unknown length on the diagram to see how the lengths compare.

In the following problem, which answer choices can you eliminate by eyeballing?

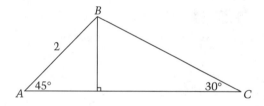

EXAMPLE

In the figure above, what is the length of BC?

(A) $\sqrt{2}$
(B) 2
(C) $2\sqrt{2}$
(D) 4
(E) $4\sqrt{2}$

Solution:

- *AB* is 2, so measure off this length on your pencil.
- Compare *BC* with this length.
- *BC* appears almost twice as long as *AB*, so *BC* is about 4.
- Since $\sqrt{2}$ is about 1.4, choices (A) and (B) are too small.
- Choice (E) is much greater than 4, so eliminate that.
- Now guess between (C) and (D). The correct answer is (C).

Angles

You can also eyeball angles. To eyeball an angle, compare the angle with a familiar angle, such as a straight angle (180°), a right angle (90°), or half a right angle (45°). The corner of a piece of paper is a right angle, so use that to see if an angle is greater or less than 90°.

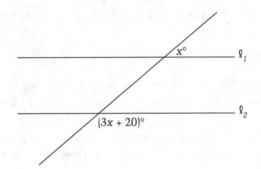

In the figure above, if $\ell_1 \parallel \ell_2$, what is the value of x?

(A) 130
(B) 100
(C) 80
(D) 50
(E) 40

Solution:

- You see that x is less than 90 degrees, so eliminate choices (A) and (B).

- Since x appears to be much less than 90 degrees, eliminate choice (C).

- Now pick between (D) and (E). In fact, the correct answer is (E).

Areas

Eyeballing an area is similar to eyeballing a length. You compare an unknown area in a diagram to an area that you do know.

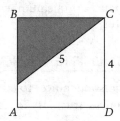

In square ABCD above, what is the area of the shaded region?

(A) 10
(B) 9
(C) 8
(D) 6
(E) 4

Solution:

- Since *ABCD* is a square, it has area 4^2, or 16.

- The shaded area is less than one-half the size of the square, so its area must be less than 8.

- Eliminate answer choices (A), (B), and (C). The correct answer is (D).

4. ON QCS, IF BOTH COLUMNS CONTAIN ONLY NUMBERS, ELIMINATE "D."

If both columns contain only concrete numbers, choice (D) — "the relationship cannot be determined" — can't be right. With no variables in either column, there must be one consistent relationship, even if you can't find it. If you don't know the answer, eliminate (D) as unreasonable and guess.

Column A	Column B
The largest prime factor of 1,224	18

Solution:

Each column contains only numbers — so eliminate choice (D) and guess. If you were extra clever you may also have seen that since 18 isn't prime, and Column A contains a prime number, the answer cannot be (C) either. The correct answer is (B).

5. ON GRID-INS, FIND THE RANGE AND GUESS

On Grid-ins, there are no answer choices to eliminate, but you won't lose points for guessing. So if you are stuck, try to estimate the general range of the answer, and guess.

Here are some examples of hard Grid-in questions. See if you can guess intelligently. Solutions follow the problems.

EXAMPLES

1. If the 3-digit number 11Q is a prime number, what digit is represented by Q?

2. The sum of 5 consecutive odd integers is 425. What is the greatest of these integers?

3. A triangle has one side of length 3 and another of length 7. If the length of the third side is a solution to the equation $x^2 - 2x = 63$, what is the length of the third side?

Solutions:

1. x is a digit, so it must be one of the integers 0 through 9. Eliminate all the even digits, since they are divisible by 2. And eliminate 5, since any number ending with 5 is divisible by 5. You are left with 1, 3, 7 and 9 to pick between. The correct answer is 3.

2. Since the integers are consecutive, they are all about the same size. So the number we are looking for is an odd number around 425 ÷ 5, which is 85. The right answer is 89.

3. Even if you can't solve that quadratic, you know that the third side is greater than the difference and less than the sum of the other two sides. So the third side is greater than 7 − 3 = 4 and less than 7 + 3 = 10. Since solutions to SAT quadratics are usually integers, pick an integer from 5 to 9. If you picked 9, you'd be right.

CHAPTER 16

WHAT DO
I DO NOW?

Is it starting to feel like your whole life is a buildup to the SAT? You've known about it for years, worried about it for months, and now spent at least a few hours in solid preparation for it. As the test gets closer, you may find your anxiety is on the rise. You shouldn't worry. After the preparation you've received from this book, you're in good shape for test day.

To calm any pre-test jitters you may have, this chapter leads you through a sane itinerary for the last week.

THE WEEK BEFORE THE TEST

Review the FastPrep checklist at the beginning of each chapter. Are there major holes in your preparation? If there are, choose a few of these areas to work on — but don't overload. You can't cram for the SAT.

Take a full-length SAT. If you haven't done so already, take the practice test at the end of this book. Actual SATs released by ETS are available in libraries and bookstores. You can also pick up Kaplan's Sneak Preview for the SAT, a full-length practice SAT written by Kaplan. All of these are good practice for the real thing.

TWO DAYS BEFORE THE TEST

Do your last studying — a few more practice problems, a few more vocabulary words and call it quits.

THE NIGHT BEFORE THE TEST

Don't study.
   Get together the following items:
   • a calculator with fresh batteries
   • a watch

THINGS NOT TO DO THE NIGHT BEFORE THE TEST
• Try to copy the dictionary onto your fingernails
• Stay up all night watching all the "Friday the 13th" movies
• Eat a large double anchovy, sausage, and pepper pizza with a case of chocolate soda
• Send away for brochures from vocational schools
• Begin prepping for the LSAT
• Start making flash cards
• Tattoo yourself

- a few #2 pencils
- erasers
- photo ID Card
- your admission ticket from ETS
- a snack — there are two breaks and you'll probably get hungry.

Know exactly where you're going and exactly how you're getting there.

Relax the night before the test. Read a good book, take a bubble bath, watch TV. Get a good night's sleep. Go to bed early and leave yourself extra time in the morning.

THE MORNING OF THE TEST

Eat breakfast. Make it something substantial, but not anything too heavy or greasy. Don't drink a lot of coffee if you're not used to it; bathroom breaks cut into your time.

Dress in layers so that you can adjust to the temperature of the test room.

Read something. Warm up your brain with a newspaper or a magazine. You shouldn't let the SAT be the first thing you read that day.

Be sure to get there early.

DURING THE TEST

Don't be shaken. If you find your confidence slipping, remind yourself how well you've prepared. You know the structure of the test; you know the instructions; you've studied for every question type.

Even if something goes really wrong, don't panic. If the test booklet is defective—two pages are stuck together or the ink has run— try to stay calm. Raise your hand, tell the proctor you need a new book. If you accidentally misgrid your answer page or put the answers in the wrong section, again don't panic. Raise your hand, tell the proctor. He or she might be able to arrange for you to regrid your test after it's over, when it won't cost you any time.

Don't think about which section is experimental. Remember, you never know for sure which section won't count. Besides, you can't work on any other section during that section's designated time slot.

AFTER THE TEST

Once the test is over, put it out of your mind. If you don't plan to take the test again, give this book away and start thinking about more interesting things.

You might walk out of the SAT thinking that you blew it. You probably didn't. You tend to remember the ones that stumped you, not the many that you knew. If you're really concerned, you can call ETS within 24 hours to find out about canceling your score. But there is usually no good reason to do so. Remember, you can retake the test as many times as you want, and most colleges consider only your highest scores.

If you want more help, or just want to know more about the SAT, college admissions, or Kaplan prep courses for the PSAT, SAT, and ACT, give us a call at 1-800-KAP-TEST. We're here to answer your questions and to help you in any way that we can.

HIGHLIGHTS

- Don't study the night before the SAT
- Make sure you know where the test center is; arrive there early
- Don't let yourself get shaken during or after the test

F·A·S·T P·R·E·P

✍ Appendix Checklist ✍

Once you've mastered a concept, check it off:

LEARNING NEW WORDS

❏ THE WORD LIST
❏ THE ROOT LIST
❏ WORD FAMILIES

PanicPlan

If you have a month or less to prep for the SAT, here's the best way to spend your time:

Learn the vocabulary strategies in Chapter 4.

WORD & ROOT LISTS

The Word List and Root List can boost your knowledge of SAT-level words, and that can help you get more questions right. No one can predict exactly which words will show up on your SAT test. But there are certain words that the testmakers favor. The more of these you know, the better.

The Word List that follows contains typical SAT words, and the Root List gives you their component parts. Knowing these words can help you because you may run across them on *your* SAT. Also, becoming comfortable with the types of words that pop up will reduce your anxiety about the test.

Knowing roots can help you in two ways. First, instead of learning one word at a time, you can learn a whole group of words which contain a certain root. They'll be related in meaning, so if you remember one, it will be easier for you to remember others. Second, roots can often help you decode an unknown SAT word. If you recognize a familiar root, you could get a good enough idea of the word to answer the question.

> ### GET TO YOUR ROOTS
>
> Most of the words you use every day have their origins in simple roots. Once you know the root, it's much easier to figure out what a strange word means.
>
> For example, the root *MAL* means bad. So *malodorous* must mean bad-smelling.
>
> Take a look through this appendix. Many of the roots are easy to learn, and they'll help you on test day.

SHORT ON TIME?

If you have less than a month to go before you take the SAT, your study time would be best spent learning the vocabulary strategies in Chapter 4. If you have over a month to go and you have at least 2 hours a week to devote to studying vocabulary, follow the plan of study outlined below. If you do memorize a lot of SAT-type words, it can only help you on test day.

MEMORIZING SAT WORDS

In general, the very best way to improve your vocabulary is to read. Choose challenging, college-level material. If you encounter an unknown word, put it on a flash card or in your vocabulary notebook.

If you are mainly concerned with honing your knowledge of SAT words, memorizing the words on the following list can help. Here's one good way to use these lists:

INTIMIDATED?

If you've got two months to prepare for the SAT, you can learn ten words a day and walk in to the exam knowing 600 words. Not a bad start.

1. Memorize 10 new words and roots a day, using one or more of the techniques below.

2. Reinforce what you've learned. Periodically quiz yourself on all the words you've learned so far.

3. Two weeks before the test, stop learning new words. Spend a week reviewing the word list. Rest up during the last week.

Here are some techniques for memorizing words.

1. Learn words in groups. You can group words by a common root they contain (see the Root list for examples of this), or you can group words that are related in meaning together. If you memorize words in groups this way, it may help you to remember them.

2. Use flash cards. Write down new words or word groups and run through them when you have a few minutes to spare. Put one new word or word group on one side of a 3 x 5 card and put a short definition or definitions on the back.

3. Make a vocabulary notebook. List words in one column and their definitions in another. Test yourself. Cover up the meanings, and see which words you can define from memory. Make a sample sentence using each word in context.

4. Think of hooks that lodge a new word in your mind — create visual images of words.

5. Use rhymes, pictures, songs, and any other devices that help you remember words.

NEED MORE HELP?

The lists that follow come from Kaplan's Verbal Workbook. For more help with the Verbal section of the SAT, the workbook is a great place to start.

To get the most out of your remaining study time, use the techniques that work for you, and stick with them.

THE KAPLAN WORD LIST

A

- ❑ ABANDON (n.) — total lack of inhibition
- ❑ ABASE — to humble, disgrace
- ❑ ABATEMENT — decrease, reduction
- ❑ ABDICATE — to give up a position, right, or power
- ❑ ABERRATION — something different from the usual or normal
- ❑ ABET — to aid, act as accomplice
- ❑ ABEYANCE — temporary suppression or suspension
- ❑ ABHOR — to loathe, detest
- ❑ ABJECT — miserable, pitiful
- ❑ ABJURE — to reject, abandon formally
- ❑ ABLUTION — act of cleansing
- ❑ ABNEGATE — to deny, renounce
- ❑ ABOLITIONIST — one who opposes the practice of slavery
- ❑ ABORTIVE — interrupted while incomplete
- ❑ ABRIDGE — to condense, shorten
- ❑ ABROGATE — to abolish or invalidate by authority
- ❑ ABSCOND — to depart secretly
- ❑ ABSOLVE — to forgive, free from blame
- ❑ ABSTEMIOUS — moderate in appetite
- ❑ ABSTRACT (adj.) — theoretical; complex, difficult
- ❑ ABSTRUSE — difficult to comprehend
- ❑ ACCEDE — to express approval; agree to
- ❑ ACCESSIBLE — attainable, available; approachable
- ❑ ACCESSORY — attachment, ornament; accomplice, partner
- ❑ ACCOLADE — praise, distinction
- ❑ ACCOST — to approach and speak to someone
- ❑ ACCRETION — growth in size or increase in amount
- ❑ ACCRUE — to accumulate, grow by additions
- ❑ ACERBIC — bitter, sharp in taste or temper
- ❑ ACME — highest point; summit
- ❑ ACQUIESCE — to agree, comply quietly
- ❑ ACQUITTAL — release from blame
- ❑ ACRID — harsh, bitter
- ❑ ACRIMONY — bitterness, animosity
- ❑ ACUITY — sharpness
- ❑ ACUMEN — sharpness of insight
- ❑ ACUTE — sharp, pointed
- ❑ ADAGE — old saying or proverb
- ❑ ADAMANT — uncompromising, unyielding

- ❑ ADAPT — to accommodate, adjust
- ❑ ADHERE — to cling or follow without deviation
- ❑ ADJACENT — next to
- ❑ ADJUNCT — something added, attached, or joined
- ❑ ADMONISH — to caution or reprimand
- ❑ ADROIT — skillful, accomplished, highly competent
- ❑ ADULATION — high praise
- ❑ ADULTERATE — to corrupt or make impure
- ❑ ADUMBRATE — to sketch, outline in a shadowy way
- ❑ ADVANTAGEOUS — favorable, useful
- ❑ ADVERSARIAL — antagonistic, competitive
- ❑ ADVERSE — unfavorable, unlucky, harmful
- ❑ AERIAL — having to do with the air
- ❑ AERIE — nook or nest built high in the air
- ❑ AERODYNAMIC — relating to objects moving through the air
- ❑ AESTHETIC — pertaining to beauty or art
- ❑ AFFABLE — friendly, easy to approach
- ❑ AFFECTED (adj.) — pretentious, phony
- ❑ AFFINITY — fondness, liking; similarity
- ❑ AFFLUENT — rich, abundant
- ❑ AFFRONT (n.) — personal offense, insult
- ❑ AGENDA — plan, schedule
- ❑ AGGRANDIZE — to make larger or greater in power
- ❑ AGGREGATE (n.) — collective mass or sum; total
- ❑ AGGRIEVE — to afflict, distress
- ❑ AGILE — well-coordinated, nimble
- ❑ AGITATION — commotion, excitement; uneasiness
- ❑ AGNOSTIC — one doubting that people can know God
- ❑ AGRARIAN — relating to farming or rural matters
- ❑ ALACRITY — cheerful willingness, eagerness; speed
- ❑ ALCHEMY — medieval chemical philosophy based on trying to change metal into gold
- ❑ ALGORITHM — mechanical problem-solving procedure
- ❑ ALIAS — assumed name
- ❑ ALIENATED — distanced, estranged
- ❑ ALIGNED — precisely adjusted; committed to one side
- ❑ ALLAY — to lessen, ease, or soothe
- ❑ ALLEGORY — symbolic representation
- ❑ ALLEVIATE — to relieve, improve partially
- ❑ ALLITERATION — repetition of the beginning sounds of words

- ❑ ALLOCATION — allowance, portion, share
- ❑ ALLURE (v.) — to entice by charm; attract
- ❑ ALLUSION — indirect reference
- ❑ ALLUSIVENESS — quality of making many indirect references
- ❑ ALOOF — detached, indifferent
- ❑ ALTERCATION — noisy dispute
- ❑ ALTRUISM — unselfish concern for others' welfare
- ❑ AMALGAM — mixture, combination, alloy
- ❑ AMBIDEXTROUS — able to use both hands equally well
- ❑ AMBIGUOUS — uncertain; subject to multiple interpretations
- ❑ AMBIVALENCE — attitude of uncertainty; conflicting emotions
- ❑ AMELIORATE — to make better, improve
- ❑ AMENABLE — agreeable, cooperative
- ❑ AMEND — to improve or correct flaws in
- ❑ AMENITY — pleasantness; something increasing comfort
- ❑ AMIABLE — friendly, pleasant, likable
- ❑ AMICABLE — friendly, agreeable
- ❑ AMITY — friendship
- ❑ AMORAL — unprincipled, unethical
- ❑ AMOROUS — strongly attracted to love; showing love
- ❑ AMORPHOUS — having no definite form
- ❑ AMORTIZE — to diminish by installment payments
- ❑ AMPHIBIAN — creature equally at home on land or in water
- ❑ AMPHITHEATER — arena theater with rising tiers around a central open space
- ❑ AMPLE — abundant, plentiful
- ❑ AMPLIFY — increase, intensify
- ❑ AMULET — ornament worn as a charm against evil spirits
- ❑ ANACHRONISM — something chronologically inappropriate
- ❑ ANACHRONISTIC — out-dated
- ❑ ANALOGOUS — comparable, parallel
- ❑ ANARCHY — absence of government or law; chaos
- ❑ ANATHEMA — ban, curse; something shunned or disliked
- ❑ ANCILLARY — accessory, subordinate, helping
- ❑ ANECDOTE — short, usually funny account of an event
- ❑ ANGULAR — characterized by sharp angles; lean and gaunt
- ❑ ANIMATION — enthusiasm, excitement
- ❑ ANIMOSITY — hatred, hostility

- ❑ ANNUL — to cancel, nullify, declare void, or make legally invalid
- ❑ ANODYNE — something that calms or soothes pain
- ❑ ANOINT — to apply oil to, esp. as a sacred rite
- ❑ ANOMALY — irregularity or deviation from the norm
- ❑ ANONYMITY — condition of having no name or an unknown name
- ❑ ANTAGONIST — foe, opponent, adversary
- ❑ ANTECEDENT (adj.) — coming before in place or time
- ❑ ANTEDILUVIAN — prehistoric, ancient beyond measure
- ❑ ANTEPENULTIMATE — third from last
- ❑ ANTERIOR — preceding, previous, before, prior (to)
- ❑ ANTHOLOGY — collection of literary works
- ❑ ANTHROPOMORPHIC — attributing human qualities to non-humans
- ❑ ANTIPATHY — dislike, hostility; extreme opposition or aversion
- ❑ ANTIQUATED — outdated, obsolete
- ❑ ANTIQUITY — ancient times; the quality of being old or ancient
- ❑ ANTITHESIS — exact opposite or direct contrast
- ❑ APATHETIC — indifferent, unconcerned
- ❑ APATHY — lack of feeling or emotion
- ❑ APHASIA — inability to speak or use words
- ❑ APHELION — point in a planet's orbit that is farthest from the sun
- ❑ APHORISM — old saying or short pithy statement
- ❑ APOCRYPHAL — not genuine; fictional
- ❑ APOSTATE — one who renounces a religious faith
- ❑ APOSTROPHE — an address to the reader or someone not present
- ❑ APOTHEOSIS — glorification; glorified ideal
- ❑ APPEASE — to satisfy, placate, calm, pacify
- ❑ APPROBATION — praise; official approval
- ❑ APPROPRIATE (v.) — to take possession of
- ❑ AQUATIC — belonging or living in water
- ❑ ARABLE — suitable for cultivation
- ❑ ARBITRARY — depending solely on individual will; inconsistent
- ❑ ARBITRATOR — mediator, negotiator
- ❑ ARBOREAL — relating to trees; living in trees
- ❑ ARBORETUM — place where trees are displayed and studied
- ❑ ARCANE — secret, obscure, known only to a few
- ❑ ARCHAIC — antiquated, from an earlier time; outdated
- ❑ ARCHIPELAGO — large group of islands
- ❑ ARDENT — passionate, enthusiastic, fervent
- ❑ ARDOR — great emotion or passion

- ❑ ARDUOUS — extremely difficult, laborious
- ❑ ARID — extremely dry or deathly boring
- ❑ ARRAIGN — to call to court to answer an indictment
- ❑ ARROGATE — to demand, claim arrogantly
- ❑ ARSENAL — ammunition storehouse
- ❑ ARTICULATE (adj.) — well-spoken, expressing oneself clearly
- ❑ ARTIFACT — historical relic, item made by human craft
- ❑ ARTISAN — craftsperson; expert
- ❑ ASCEND — to rise or climb
- ❑ ASCENDANCY — state of rising, ascending; power or control
- ❑ ASCERTAIN — to determine, discover, make certain of
- ❑ ASCETIC — self-denying, abstinent, austere
- ❑ ASCRIBE — to attribute to, assign
- ❑ ASHEN — resembling ashes; deathly pale
- ❑ ASKEW — crooked, tilted
- ❑ ASPERSION — false rumor, damaging report, slander
- ❑ ASPIRE — to have great hopes; to aim at a goal
- ❑ ASSAIL — to attack, assault
- ❑ ASSENT — to express agreement
- ❑ ASSERT — to affirm, attest
- ❑ ASSIDUOUS — diligent, persistent, hard-working
- ❑ ASSIGNATION — appointment for lovers' meeting; assignment
- ❑ ASSIMILATION — act of blending in, becoming similar
- ❑ ASSONANCE — resemblance in sound, especially in vowel sounds; partial rhyme
- ❑ ASSUAGE — to make less severe, ease, relieve
- ❑ ASTRINGENT — harsh, severe, stern
- ❑ ASTUTE — having good judgment
- ❑ ASUNDER (adv.) — into different parts
- ❑ ASYMMETRICAL — not corresponding in size, shape, position, etc.
- ❑ ATONE — to make amends for a wrong
- ❑ ATROCIOUS — monstrous, shockingly bad, wicked
- ❑ ATROPHY — to waste away, wither from disuse
- ❑ ATTAIN — to accomplish, gain
- ❑ ATTENUATE — to make thin or slender; weaken
- ❑ ATTEST — to testify, stand as proof of, bear witness
- ❑ AUDACIOUS — bold, daring, fearless
- ❑ AUDIBLE — capable of being heard
- ❑ AUDIT — formal examination of financial records
- ❑ AUDITORY — having to do with hearing
- ❑ AUGMENT — to expand, extend
- ❑ AUGURY — prophecy, prediction of events
- ❑ AUGUST — dignified, awe-inspiring, venerable

- ❑ AUSPICIOUS — having favorable prospects, promising
- ❑ AUSTERE — stern, strict, unadorned
- ❑ AUTHORITARIAN — extremely strict, bossy
- ❑ AUTOCRAT — dictator
- ❑ AUTONOMOUS — separate, independent
- ❑ AUXILIARY — supplementary, reserve
- ❑ AVARICE — greed
- ❑ AVENGE — to retaliate, take revenge for an injury or crime
- ❑ AVER — to declare to be true, affirm
- ❑ AVERSION — intense dislike
- ❑ AVERT — to turn (something) away; prevent, hinder
- ❑ AVIARY — large enclosure housing birds
- ❑ AVOW — to state openly or declare
- ❑ AWRY — crooked, askew, amiss
- ❑ AXIOM — premise, postulate, self-evident truth

B

- ❑ BALEFUL — harmful, with evil intentions
- ❑ BALK — to refuse, shirk; prevent
- ❑ BALLAD — folk song, narrative poem
- ❑ BALM — soothing, healing influence
- ❑ BAN — to forbid, outlaw
- ❑ BANAL — trite and overly common
- ❑ BANE — something causing death, destruction, or ruin
- ❑ BANTER — playful conversation
- ❑ BASTION — fortification, stronghold
- ❑ BAY (v.) — to bark, especially in a deep, prolonged way
- ❑ BECALM — to make calm or still; keep motionless by lack of wind
- ❑ BECLOUD — to confuse; darken with clouds
- ❑ BEGUILE — to deceive, mislead; charm
- ❑ BEHEMOTH — huge creature
- ❑ BELABOR — to insist repeatedly or harp on
- ❑ BELATED — late
- ❑ BELEAGUER — to harass, plague
- ❑ BELFRY — bell tower, room in which a bell is hung
- ❑ BELIE — to misrepresent; expose as false
- ❑ BELITTLE — to represent as unimportant, make light of
- ❑ BELLICOSE — warlike, aggressive
- ❑ BELLIGERENT — hostile, tending to fight
- ❑ BELLOW — to roar, shout
- ❑ BEMUSE — to confuse, stupefy; plunge deep into thought

- ❏ BENCHMARK — standard of measure
- ❏ BENEFACTOR — someone giving aid or money
- ❏ BENEFICENT — kindly, charitable; doing good deeds; producing good effects
- ❏ BENIGHTED — unenlightened
- ❏ BENIGN — kindly, gentle or harmless
- ❏ BEQUEATH — to give or leave through a will; to hand down
- ❏ BERATE — to scold harshly
- ❏ BESEECH — to beg, plead, implore
- ❏ BESTIAL — beastly, animal-like
- ❏ BESTOW — to give as a gift
- ❏ BETOKEN — to indicate, signify, give evidence of
- ❏ BEVY — group
- ❏ BIAS — prejudice, slant
- ❏ BIBLIOGRAPHY — list of books
- ❏ BIBLIOPHILE — book lover
- ❏ BILATERAL — two-sided
- ❏ BILK — to cheat, defraud
- ❏ BILLET — board and lodging for troops
- ❏ BIPED — two-footed animal
- ❏ BISECT — to cut into two (usually equal) parts
- ❏ BLANCH — to pale; take the color out of
- ❏ BLANDISH — to coax with flattery
- ❏ BLASPHEMOUS — cursing, profane, irreverent
- ❏ BLATANT — glaring, obvious, showy
- ❏ BLIGHT (v.) — to afflict, destroy
- ❏ BLITHE — joyful, cheerful, or without appropriate thought
- ❏ BLUDGEON — to hit as with a short, heavy club
- ❏ BOISTEROUS — rowdy, loud, unrestrained
- ❏ BOMBASTIC — using high-sounding but meaningless language
- ❏ BONANZA — extremely large amount; something profitable
- ❏ BONHOMIE — good-natured geniality; atmosphere of good cheer
- ❏ BOON — blessing, something to be thankful for
- ❏ BOOR — crude person, one lacking manners or taste
- ❏ BOTANIST — scientist who studies plants
- ❏ BOUNTIFUL — plentiful
- ❏ BOURGEOIS — middle-class
- ❏ BOVINE — cow-like; relating to cows
- ❏ BRAZEN — bold, shameless, impudent; of or like brass
- ❏ BREACH — act of breaking, violation
- ❏ BRIGAND — bandit, outlaw
- ❏ BROACH — to mention or suggest for the first time
- ❏ BRUSQUE — rough and abrupt in manner

- ❏ BUFFET (v.) — to strike, hit
- ❏ BUFFOON — clown or fool
- ❏ BULWARK — defense wall; anything serving as defense
- ❏ BURGEON — to sprout or flourish
- ❏ BURLY — brawny, husky
- ❏ BURNISH — to polish, make smooth and bright
- ❏ BURSAR — treasurer
- ❏ BUSTLE — commotion, energetic activity
- ❏ BUTT — person or thing that is object of ridicule
- ❏ BUTTRESS (n.) — to reinforce or support
- ❏ BYWAY — back road

C

- ❏ CACOPHONOUS — jarring, unpleasantly noisy
- ❏ CADENCE — rhythmic flow of poetry; marching beat
- ❏ CAJOLE — to flatter, coax, persuade
- ❏ CALAMITOUS — disastrous, catastrophic
- ❏ CALLOUS — thick-skinned, insensitive
- ❏ CALLOW — immature, lacking sophistication
- ❏ CALUMNY — false and malicious accusation, misrepresentation, slander
- ❏ CANDOR — honesty of expression
- ❏ CANNY — smart; founded on common sense
- ❏ CANONIZE — to declare a person a saint; raise to highest honors
- ❏ CANVASS — to examine thoroughly; conduct a poll
- ❏ CAPACIOUS — large, roomy; extensive
- ❏ CAPITULATE — to submit completely, surrender
- ❏ CAPRICIOUS — impulsive, whimsical, without much thought
- ❏ CARDIOLOGIST — physician specializing in diseases of the heart
- ❏ CARICATURE — exaggerated portrait, cartoon
- ❏ CARNAL — of the flesh
- ❏ CARNIVOROUS — meat-eating
- ❏ CARP (v.) — to find fault, complain constantly
- ❏ CARTOGRAPHY — science or art of making maps
- ❏ CAST (n.) — copy, replica
- ❏ CAST (v.) — to fling, to throw
- ❏ CASTIGATE — to punish, chastise, criticize severely
- ❏ CATALYST — something causing change without being changed
- ❏ CATEGORICAL — absolute, without exception
- ❏ CATHARSIS — purification, cleansing
- ❏ CATHOLIC — universal; broad and comprehensive

❑ CAUCUS — smaller group within an organization; a meeting of such a group

❑ CAULK — to make watertight

❑ CAUSALITY — cause-and-effect relationship

❑ CAUSTIC — biting, sarcastic; able to burn

❑ CAVALIER — carefree, happy; with lordly disdain

❑ CAVORT — to frolic, frisk

❑ CEDE — to surrender possession of something

❑ CELEBRITY — fame, widespread acclaim

❑ CENSORIOUS — severely critical

❑ CENTRIPETAL — directed or moving toward the center

❑ CERTITUDE — assurance, certainty

❑ CESSATION — temporary or complete halt

❑ CESSION — act of surrendering something

❑ CHAGRIN — shame, embarrassment, humiliation

❑ CHALICE — goblet, cup

❑ CHAMPION (v.) — to defend or support

❑ CHAOTIC — extremely disorderly

❑ CHARLATAN — quack, fake

❑ CHARY — watchful, cautious, extremely shy

❑ CHASTISE — to punish, discipline, scold

❑ CHERUBIC — sweet, innocent, resembling a cherub angel

❑ CHICANERY — trickery, fraud, deception

❑ CHIDE — to scold, express disapproval

❑ CHIMERICAL — fanciful, imaginary, visionary, impossible

❑ CHOLERIC — easily angered, short-tempered

❑ CHOICE (adj.) — specially selected, preferred

❑ CHORTLE — to chuckle

❑ CHROMATIC — relating to color

❑ CHRONICLER — one who keeps records of historical events

❑ CIRCUITOUS — roundabout

❑ CIRCUMFERENCE — boundary or distance around a circle or sphere

❑ CIRCUMLOCUTION — roundabout, lengthy way of saying something

❑ CIRCUMNAVIGATE — to sail completely around

❑ CIRCUMSCRIBE — to encircle; set limits on, confine

❑ CIRCUMSPECT — cautious, wary

❑ CIRCUMVENT — to go around; avoid

❑ CISTERN — tank for rainwater

❑ CITADEL — fortress or stronghold

❑ CIVIL — polite; relating to citizens

❑ CIVILITY — courtesy, politeness

❑ CLAIRVOYANT (adj.) — having ESP, psychic

❑ CLAMOR (v.) — to make a noisy outcry

❑ CLAMOR (n.) — noisy outcry

❑ CLANDESTINE — secretive, concealed for a darker purpose

❑ CLARITY — clearness; clear understanding

❑ CLAUSTROPHOBIA — fear of small, confined places

❑ CLEAVE — to split or separate or to stick, cling, adhere

❑ CLEMENCY — merciful leniency

❑ CLOISTER (v.) — to confine, seclude

❑ COAGULATE — to clot or change from a liquid to a solid

❑ COALESCE — to grow together or cause to unite as one

❑ CODDLE — to baby, treat indulgently

❑ COERCE — to compel by force or intimidation

❑ COFFER — strongbox, large chest for money

❑ COGENT — logically forceful, compelling, convincing

❑ COGNATE — related, similar, akin

❑ COGNITION — mental process by which knowledge is acquired

❑ COGNOMEN — family name; any name, especially a nickname

❑ COHABIT — to live together

❑ COHERENT — intelligible, lucid, understandable

❑ COLLATERAL — accompanying

❑ COLLOQUIAL — characteristic of informal speech

❑ COLLOQUY — dialogue or conversation, conference

❑ COLLUSION — collaboration, complicity, conspiracy

❑ COMELINESS — physical grace and beauty

❑ COMMEND — to compliment, praise

❑ COMMENSURATE — proportional

❑ COMMISSION — fee payable to an agent; authorization

❑ COMMODIOUS — roomy, spacious

❑ COMMONPLACE — ordinary, found every day

❑ COMMUNICABLE — transmittable

❑ COMMUTE — to change a penalty to a less severe one

❑ COMPATRIOT — fellow countryman

❑ COMPELLING (adj.) — having a powerful and irresistible effect

❑ COMPENSATE — to repay or reimburse

❑ COMPLACENT — self-satisfied, smug

❑ COMPLEMENT — to complete, perfect

❑ COMPLIANT — submissive and yielding

❑ COMPLICITY — knowing partnership in wrongdoing

❑ COMPOUND (adj.) — complex; composed of several parts

❑ COMPOUND (v.) — to combine, augment

- ❑ COMPRESS — to reduce, squeeze
- ❑ COMPULSIVE — obsessive, fanatic
- ❑ COMPUNCTION — feeling of uneasiness caused by guilt or regret
- ❑ CONCAVE — curving inward
- ❑ CONCEDE — to yield, admit
- ❑ CONCEPTUALIZE — to envision, imagine
- ❑ CONCERTO — musical composition for orchestra and soloist(s)
- ❑ CONCILIATORY — overcoming distrust or hostility
- ❑ CONCORD — agreement
- ❑ CONCUR — to agree
- ❑ CONDONE — to pardon or forgive; overlook, justify, or excuse a fault
- ❑ CONDUIT — tube, pipe, or similar passage
- ❑ CONFECTION — something sweet to eat
- ❑ CONFISCATE — to appropriate, seize
- ❑ CONFLAGRATION — big, destructive fire
- ❑ CONFLUENCE — meeting place; meeting of two streams
- ❑ CONFOUND — to baffle, perplex
- ❑ CONGEAL — to become thick or solid, as a liquid freezing
- ❑ CONGENIAL — similar in tastes and habits
- ❑ CONGENITAL — existing since birth
- ❑ CONGLOMERATE — collected group of varied things
- ❑ CONGRESS — formal meeting or assembly
- ❑ CONGRUITY — correspondence, harmony, agreement
- ❑ CONJECTURE — speculation, prediction
- ❑ CONJUGAL — pertaining to marriage
- ❑ CONJURE — to evoke a spirit, cast a spell
- ❑ CONNIVE — to conspire, scheme
- ❑ CONSANGUINEOUS — of the same origin; related by blood
- ❑ CONSCIENTIOUS — governed by conscience; careful and thorough
- ❑ CONSECRATE — to declare sacred; dedicate to a goal
- ❑ CONSENSUS — unanimity, agreement of opinion or attitude
- ❑ CONSIGN — to commit, entrust
- ❑ CONSOLATION — something providing comfort or solace for a loss or hardship
- ❑ CONSOLIDATE — to combine, incorporate
- ❑ CONSONANT (adj.) — consistent with, in agreement with
- ❑ CONSTITUENT — component, part; citizen, voter
- ❑ CONSTRAINED — forced, compelled; confined, restrained

- ❑ CONSTRAINT — something that forces or compels; something which restrains or confines
- ❑ CONSTRUE — to explain or interpret
- ❑ CONSUMMATE (adj.) — accomplished, complete, perfect
- ❑ CONSUMMATE (v.) — to complete, fulfill
- ❑ CONTEND — to battle, clash; compete
- ❑ CONTENTIOUS — quarrelsome, disagreeable, belligerent
- ❑ CONTINENCE — self-control, self-restraint
- ❑ CONTRAVENE — to contradict, deny, act contrary to
- ❑ CONTRITE — deeply sorrowful and repentant for a wrong
- ❑ CONTUSION — bruise
- ❑ CONUNDRUM — riddle, puzzle or problem with no solution
- ❑ CONVALESCENCE — gradual recovery after an illness
- ❑ CONVENE — to meet, come together, assemble
- ❑ CONVENTIONAL — typical, customary, commonplace
- ❑ CONVEX — curved outward
- ❑ CONVIVIAL — sociable; fond of eating, drinking, and people
- ❑ CONVOKE — to call together, summon
- ❑ CONVOLUTED — twisted, complicated, involved
- ❑ COPIOUS — abundant, plentiful
- ❑ COQUETTE — woman who flirts
- ❑ CORPOREAL — having to do with the body; tangible, material
- ❑ CORPULENCE — obesity, fatness, bulkiness
- ❑ CORRELATION — association, mutual relation of two or more things
- ❑ CORROBORATE — to confirm, verify
- ❑ CORRUGATE — to mold in a shape with parallel grooves and ridges
- ❑ COSMETIC (adj.) — relating to beauty; affecting the surface of something
- ❑ COSMOGRAPHY — science that deals with the nature of the universe
- ❑ COSMOPOLITAN — sophisticated, free from local prejudices
- ❑ COSSET — to pamper, treat with great care
- ❑ COTERIE — small group of persons with a similar purpose
- ❑ COUNTENANCE (n.) — facial expression; look of approval or support
- ❑ COUNTENANCE (v.) — to favor, support
- ❑ COUNTERMAND — to annul, cancel, make a contrary order
- ❑ COUNTERVAIL — to counteract, to exert force against
- ❑ COVEN — group of witches

❑ COVERT — hidden; secret

❑ COVET — to desire strongly something possessed by another

❑ CRASS — crude, unrefined

❑ CRAVEN — cowardly

❑ CREDENCE — acceptance of something as true or real

❑ CREDIBLE — plausible, believable

❑ CREDULOUS — gullible, trusting

❑ CREED — statement of belief or principle

❑ CRESCENDO — gradual increase in volume of sound

❑ CRITERION — standard for judging, rule for testing

❑ CRYPTIC — puzzling

❑ CUISINE — characteristic style of cooking

❑ CULMINATION — climax, final stage

❑ CULPABLE — guilty, responsible for wrong

❑ CULPRIT — guilty person

❑ CUMULATIVE — resulting from gradual increase

❑ CUPIDITY — greed

❑ CURATOR — caretaker and overseer of an exhibition, esp. in a museum

❑ CURMUDGEON — cranky person

❑ CURSORY — hastily done, superficial

❑ CURT — abrupt, blunt

❑ CURTAIL — to shorten

❑ CUTLERY — cutting instruments; tableware

❑ CYGNET — young swan

❑ CYNIC — person who distrusts the motives of others

D

❑ DAINTY — delicate, sweet

❑ DAUNT — to discourage, intimidate

❑ DEARTH — lack, scarcity, insufficiency

❑ DEBASE — to degrade or lower in quality or stature

❑ DEBAUCH — to corrupt, seduce from virtue or duty; indulge

❑ DEBILITATE — to weaken, enfeeble

❑ DEBUNK — to discredit, disprove

❑ DEBUTANTE — young woman making debut in high society

❑ DECAPITATE — to behead

❑ DECATHLON — athletic contest with ten events

❑ DECIDUOUS — losing leaves in the fall; short-lived, temporary

❑ DECLIVITY — downward slope

❑ DECOROUS — proper, tasteful, socially correct

❑ DECORUM — proper behavior, etiquette

❑ DECRY — to belittle, openly condemn

❑ DEFACE — to mar the appearance of, vandalize

❑ DEFAMATORY — slanderous, injurious to the reputation

❑ DEFENDANT — person required to answer a legal action or suit

❑ DEFERENTIAL — respectful and polite in a submissive way

❑ DEFILE — to dirty, spoil; to disgrace, dishonor

❑ DEFINITIVE — clear-cut, explicit or decisive

❑ DEFLATION — decrease, depreciation

❑ DEFORM — to disfigure, distort

❑ DEFT — skillful, dexterous

❑ DEFUNCT — no longer existing, dead, extinct

❑ DELECTABLE — appetizing, delicious

❑ DELEGATE (v.) — to give powers to another

❑ DELETERIOUS — harmful, destructive, detrimental

❑ DELINEATION — depiction, representation

❑ DELTA — tidal deposit at the mouth of a river

❑ DELUGE (n.) — flood

❑ DELUGE (v.) — to submerge, overwhelm

❑ DEMAGOGUE — leader, rabble-rouser, usually using appeals to emotion or prejudice

❑ DEMARCATION — borderline; act of defining or marking a boundary or distinction

❑ DEMEAN — to degrade, humiliate, humble

❑ DEMOGRAPHICS — data relating to study of human population

❑ DEMOTE — to reduce to a lower grade or rank

❑ DEMOTION — lowering in rank or grade

❑ DEMUR — to express doubts or objections

❑ DEMYSTIFY — to remove mystery from, clarify

❑ DENIGRATE — to slur or blacken someone's reputation

❑ DENOUNCE — to accuse, blame

❑ DENUDE — to make bare, uncover, undress

❑ DENUNCIATION — public condemnation

❑ DEPICT — to describe, represent

❑ DEPLETE — to use up, exhaust

❑ DEPLORE — to express or feel disapproval of; regret strongly

❑ DEPLOY — to spread out strategically over an area

❑ DEPOSE — to remove from a high position, as from a throne

❑ DEPRAVITY — sinfulness, moral corruption

❑ DEPRECATE — to lessen in value, belittle, disparage

❑ DEPRECIATE — to lose value gradually

- DERIDE — to mock, ridicule, make fun of
- DERIVATIVE — copied or adapted; not original
- DERIVE — to originate; take from a certain source
- DEROGATE — to belittle, disparage
- DESECRATE — to abuse something sacred
- DESICCATE — to dry completely, dehydrate
- DESIST — to stop doing something
- DESPONDENT — feeling discouraged and dejected
- DESPOT — tyrannical ruler
- DESTITUTE — very poor, poverty-stricken
- DESULTORY — at random, rambling, unmethodical
- DETER — to discourage; prevent from happening
- DETERMINATE — having defined limits; conclusive
- DETRIMENTAL — causing harm or injury
- DEVIATE — to stray, wander
- DEVIATION — departure, exception, anomaly
- DEVOID — totally lacking
- DEVOUT — deeply religious
- DEXTEROUS — skilled physically or mentally
- DIABOLICAL — fiendish; wicked
- DIALECT — regional style of speaking
- DIAPHANOUS — allowing light to show through; delicate
- DIATRIBE — bitter verbal attack
- DICHOTOMY — division into two parts
- DICTUM — authoritative statement; popular saying
- DIDACTIC — excessively instructive
- DIFFERENTIATE — to distinguish between two items
- DIFFIDENCE — shyness, lack of confidence
- DIFFRACT — to cause to separate into parts, esp. light
- DIFFUSE — widely spread out
- DIGRESS — to turn aside; to stray from the main point
- DILAPIDATED — in disrepair, run down, neglected
- DILATE — to enlarge, swell, extend
- DILATORY — slow, tending to delay
- DILUVIAL — relating to a flood
- DIMINUTIVE — small
- DIPLOMACY — discretion, tact
- DIRGE — funeral hymn
- DISAFFECTED — discontented and disloyal
- DISARRAY — clutter, disorder
- DISBAND — to break up
- DISBAR — to expel from legal profession
- DISBURSE — to pay out
- DISCERN — to perceive something obscure
- DISCLAIM — to deny, disavow

- DISCLOSE — to confess, divulge
- DISCONCERTING — bewildering, perplexing, slightly disturbing
- DISCORDANT — harsh-sounding, badly out of tune
- DISCREDIT — to dishonor or disgrace
- DISCREDITED — disbelieved, discounted; disgraced, dishonored
- DISCREPANCY — difference between
- DISCRETIONARY — subject to one's own judgment
- DISCURSIVE — wandering from topic to topic
- DISDAIN — to regard with scorn and contempt
- DISDAINFUL — contemptuous, scornful
- DISENGAGED — disconnected, disassociated
- DISGORGE — to vomit, discharge violently
- DISHEVELED — untidy, disarranged, unkempt
- DISINCLINED — averse, unwilling, lacking desire
- DISPARAGE — to belittle, speak disrespectfully about
- DISPARATE — dissimilar, different in kind
- DISPARITY — contrast, dissimilarity
- DISPASSIONATE — free from emotion; impartial, unbiased
- DISPEL — to drive out or scatter
- DISPENSE — to distribute, administer
- DISPENSE WITH — to suspend the operation of, do without
- DISPERSE — to break up, scatter
- DISPIRIT — to dishearten, make dejected
- DISREPUTE — disgrace, dishonor
- DISSEMBLE — to pretend, disguise one's motives
- DISSEMINATE — to spread far and wide
- DISSENSION — difference of opinion
- DISSIPATE — to scatter; to pursue pleasure to excess
- DISSOCIATE — to separate; remove from an association
- DISSONANT — harsh and unpleasant sounding
- DISSUADE — to persuade someone to alter original intentions
- DISTEND — to swell, inflate, bloat
- DISTRAUGHT — very worried and distressed
- DISTRUST (n.) — disbelief and suspicion
- DITHER — to move or act confusedly or without clear purpose
- DIURNAL — daily
- DIVINE (v.) — to foretell or know by inspiration
- DIVISIVE — creating disunity or conflict
- DOCILE — tame, willing to be taught
- DOCTRINAIRE — rigidly devoted to theories
- DOGMATIC — rigidly fixed in opinion, opinionated
- DOLEFUL — sad, mournful

- DOLT — idiot, dimwit, foolish person
- DOMINEER — to rule over something in a tyrannical way
- DONOR — benefactor, contributor
- DORMANT — at rest, inactive, in suspended animation
- DOTARD — senile old person
- DOTING — excessively fond, loving to excess
- DOUR — sullen and gloomy; stern and severe
- DOWRY — money or property given by a bride to her husband
- DRAFT (v.) — to plan, outline; to recruit, conscript
- DRIVEL — stupid talk; slobber
- DROLL — amusing in a wry, subtle way
- DROSS — waste produced during metal smelting; garbage
- DULCET — pleasant sounding, soothing to the ear
- DUPE (v.) — to deceive, trick
- DUPE (n.) — fool, pawn
- DUPLICITY — deception, dishonesty, double-dealing
- DURABILITY — strength, sturdiness
- DURATION — period of time that something lasts
- DURESS — threat of force or intimidation; imprisonment
- DYSPEPTIC — suffering from indigestion; gloomy and irritable

E

- EBB — to fade away, recede
- EBULLIENT — exhilarated, full of enthusiasm and high spirits
- ECLECTIC — selecting from various sources
- ECSTATIC — joyful
- EDDY — air or wind current
- EDICT — law, command, official public order
- EDIFICE — building
- EDIFY — to instruct morally and spiritually
- EDITORIALIZE — to express an opinion on an issue
- EFFACE — to erase or make illegible
- EFFERVESCENT — bubbly, lively
- EFFICACIOUS — effective, efficient
- EFFIGY — stuffed doll; likeness of a person
- EFFLUVIA — outpouring of gases or vapors
- EFFRONTERY — impudent boldness; audacity
- EFFULGENT — brilliantly shining

- EFFUSIVE — expressing emotion without restraint
- EGOCENTRIC — acting as if things are centered around oneself
- EGREGIOUS — conspicuously bad
- EGRESS — exit
- ELATION — exhilaration, joy
- ELEGY — mournful poem, usually about the dead
- ELICIT — to draw out, provoke
- ELOQUENCE — fluent and effective speech
- ELUCIDATE — to explain, clarify
- EMACIATED — skinny, scrawny, gaunt, esp. from hunger
- EMANCIPATION — to set free, liberate
- EMBELLISH — to ornament; make attractive with decoration or details; add details to a statement
- EMBEZZLE — to steal money in violation of a trust
- EMBROIL — to involve in; cause to fall into disorder
- EMEND — to correct a text
- EMINENT — celebrated, distinguished; outstanding, towering
- EMOLLIENT — having soothing qualities, especially for skin
- EMOTIVE — appealing to or expressing emotion
- EMPATHY — sympathy, identification with another's feelings
- EMULATE — to copy, imitate
- ENCIPHER — to translate a message into code
- ENCORE — additional performance, often demanded by audience
- ENCUMBER — to hinder, burden, restrict motion
- ENDEMIC — belonging to a particular area, inherent
- ENDURANCE — ability to withstand hardships
- ENERVATE — to weaken, sap strength from
- ENGENDER — to produce, cause, bring about
- ENIGMATIC — puzzling, inexplicable
- ENJOIN — to urge, order, command; forbid or prohibit, as by judicial order
- ENMITY — hostility, antagonism, ill-will
- ENNUI — boredom, lack of interest and energy
- ENORMITY — state of being gigantic or terrible
- ENSCONCE — to settle comfortably into a place
- ENSHROUD — to cover, enclose with a dark cover
- ENTAIL — to involve as a necessary result, necessitate
- ENTHRALL — to captivate, enchant, enslave
- ENTITY — something with its own existence or form
- ENTOMOLOGIST — scientist who studies insects
- ENTREAT — to plead, beg
- ENUMERATE — to count, list, itemize

- ❏ ENUNCIATE — to pronounce clearly
- ❏ EPHEMERAL — momentary, transient, fleeting
- ❏ EPICURE — person with refined taste in food and wine
- ❏ EPIGRAM — short, witty saying or poem
- ❏ EPIGRAPH — quotation at the beginning of a literary work
- ❏ EPILOGUE — concluding section of a literary work
- ❏ EPITOME — representative of an entire group; summary
- ❏ EPOCHAL — very significant or influential; defining an epoch or time-period
- ❏ EQUANIMITY — calmness, composure
- ❏ EQUESTRIAN — one who rides on horseback
- ❏ EQUINE — relating to horses
- ❏ EQUIVOCAL — ambiguous, open to two interpretations
- ❏ EQUIVOCATE — to use vague or ambiguous language intentionally
- ❏ ERADICATE — to erase or wipe out
- ❏ ERRANT — straying, mistaken, roving
- ❏ ERUDITE — learned, scholarly
- ❏ ESCHEW — to abstain from, avoid
- ❏ ESOTERIC — understood only by a learned few
- ❏ ESPOUSE — to support or advocate; to marry
- ❏ ESTRANGE — to alienate, keep at a distance
- ❏ ETHEREAL — not earthly, spiritual, delicate
- ❏ ETHOS — beliefs or character of a group
- ❏ ETYMOLOGY — origin and history of a word; study of words
- ❏ EULOGY — high praise, often in a public speech
- ❏ EUPHEMISM — use of an inoffensive word or phrase in place of a more distasteful one
- ❏ EUPHONY — pleasant, harmonious sound
- ❏ EUPHORIA — feeling of well-being or happiness
- ❏ EURYTHMICS — art of harmonious bodily movement
- ❏ EUTHANASIA — mercy-killing; intentional, easy and painless death
- ❏ EVADE — to avoid, dodge
- ❏ EVANESCENT — momentary, transitory, short-lived
- ❏ EVICT — to put out or force out
- ❏ EVINCE — to show clearly, display, signify
- ❏ EVOKE — to inspire memories; to produce a reaction
- ❏ EXACERBATE — to aggravate, intensify the bad qualities of
- ❏ EXASPERATION — irritation
- ❏ EXCERPT (n.) — selection from a book or play
- ❏ EXCOMMUNICATE — to bar from membership in the church
- ❏ EXCRUCIATING — agonizing, intensely painful

- ❏ EXCULPATE — to clear of blame or fault, vindicate
- ❏ EXECRABLE — utterly detestable, abhorrent
- ❏ EXHILARATION — state of being energetic or filled with happiness
- ❏ EXHORT — to urge or incite by strong appeals
- ❏ EXHUME — to remove from a grave; uncover a secret
- ❏ EXIGENT — urgent; excessively demanding
- ❏ EXONERATE — to clear of blame, absolve
- ❏ EXORBITANT — extravagant, greater than reasonable
- ❏ EXORCISE — to expel evil spirits
- ❏ EXOTIC — foreign; romantic, excitingly strange
- ❏ EXPANSIVE — sweeping, comprehensive; tending to expand
- ❏ EXPATRIATE (n.) — one who lives outside one's native land
- ❏ EXPATRIATE (v.) — to drive someone from his/her native land
- ❏ EXPEDIENT (adj.) — convenient, efficient, practical
- ❏ EXPIATE — to atone for, make amends for
- ❏ EXPIRE — to come to an end; die; breathe out
- ❏ EXPLICABLE — capable of being explained
- ❏ EXPLICIT — clearly defined, specific; forthright in expression
- ❏ EXPLODE — to debunk, disprove; blow up, burst
- ❏ EXPONENT — one who champions or advocates
- ❏ EXPOUND — to elaborate; to expand or increase
- ❏ EXPUNGE — to erase, eliminate completely
- ❏ EXPURGATE — to censor
- ❏ EXTEMPORANEOUS — unrehearsed, on the spur of the moment
- ❏ EXTENUATE — to lessen the seriousness, strength or effect of
- ❏ EXTINCTION — end of a living thing or species
- ❏ EXTOL — to praise
- ❏ EXTORT — to obtain something by threats
- ❏ EXTRANEOUS — irrelevant, unrelated, unnecessary
- ❏ EXTREMITY — outermost or farthest point
- ❏ EXTRICATE — to free from, disentangle, free
- ❏ EXTRINSIC — not inherent or essential, coming from without
- ❏ EXUBERANT — lively, happy, and full of good spirits
- ❏ EXUDE — to give off, ooze
- ❏ EXULT — to rejoice

F

- ❏ FABRICATE — to make or devise; construct

- ❑ FABRICATED — constructed, invented; faked, falsified
- ❑ FACADE — face, front; mask, superficial appearance
- ❑ FACILE — very easy
- ❑ FACILITATE — to aid, assist
- ❑ FACILITY — aptitude, ease in doing something
- ❑ FALLACIOUS — wrong, unsound, illogical
- ❑ FALLOW — uncultivated, unused
- ❑ FANATICISM — extreme devotion to a cause
- ❑ FARCICAL — absurd, ludicrous
- ❑ FASTIDIOUS — careful with details
- ❑ FATHOM (v.) — to measure the depth of, gauge
- ❑ FATUOUS — stupid; foolishly self-satisfied
- ❑ FAULT — break in a rock formation; mistake or error
- ❑ FAWN (v.) — to flatter excessively, seek the favor of
- ❑ FAZE — to bother, upset, or disconcert
- ❑ FEASIBLE — possible, capable of being done
- ❑ FECKLESS — ineffective, careless, irresponsible
- ❑ FECUND — fertile, fruitful, productive
- ❑ FEDERATION — union of organizations; union of several states, each of which retains local power
- ❑ FEIGN — to pretend, give a false impression; to invent falsely
- ❑ FEISTY — excitable, easily drawn into quarrels
- ❑ FELICITOUS — suitable, appropriate; well-spoken
- ❑ FELL (v.) — to chop, cut down
- ❑ FERVID — passionate, intense, zealous
- ❑ FETID — foul-smelling, putrid
- ❑ FETTER — to bind, chain, confine
- ❑ FIASCO — disaster, utter failure
- ❑ FICTIVE — fictional, imaginary
- ❑ FIDELITY — loyalty
- ❑ FILCH — to steal
- ❑ FILIBUSTER — use of obstructive tactics in a legislative assembly to prevent adoption of a measure
- ❑ FINICKY — fussy, difficult to please
- ❑ FISSION — process of splitting into two parts
- ❑ FITFUL — intermittent, irregular
- ❑ FLACCID — limp, flabby, weak
- ❑ FLAGRANT — outrageous, shameless
- ❑ FLAMBOYANT — flashy, garish; exciting, dazzling
- ❑ FLAMMABLE — combustible, being easily burned
- ❑ FLAUNT — to show off
- ❑ FLEDGLING — young bird just learning to fly; beginner, novice
- ❑ FLORA — plants
- ❑ FLORID — gaudy, extremely ornate; ruddy, flushed
- ❑ FLOUNDER — to falter, waver; to muddle, struggle

- ❑ FLOUT — to treat contemptuously, scorn
- ❑ FLUCTUATE — to alternate, waver
- ❑ FODDER — raw material; feed for animals
- ❑ FOIBLE — minor weakness or character flaw
- ❑ FOIL (v.) — to defeat, frustrate
- ❑ FOLIATE — to grow, sprout leaves
- ❑ FOMENT — to arouse or incite
- ❑ FORBEARANCE — patience, restraint, leniency
- ❑ FORECLOSE — to rule out; to seize debtor's property for lack of payments
- ❑ FORD (v.) — to cross a body of water at a shallow place
- ❑ FOREBODING — dark sense of evil to come
- ❑ FORENSIC — relating to legal proceedings; relating to debates
- ❑ FORSAKE — to abandon, withdraw from
- ❑ FORESTALL — to prevent, delay; anticipate
- ❑ FORETHOUGHT — anticipation, foresight
- ❑ FORGO — to go without, refrain from
- ❑ FORLORN — dreary, deserted; unhappy; hopeless, despairing
- ❑ FORMULATE — to conceive, devise; to draft, plan; to express, state
- ❑ FORSWEAR — to repudiate, renounce, disclaim, reject
- ❑ FORTE — strong point, something a person does well
- ❑ FORTUITOUS — happening by luck, fortunate
- ❑ FOSTER — to nourish, cultivate, promote
- ❑ FOUNDATION — groundwork, support; institution established by donation to aid a certain cause
- ❑ FOUNDER (v.) — to fall helplessly; sink
- ❑ FRACAS — noisy dispute
- ❑ FRACTIOUS — unruly, rebellious
- ❑ FRAGMENTATION — division, separation into parts, disorganization
- ❑ FRANK — honest and straightforward
- ❑ FRAUD — deception, hoax
- ❑ FRAUDULENT — deceitful, dishonest, unethical
- ❑ FRAUGHT — full of, accompanied by
- ❑ FRENETIC — wildly frantic, frenzied, hectic
- ❑ FRENZIED — feverishly fast, hectic, and confused
- ❑ FRIVOLOUS — petty, trivial; flippant, silly
- ❑ FROND — leaf
- ❑ FULSOME — excessive, overdone, sickeningly abundant
- ❑ FUNEREAL — mournful, appropriate to a funeral
- ❑ FURTIVE — secret, stealthy
- ❑ FUSION — process of merging things into one

G

- ❏ GALL (n.) — bitterness; careless nerve
- ❏ GALL (v.) — to exasperate and irritate
- ❏ GAMBOL — to dance or skip around playfully
- ❏ GAMELY — courageously
- ❏ GARGANTUAN — giant, tremendous
- ❏ GARNER — to gather and store
- ❏ GARRULOUS — very talkative
- ❏ GAUNT — thin and bony
- ❏ GAVEL — mallet used for commanding attention
- ❏ GENRE — type, class, category
- ❏ GERMINATE — to begin to grow (used of a seed or idea)
- ❏ GESTATION — growth process from conception to birth
- ❏ GIBE — to make heckling, taunting remarks
- ❏ GIRTH — distance around something
- ❏ GLIB — fluent in an insincere manner; off-hand, casual
- ❏ GLOBAL — involving the entire world; relating to a whole
- ❏ GLOWER — to glare, stare angrily and intensely
- ❏ GLUTTONY — eating and drinking to excess
- ❏ GNARL — to make knotted, deform
- ❏ GNOSTIC — having to do with knowledge
- ❏ GOAD — to prod or urge
- ❏ GRADATION — process occurring by regular degrees or stages; variation in color
- ❏ GRANDILOQUENCE — pompous talk, fancy but meaningless language
- ❏ GRANDIOSE — magnificent and imposing; exaggerated and pretentious
- ❏ GRANULAR — having a grainy texture
- ❏ GRASP (v.) — to perceive and understand; to hold securely
- ❏ GRATIS — free, costing nothing
- ❏ GRATUITOUS — free, voluntary; unnecessary and unjustified
- ❏ GRATUITY — something given voluntarily, tip
- ❏ GREGARIOUS — outgoing, sociable
- ❏ GRIEVOUS — causing grief or sorrow; serious and distressing
- ❏ GRIMACE — facial expression showing pain or disgust
- ❏ GRIMY — dirty, filthy
- ❏ GROSS (adj.) — obscene; blatant, flagrant
- ❏ GROSS (n.) — total before deductions
- ❏ GROVEL — to humble oneself in a demeaning way
- ❏ GUILE — trickery, deception
- ❏ GULLIBLE — easily deceived
- ❏ GUSTATORY — relating to sense of taste

H

- ❏ HABITAT — dwelling place
- ❏ HACKNEYED — worn out by over-use
- ❏ HALLOW — to make holy; treat as sacred
- ❏ HAMLET — small village
- ❏ HAPLESS — unfortunate, having bad luck
- ❏ HARBINGER — precursor, sign of something to come
- ❏ HARDY — robust, vigorous
- ❏ HARROWING — extremely distressing, terrifying
- ❏ HASTEN — to hurry, to speed up
- ❏ HAUGHTY — arrogant and condescending
- ❏ HEADSTRONG — reckless; insisting on one's own way
- ❏ HEATHEN — pagan; uncivilized and irreligious
- ❏ HECTIC — hasty, hurried, confused
- ❏ HEDONISM — pursuit of pleasure as a goal
- ❏ HEGEMONY — leadership, domination, usually by a country
- ❏ HEIGHTEN — to raise
- ❏ HEINOUS — shocking, wicked, terrible
- ❏ HEMICYCLE — semicircular form or structure
- ❏ HEMORRHAGE (n.) — heavy bleeding
- ❏ HEMORRHAGE (v.) — to bleed heavily
- ❏ HERETICAL — opposed to an established religious orthodoxy
- ❏ HERMETIC — tightly sealed
- ❏ HETERODOX — unorthodox, not widely accepted
- ❏ HETEROGENEOUS — composed of unlike parts, different, diverse
- ❏ HEW — to cut with an ax
- ❏ HIATUS — break, interruption, vacation
- ❏ HIDEBOUND — excessively rigid; dry and stiff
- ❏ HINDSIGHT — perception of events after they happen
- ❏ HINTERLAND — wilderness
- ❏ HOARY — very old; whitish or gray from age
- ❏ HOLISTIC — emphasizing importance of the whole and interdependence of its parts
- ❏ HOLOCAUST — widespread destruction, usually by fire
- ❏ HOMAGE — public honor and respect
- ❏ HOMOGENEOUS — composed of identical parts
- ❏ HOMONYM — word identical in pronunciation and spelling but different in meaning
- ❏ HONE — to sharpen

❑ HONOR — to praise, glorify, pay tribute to

❑ HUMANE — merciful, kindly

❑ HUSBAND (v.) — to farm, manage carefully and thriftily

❑ HUTCH — pen or coop for animal; shack, shanty

❑ HYDRATE — to add water to

❑ HYGIENIC — clean, sanitary

❑ HYMN — religious song, usually of praise or thanks

❑ HYPERBOLE — purposeful exaggeration for effect

❑ HYPERVENTILATE — to breathe abnormally fast

❑ HYPOCHONDRIA — unfounded belief that one is often ill

❑ HYPOCRITE — person claiming beliefs or virtues he or she doesn't really possess

❑ HYPOTHERMIA — abnormally low body temperature

❑ HYPOTHESIS — assumption subject to proof

❑ HYPOTHETICAL — theoretical, speculative

I

❑ ICONOCLAST — one who attacks traditional beliefs

❑ IDEALISM — pursuit of noble goals

❑ IDIOSYNCRASY — peculiarity of temperament, eccentricity

❑ IGNOBLE — dishonorable, not noble in character

❑ IGNOMINIOUS — disgraceful and dishonorable

❑ ILK — type or kind

❑ ILLICIT — illegal, improper

❑ ILLIMITABLE — limitless

❑ ILLUSORY — unreal, deceptive

❑ ILLUSTRIOUS — famous, renowned

❑ IMBUE — to infuse; dye, wet, moisten

❑ IMMACULATE — spotless; free from error

❑ IMMATERIAL — extraneous, inconsequential, nonessential; not consisting of matter

❑ IMMENSE — enormous, huge

❑ IMMERSE — to bathe, dip; to engross, preoccupy

❑ IMMOBILE — not moveable; still

❑ IMMUNE — exempt; protected from harm or disease; unresponsive to

❑ IMMUNOLOGICAL — relating to immune system

❑ IMMUTABLE — unchangeable, invariable

❑ IMPAIR — to damage, injure

❑ IMPASSE — blocked path, dilemma with no solution

❑ IMPASSIONED — with passion

❑ IMPASSIVE — showing no emotion

❑ IMPEACH — to charge with misdeeds in public office; accuse

❑ IMPECCABLE — flawless, without fault

❑ IMPECUNIOUS — poor, having no money

❑ IMPEDIMENT — barrier, obstacle; speech disorder

❑ IMPERATIVE — essential; mandatory

❑ IMPERIOUS — arrogantly self-assured, domineering, overbearing

❑ IMPERTINENT — rude

❑ IMPERTURBABLE — not capable of being disturbed

❑ IMPERVIOUS — impossible to penetrate; incapable of being affected

❑ IMPETUOUS — quick to act without thinking

❑ IMPIOUS — not devout in religion

❑ IMPLACABLE — inflexible, incapable of being pleased

❑ IMPLANT — to set securely or deeply; to instill

❑ IMPLAUSIBLE — improbable, inconceivable

❑ IMPLICATE — to involve in a crime, incriminate

❑ IMPLICIT — implied, not directly expressed

❑ IMPORTUNE — to ask repeatedly, beg

❑ IMPOSE — to inflict, force upon

❑ IMPOSING — dignified, grand

❑ IMPOTENT — powerless, ineffective, lacking strength

❑ IMPOUND — to seize and confine

❑ IMPOVERISH — to make poor or bankrupt

❑ IMPRECATION — curse

❑ IMPREGNABLE — totally safe from attack, able to resist defeat

❑ IMPRESSIONABLE — easily influenced or affected

❑ IMPROMPTU — spontaneous, without rehearsal

❑ IMPROVIDENT — without planning or foresight, negligent

❑ IMPUDENT — arrogant, audacious

❑ IMPUGN — to call into question, attack verbally

❑ IMPULSE — sudden tendency, inclination

❑ IMPULSIVE — spontaneous, unpredictable

❑ INADVERTENTLY — unintentionally

❑ INANE — foolish, silly, lacking significance

❑ INAUGURATE — to begin or start officially; to induct into office

❑ INCANDESCENT — shining brightly

❑ INCARCERATE — to put in jail; to confine

❑ INCARCERATION — imprisonment

❑ INCARNADINE — blood-red in color

❑ INCARNATE — having bodily form

❑ INCENDIARY — combustible, flammable, burning easily

- ❏ INCENSE — to infuriate, enrage
- ❏ INCEPTION — beginning
- ❏ INCESSANT — continuous, never ceasing
- ❏ INCHOATE — imperfectly formed or formulated
- ❏ INCIPIENT — beginning to exist or appear; in an initial stage
- ❏ INCISIVE — perceptive, penetrating
- ❏ INCLINATION — tendency towards
- ❏ INCLUSIVE — comprehensive, all-encompassing
- ❏ INCOGNITO — in disguise, concealing one's identity
- ❏ INCONCEIVABLE — impossible, unthinkable
- ❏ INCONSEQUENTIAL — unimportant, trivial
- ❏ INCONTROVERTIBLE — unquestionable, beyond dispute
- ❏ INCORRIGIBLE — incapable of being corrected
- ❏ INCREDULOUS — skeptical, doubtful
- ❏ INCULCATE — to teach, impress in the mind
- ❏ INCULPATE — to blame, charge with a crime
- ❏ INCUMBENT — holding a specified office, often political
- ❏ INCURSION — sudden invasion
- ❏ INDEFATIGABLE — never tired
- ❏ INDEFENSIBLE — inexcusable, unforgivable
- ❏ INDELIBLE — permanent, not erasable
- ❏ INDICATIVE — showing or pointing out, suggestive of
- ❏ INDICT — to accuse formally, charge with a crime
- ❏ INDIGENOUS — native, occurring naturally in an area
- ❏ INDIGENT — very poor
- ❏ INDIGNANT — angry, incensed, offended
- ❏ INDOLENT — habitually lazy, idle
- ❏ INDOMITABLE — fearless, unconquerable
- ❏ INDUBITABLE — unquestionable
- ❏ INDUCE — to persuade; bring about
- ❏ INDUCT — to place ceremoniously in office
- ❏ INDULGE — to give in to a craving or desire
- ❏ INDUSTRY — business or trade; diligence, energy
- ❏ INEBRIATED — drunk, intoxicated
- ❏ INEPT — clumsy, awkward
- ❏ INERT — unable to move, tending to inactivity
- ❏ INESTIMABLE — too great to be estimated
- ❏ INEVITABLE — certain, unavoidable
- ❏ INEXORABLE — inflexible, unyielding
- ❏ INEXTRICABLE — incapable of being disentangled
- ❏ INFALLIBLE — incapable of making a mistake
- ❏ INFAMY — reputation for bad deeds
- ❏ INFANTILE — childish, immature

- ❏ INFATUATED — strongly or foolishly attached to, inspired with foolish passion, overly in love
- ❏ INFER — to conclude, deduce
- ❏ INFILTRATE — to pass secretly into enemy territory
- ❏ INFINITESIMAL — extremely tiny
- ❏ INFIRMITY — disease, ailment
- ❏ INFRINGE — to encroach, trespass; to transgress, violate
- ❏ INFURIATE — to anger, provoke, outrage
- ❏ INFURIATING — provoking anger or outrage
- ❏ INGENIOUS — original, clever, inventive
- ❏ INGENUOUS — straightforward, open; naive and unsophisticated
- ❏ INGRATE — ungrateful person
- ❏ INGRATIATE — to bring oneself purposely into another's good graces
- ❏ INGRESS — entrance
- ❏ INHIBIT — to hold back, prevent, restrain
- ❏ INIMICAL — hostile, unfriendly
- ❏ INIQUITY — sin, evil act
- ❏ INITIATE — to begin, introduce; to enlist, induct
- ❏ INJECT — to force into; to introduce into conversation
- ❏ INJUNCTION — command, order
- ❏ INKLING — hint; vague idea
- ❏ INNATE — natural, inborn
- ❏ INNATENESS — state of being natural or inborn
- ❏ INNOCUOUS — harmless; inoffensive
- ❏ INNOVATE — to invent, modernize, revolutionize
- ❏ INNUENDO — indirect and subtle criticism, insinuation
- ❏ INNUMERABLE — too many to be counted
- ❏ INOFFENSIVE — harmless, innocent
- ❏ INOPERABLE — not operable; incurable by surgery
- ❏ INQUEST — investigation; court or legal proceeding
- ❏ INSATIABLE — never satisfied
- ❏ INSCRUTABLE — impossible to understand fully
- ❏ INSENTIENT — unfeeling, unconscious
- ❏ INSIDIOUS — sly, treacherous, devious
- ❏ INSINUATE — to suggest, say indirectly, imply
- ❏ INSIPID — bland, lacking flavor; lacking excitement
- ❏ INSOLENT — insulting and arrogant
- ❏ INSOLUBLE — not able to be solved or explained
- ❏ INSOLVENT — bankrupt, unable to pay one's debts
- ❏ INSTIGATE — to incite, urge, agitate
- ❏ INSUBSTANTIAL — modest, insignificant
- ❏ INSULAR — isolated, detached
- ❏ INSUPERABLE — insurmountable, unconquerable
- ❏ INSURGENT — rebellious, insubordinate

❏ INSURRECTION — rebellion
❏ INTEGRAL — central, indispensable
❏ INTEGRITY — decency, honest; wholeness
❏ INTEMPERATE — not moderate
❏ INTER — to bury
❏ INTERDICT — to forbid, prohibit
❏ INTERJECT — to interpose, insert
❏ INTERLOCUTOR — someone taking part in a dialogue
❏ INTERLOPER — trespasser; meddler in others' affairs
❏ INTERMINABLE — endless
❏ INTERMITTENT — starting and stopping
❏ INTERNECINE — deadly to both sides
❏ INTERPOLATE — to insert; change by adding new words or material
❏ INTERPOSE — to insert; to intervene
❏ INTERREGNUM — interval between reigns
❏ INTERROGATE — to question formally
❏ INTERSECT — to divide by passing through or across
❏ INTERSPERSE — to distribute among, mix with
❏ INTIMATION — clue, suggestion
❏ INTRACTABLE — not easily managed
❏ INTRAMURAL — within an institution like a school
❏ INTRANSIGENT — uncompromising, refusing to be reconciled
❏ INTREPID — fearless
❏ INTRINSIC — inherent, internal
❏ INTROSPECTIVE — contemplating one's own thoughts and feelings
❏ INTROVERT — someone given to self-analysis
❏ INTRUSION — trespass, invasion of another's privacy
❏ INTUITIVE — instinctive, untaught
❏ INUNDATE — to cover with water; overwhelm
❏ INURE — to harden; accustom; become used to
❏ INVALIDATE — to negate or nullify
❏ INVECTIVE — verbal abuse
❏ INVESTITURE — ceremony conferring authority
❏ INVETERATE — confirmed, long-standing, deeply rooted
❏ INVIDIOUS — likely to provoke ill-will, offensive
❏ INVINCIBLE — invulnerable, unbeatable
❏ INVIOLABLE — safe from violation or assault
❏ INVOKE — to call upon, request help
❏ IOTA — very tiny amount
❏ IRASCIBLE — easily angered
❏ IRIDESCENT — showing many colors
❏ IRRESOLVABLE — unable to be resolved; not analyzable

❏ IRREVERENT — disrespectful
❏ IRREVOCABLE — conclusive, irreversible
❏ ITINERANT — wandering from place to place, unsettled
❏ ITINERARY — route of a traveler's journey

J

❏ JADED — tired by excess or over-use; slightly cynical
❏ JANGLING — clashing, jarring; harshly unpleasant (in sound)
❏ JARGON — nonsensical talk; specialized language
❏ JAUNDICE — yellowish discoloration of skin
❏ JAUNDICED — affected by jaundice; prejudiced or embittered
❏ JETTISON — to cast off, throw cargo overboard
❏ JINGOISM — belligerent support of one's country
❏ JOCULAR — jovial, playful, humorous
❏ JUBILEE — special anniversary
❏ JUDICIOUS — sensible, showing good judgment
❏ JUGGERNAUT — huge force destroying everything in its path
❏ JUNCTURE — point where two things are joined
❏ JURISPRUDENCE — philosophy of law
❏ JUXTAPOSITION — side-by-side placement

K

❏ KEEN — having a sharp edge; intellectually sharp, perceptive
❏ KERNEL — innermost, essential part; seed grain, often in a shell
❏ KEYNOTE — note or tone on which a musical key is founded; main idea of a speech, program, etc.
❏ KINDLE — to set fire to or ignite; excite or inspire
❏ KINETIC — relating to motion; characterized by movement
❏ KNELL — sound of a funeral bell; omen of death or failure
❏ KUDOS — fame, glory, honor

L

❏ LABYRINTH — maze

- LACERATION — cut or wound
- LACHRYMOSE — tearful
- LACKADAISICAL — idle, lazy; apathetic, indifferent
- LACONIC — using few words
- LAGGARD — dawdler, loafer, lazy person
- LAMENT (v.) — to deplore, grieve
- LAMPOON — to attack with satire, mock harshly
- LANGUID — lacking energy, indifferent, slow
- LAP (v.) — to drink using the tongue; to wash against
- LAPIDARY — relating to precious stones
- LARCENY — theft of property
- LARDER — place where food is stored
- LARGESS — generosity; gift
- LARYNX — organ containing vocal cords
- LASSITUDE — lethargy, sluggishness
- LATENT — present but hidden; potential
- LAUDABLE — deserving of praise
- LAXITY — carelessness
- LEERY — suspicious
- LEGERDEMAIN — trickery
- LEGIBLE — readable
- LEGISLATE — to decree, mandate, make laws
- LENIENT — easygoing, permissive
- LETHARGY — indifferent inactivity
- LEVITATE — to rise in the air or cause to rise
- LEVITY — humor, frivolity, gaiety
- LEXICON — dictionary, list of words
- LIBERAL — tolerant, broad-minded; generous, lavish
- LIBERATION — freedom, emancipation
- LIBERTARIAN — one who believes in unrestricted freedom
- LIBERTINE — one without moral restraint
- LICENTIOUS — immoral; unrestrained by society
- LIEN — right to possess and sell the property of a debtor
- LIMPID — clear, transparent
- LINEAGE — ancestry
- LINGUISTICS — study of language
- LINIMENT — medicinal liquid used externally to ease pain
- LIONIZE — to treat as a celebrity
- LISSOME — easily flexed, limber, agile
- LISTLESS — lacking energy and enthusiasm
- LITERATE — able to read and write; well-read and educated
- LITHE — moving and bending with ease; graceful
- LITIGATION — lawsuit
- LIVID — discolored from a bruise; reddened with anger

- LOATHE — to abhor, despise, hate
- LOCOMOTION — movement from place to place
- LOGO — corporate symbol
- LOITER — to stand around idly
- LOQUACIOUS — talkative
- LOW (v.) — to make a sound like a cow, moo
- LUCID — clear and easily understood
- LUDICROUS — laughable, ridiculous
- LUGUBRIOUS — sorrowful, mournful
- LUMBER (v.) — to move slowly and awkwardly
- LUMINARY — bright object; celebrity; source of inspiration
- LUMINOUS — bright, brilliant, glowing
- LUNAR — relating to the moon
- LURID — harshly shocking, sensational; glowing
- LURK — to prowl, sneak
- LUSCIOUS — very good-tasting
- LUXURIANCE — elegance, lavishness
- LYRICAL — suitable for poetry and song; expressing feeling

M

- MACHINATION — plot or scheme
- MACROBIOTICS — art of prolonging life by special diet of organic non-meat substances
- MACROCOSM — system regarded as an entity with subsystems
- MAELSTROM — whirlpool; turmoil; agitated state of mind
- MAGNANIMOUS — generous, noble in spirit
- MAGNATE — powerful or influential person
- MAGNITUDE — extent, greatness of size
- MALADROIT — clumsy, tactless
- MALADY — illness
- MALAPROPISM — humorous misuse of a word
- MALCONTENT — discontented person, one who holds a grudge
- MALEDICTION — curse
- MALEFACTOR — evil-doer; culprit
- MALEVOLENT — ill-willed; causing evil or harm to others
- MALFUNCTION (v.) — to fail to work
- MALFUNCTION (n.) — breakdown, failure
- MALICE — animosity, spite, hatred
- MALINGER — to evade responsibility by pretending to be ill

❑ MALNUTRITION — under-nourishment

❑ MALODOROUS — foul-smelling

❑ MANDATORY — necessary, required

❑ MANIFEST (adj.) — obvious

❑ MANIFOLD — diverse, varied, comprised of many parts

❑ MANNERED — artificial or stilted in character

❑ MANUAL (adj.) — hand-operated; physical

❑ MAR — to damage, deface; spoil

❑ MARGINAL — barely sufficient

❑ MARITIME — relating to the sea or sailing

❑ MARTIAL — war-like, pertaining to the military

❑ MARTINET — strict disciplinarian, one who rigidly follows rules

❑ MARTYR — person dying for his/her beliefs

❑ MASOCHIST — one who enjoys pain or humiliation

❑ MASQUERADE — disguise; action that conceals the truth

❑ MATERIALISM — preoccupation with material things

❑ MATRICULATE — to enroll as a member of a college or university

❑ MATRILINEAL — tracing ancestry through mother's line rather than father's

❑ MAUDLIN — overly sentimental

❑ MAWKISH — sickeningly sentimental

❑ MEDDLER — person interfering in others' affairs

❑ MEDIEVAL — relating to the Middle Ages

❑ MEGALITH — huge stone used in prehistoric structures

❑ MEGALOMANIA — mental state with delusions of wealth and power

❑ MELANCHOLY — sadness, depression

❑ MELODY — pleasing musical harmony; related musical tunes

❑ MENAGERIE — various animals kept together for exhibition

❑ MENDACIOUS — dishonest

❑ MENDICANT — beggar

❑ MENTOR — experienced teacher and wise adviser

❑ MERCENARY (n.) — soldier for hire in foreign countries

❑ MERCENARY (adj.) — motivated only by greed

❑ MERCURIAL — quick, shrewd, and unpredictable

❑ MERETRICIOUS — gaudy, falsely attractive

❑ MERIDIAN — circle passing through the two poles of the earth

❑ MERITORIOUS — deserving reward or praise

❑ METAMORPHOSIS — change, transformation

❑ METAPHOR — figure of speech comparing two different things

❑ METICULOUS — extremely careful, fastidious, painstaking

❑ METRONOME — time-keeping device used in music

❑ METTLE — courageousness; endurance

❑ MICROBE — microorganism

❑ MICROCOSM — tiny system used as analogy for larger system

❑ MIGRATORY — wandering from place to place with the seasons

❑ MILITATE — to operate against, work against

❑ MINIMAL — smallest in amount, least possible

❑ MINUSCULE — very small

❑ MIRTH — frivolity, gaiety, laughter

❑ MISANTHROPE — person who hates human beings

❑ MISAPPREHEND — to misunderstand, fail to know

❑ MISCONSTRUE — to misunderstand, fail to discover

❑ MISERLINESS — extreme stinginess

❑ MISGIVING — apprehension, doubt, sense of foreboding

❑ MISHAP — accident; misfortune

❑ MISNOMER — an incorrect name or designation

❑ MISSIVE — note or letter

❑ MITIGATE — to soften, or make milder

❑ MNEMONIC — relating to memory; designed to assist memory

❑ MOBILITY — ease of movement

❑ MOCK — to deride, ridicule

❑ MODERATE (adj.) — reasonable, not extreme

❑ MODERATE (v.) — to make less excessive, restrain; regulate

❑ MOLLIFY — to calm or make less severe

❑ MOLLUSK — sea animal with soft body

❑ MOLT (v.) — to shed hair, skin, or an outer layer periodically

❑ MONASTIC — extremely plain or secluded, as in a monastery

❑ MONOCHROMATIC — having one color

❑ MONOGAMY — custom of marriage to one person at a time

❑ MONOLITH — large block of stone

❑ MONOLOGUE — dramatic speech performed by one actor

❑ MONTAGE — composite picture

❑ MOOT — debatable; previously decided

❑ MORBID — gruesome; relating to disease; abnormally gloomy

❑ MORES — customs or manners

❑ MORIBUND — dying, decaying

❑ MOROSE — gloomy, sullen, or surly

- MORSEL — small bit of food
- MOTE — small particle, speck
- MOTLEY — many-colored; composed of diverse parts
- MOTTLE — to mark with spots
- MULTIFACETED — having many parts, many-sided
- MULTIFARIOUS — diverse
- MUNDANE — worldly; commonplace
- MUNIFICENT — generous
- MUNITIONS — ammunition
- MUTABILITY — changeability
- MYOPIC — near-sighted
- MYRIAD — immense number, multitude

N

- NADIR — lowest point
- NARRATIVE — account, story
- NASCENT — starting to develop, coming into existence
- NATAL — relating to birth
- NEBULOUS — vague, cloudy
- NECROMANCY — black magic
- NEFARIOUS — vicious, evil
- NEGLIGENT — careless, inattentive
- NEGLIGIBLE — not worth considering
- NEOLOGISM — new word or expression
- NEONATE — newborn child
- NEOPHYTE — novice, beginner
- NETHER — located under or below
- NETTLE (v.) — to irritate
- NEUTRALITY — disinterest, impartiality
- NEUTRALIZE — to balance, offset
- NICETY — elegant or delicate feature; minute distinction
- NICHE — recess in a wall; best position for something
- NIGGARDLY — stingy
- NIHILISM — belief that existence and all traditional values are meaningless
- NOCTURNAL — pertaining to night; active at night
- NOISOME — stinking, putrid
- NOMADIC — moving from place to place
- NOMENCLATURE — terms used in a particular science or discipline
- NOMINAL — existing in name only; negligible
- NON SEQUITUR — conclusion not following from apparent evidence

- NONDESCRIPT — lacking interesting or distinctive qualities; dull
- NOTORIETY — unfavorable fame
- NOVICE — apprentice, beginner
- NOVITIATE — state of being a beginner or novice
- NOXIOUS — harmful, unwholesome
- NUANCE — shade of meaning
- NULLIFY — to make legally invalid; to counteract the effect of
- NUMISMATICS — coin collecting
- NUPTIAL — relating to marriage
- NUTRITIVE — relating to nutrition or health

O

- OBDURATE — stubborn
- OBFUSCATE — to confuse, obscure
- OBLIQUE — indirect, evasive; misleading, devious
- OBLITERATE — demolish, wipe out
- OBLIVIOUS — unaware, inattentive
- OBSCURE (adj.) — dim, unclear; not well-known
- OBSCURITY — place or thing that's hard to perceive
- OBSEQUIOUS — overly submissive, brown-nosing
- OBSEQUIES — funeral ceremony
- OBSESSIVE — preoccupying, all-consuming
- OBSOLETE — no longer in use
- OBSTINATE — stubborn
- OBSTREPEROUS — troublesome, boisterous, unruly
- OBTRUSIVE — pushy, too conspicuous
- OBTUSE — insensitive, stupid, dull
- OBVIATE — to make unnecessary; to anticipate and prevent
- OCCLUDE — to shut, block
- ODIOUS — hateful, contemptible
- OFFICIOUS — too helpful, meddlesome
- OFFSHOOT — branch
- OMINOUS — menacing, threatening, indicating misfortune
- OMNIPOTENT — having unlimited power
- OMNISCIENT — having infinite knowledge
- OMNIVOROUS — eating everything; absorbing everything
- ONEROUS — burdensome
- ONTOLOGY — theory about the nature of existence
- OPALESCENT — iridescent, displaying colors
- OPAQUE — impervious to light; difficult to understand

❏ OPERATIVE — functioning, working
❏ OPINE — to express an opinion
❏ OPPORTUNE — appropriate, fitting
❏ OPPORTUNIST — one who takes advantage of circumstances
❏ OPPROBRIOUS — disgraceful, contemptuous
❏ OPULENCE — wealth
❏ ORACLE — person who foresees the future and gives advice
❏ ORATION — lecture, formal speech
❏ ORATOR — lecturer, speaker
❏ ORB — spherical body; eye
❏ ORCHESTRATE — to arrange music for performance; to coordinate, organize
❏ ORDAIN — to make someone a priest or minister; to order
❏ ORNITHOLOGIST — scientist who studies birds
❏ OSCILLATE — to move back and forth
❏ OSSIFY — to turn to bone; to become rigid
❏ OSTENSIBLE — apparent
❏ OSTENTATIOUS — showy
❏ OSTRACISM — exclusion, temporary banishment
❏ OUSTER — expulsion, ejection
❏ OVERSTATE — to embellish, exaggerate
❏ OVERTURE — musical introduction; proposal, offer
❏ OVERWROUGHT — agitated, overdone

P

❏ PACIFIC — calm, peaceful
❏ PACIFIST — one opposed to war
❏ PACIFY — to restore calm, bring peace
❏ PALATIAL — like a palace, magnificent
❏ PALAVER — idle talk
❏ PALEONTOLOGY — study of past geological eras through fossil remains
❏ PALETTE — board for mixing paints; range of colors
❏ PALISADE — fence made up of stakes
❏ PALL (n.) — covering that darkens or obscures; coffin
❏ PALL (v.) — to lose strength or interest
❏ PALLIATE — to make less serious, ease
❏ PALLID — lacking color or liveliness
❏ PALPABLE — obvious, real, tangible
❏ PALPITATION — trembling, shaking
❏ PALTRY — pitifully small or worthless

❏ PANACEA — cure-all
❏ PANACHE — flamboyance, verve
❏ PANDEMIC — spread over a whole area or country
❏ PANEGYRIC — elaborate praise; formal hymn of praise
❏ PANOPLY — impressive array
❏ PANORAMA — broad view; comprehensive picture
❏ PARADIGM — ideal example, model
❏ PARADOX — contradiction, incongruity; dilemma, puzzle
❏ PARADOXICAL — self-contradictory but true
❏ PARAGON — model of excellence or perfection
❏ PARAMOUNT — supreme, dominant, primary
❏ PARAPHRASE — to reword, usually in simpler terms
❏ PARASITE — person or animal that lives at another's expense
❏ PARCH — to dry or shrivel
❏ PARE — to trim
❏ PARIAH — outcast
❏ PARITY — equality
❏ PARLEY — discussion, usually between enemies
❏ PAROCHIAL — of limited scope or outlook, provincial
❏ PARODY — humorous imitation
❏ PAROLE — conditional release of a prisoner
❏ PARRY — to ward off or deflect
❏ PARSIMONY — stinginess
❏ PARTISAN (n.) — strong supporter
❏ PARTISAN (adj.) — biased in favor of
❏ PASTICHE — piece of literature or music imitating other works
❏ PATENT (adj.) — obvious, unconcealed
❏ PATENT (n.) — official document giving exclusive right to sell an invention
❏ PATERNITY — fatherhood; descent from father's ancestors
❏ PATHOGENIC — causing disease
❏ PATHOS — pity, compassion
❏ PATRICIAN — aristocrat
❏ PATRICIDE — murder of one's father
❏ PATRIMONY — inheritance or heritage derived from one's father
❏ PATRONIZE — to condescend to, disparage; to buy from
❏ PAUCITY — scarcity, lack
❏ PAUPER — very poor person
❏ PAVILION — tent or light building used for shelter or exhibitions
❏ PECCADILLO — minor sin or offense
❏ PECULATION — theft of money or goods

❑ PEDAGOGUE — teacher

❑ PEDANT — uninspired, boring academic

❑ PEDESTRIAN (adj.) — commonplace

❑ PEDIATRICIAN — doctor specializing in children and their ailments

❑ PEDIMENT — triangular gable on a roof or facade

❑ PEER (n.) — contemporary, equal, match

❑ PEERLESS — unequaled

❑ PEJORATIVE — having bad connotations; disparaging

❑ PELLUCID — transparent; translucent; easily understood

❑ PENANCE — voluntary suffering to repent for a wrong

❑ PENCHANT — inclination

❑ PENDING (adj.) — not yet decided, awaiting decision

❑ PENITENT — expressing sorrow for sins or offenses, repentant

❑ PENSIVE — thoughtful

❑ PENULTIMATE — next to last

❑ PENUMBRA — partial shadow

❑ PENURY — extreme poverty

❑ PERAMBULATOR — baby carriage

❑ PERCIPIENT — discerning, able to perceive

❑ PERDITION — complete and utter loss; damnation

❑ PEREGRINATE — to wander from place to place

❑ PERENNIAL — present throughout the years; persistent

❑ PERFIDIOUS — faithless, disloyal, untrustworthy

❑ PERFUNCTORY — done in a routine way; indifferent

❑ PERIHELION — point in orbit nearest to the sun

❑ PERIPATETIC — moving from place to place

❑ PERJURE — to tell a lie under oath

❑ PERMEABLE — penetrable

❑ PERNICIOUS — very harmful

❑ PERPETUAL — endless, lasting

❑ PERSONIFICATION — act of attributing human qualities to objects or abstract qualities

❑ PERSPICACIOUS — shrewd, astute, keen-witted

❑ PERT — lively and bold

❑ PERTINACIOUS — persistent, stubborn

❑ PERTINENT — applicable, appropriate

❑ PERTURBATION — disturbance

❑ PERUSAL — close examination

❑ PERVERT (v.) — to cause to change in immoral way; to misuse

❑ PESTILENCE — epidemic, plague

❑ PETULANCE — rudeness, peevishness

❑ PHALANX — massed group of soldiers, people, or things

❑ PHILANDERER — pursuer of casual love affairs

❑ PHILANTHROPY — love of humanity; generosity to worthy causes

❑ PHILISTINE — narrow-minded person, someone lacking appreciation for art or culture

❑ PHILOLOGY — study of words

❑ PHLEGMATIC — calm in temperament; sluggish

❑ PHOBIA — anxiety, horror

❑ PHOENIX — mythical, immortal bird which lives for 500 years, burns itself to death, and rises from its ashes

❑ PHONETICS — study of speech sounds

❑ PHONIC — relating to sound

❑ PIETY — devoutness

❑ PILFER — to steal

❑ PILLAGE — to loot, especially during a war

❑ PINNACLE — peak, highest point of development

❑ PIOUS — dedicated, devout, extremely religious

❑ PIQUE — fleeting feeling of hurt pride

❑ PITHY — profound, substantial; concise, succinct, to the point

❑ PITTANCE — meager amount or wage

❑ PLACATE — to soothe or pacify

❑ PLACID — calm

❑ PLAGIARIST — one who steals words or ideas

❑ PLAINTIFF — injured person in a lawsuit

❑ PLAIT — to braid

❑ PLATITUDE — stale, overused expression

❑ PLEBEIAN — crude, vulgar, low-class

❑ PLENITUDE — abundance, plenty

❑ PLETHORA — excess, overabundance

❑ PLIANT — pliable, yielding

❑ PLUCK — to pull strings on musical instrument

❑ PLUCKY — courageous, spunky

❑ PLUMMET — to fall, plunge

❑ PLURALISTIC — including a variety of groups

❑ PLY (v.) — to use diligently; to engage; to join together

❑ PNEUMATIC — relating to air; worked by compressed air

❑ POACH — to steal game or fish; cook in boiling liquid

❑ PODIUM — platform or lectern for orchestra conductors or speakers

❑ POIGNANT — emotionally moving

❑ POLAR — relating to a geographic pole; exhibiting contrast

❑ POLARIZE — to tend towards opposite extremes

❑ POLEMIC — controversy, argument; verbal attack

❑ POLITIC — discreet, tactful

❑ POLYGLOT — speaker of many languages

❑ PONDEROUS — weighty, heavy, large

- ❑ PONTIFICATE — to speak in a pretentious manner
- ❑ PORE (v.) — to study closely or meditatively
- ❑ POROUS — full of holes, permeable to liquids
- ❑ PORTENT — omen
- ❑ PORTLY — stout, dignified
- ❑ POSIT — to put in position; to suggest an idea
- ❑ POSTERIOR — bottom, rear
- ❑ POSTERITY — future generations; all of a person's descendants
- ❑ POTABLE — drinkable
- ❑ POTENTATE — monarch or ruler with great power
- ❑ PRAGMATIC — practical; moved by facts rather than abstract ideals
- ❑ PRATTLE — meaningless, foolish talk
- ❑ PRECARIOUS — uncertain
- ❑ PRECEPT — principle; law
- ❑ PRECIPICE — edge, steep overhang
- ❑ PRECIPITATE (adj.) — sudden and unexpected
- ❑ PRECIPITATE (v.) — to throw down from a height; to cause to happen
- ❑ PRECIPITOUS — hasty, quickly, with too little caution
- ❑ PRÉCIS — short summary of facts
- ❑ PRECISION — state of being precise
- ❑ PRECLUDE — to rule out
- ❑ PRECOCIOUS — unusually advanced at an early age
- ❑ PRECURSOR — forerunner, predecessor
- ❑ PREDATOR — one that preys on others, destroyer, plunderer
- ❑ PREDICAMENT — difficult situation
- ❑ PREDICATE (v.) — to found or base on
- ❑ PREDICTIVE — relating to prediction, indicative of the future
- ❑ PREDILECTION — preference, liking
- ❑ PREDISPOSITION — tendency, inclination
- ❑ PREEMINENT — celebrated, distinguished
- ❑ PREFACE — introduction to a book; introductory remarks to a speech
- ❑ PREMEDITATE — to consider, plan beforehand
- ❑ PREMONITION — forewarning; presentiment
- ❑ PREPONDERANCE — majority in number; dominance
- ❑ PREPOSSESSING — attractive, engaging, appealing
- ❑ PREPOSTEROUS — absurd, illogical
- ❑ PRESAGE — to foretell, indicate in advance
- ❑ PRESCIENT — having foresight
- ❑ PRESCRIBE — to set down a rule; to recommend a treatment
- ❑ PRESENTIMENT — premonition, sense of foreboding

- ❑ PRESTIDIGITATION — sleight of hand
- ❑ PRESUMPTUOUS — rude, improperly bold
- ❑ PRETEXT — excuse, pretended reason
- ❑ PREVALENT — widespread
- ❑ PREVARICATE — to quibble, evade the truth
- ❑ PRIMEVAL — ancient, primitive
- ❑ PRIMORDIAL — original, existing from the beginning
- ❑ PRISTINE — untouched, uncorrupted
- ❑ PRIVATION — lack of usual necessities or comforts
- ❑ PROBITY — honesty, high-mindedness
- ❑ PROCLIVITY — tendency, inclination
- ❑ PROCRASTINATOR — one who continually and unjustifiably postpones
- ❑ PROCURE — to obtain
- ❑ PRODIGAL — wasteful, extravagant, lavish
- ❑ PRODIGIOUS — vast, enormous, extraordinary
- ❑ PROFANE — impure; contrary to religion; sacrilegious
- ❑ PROFICIENT — expert, skilled in a certain subject
- ❑ PROFLIGATE — corrupt, degenerate
- ❑ PROFUSE — lavish, extravagant
- ❑ PROGENITOR — originator, forefather, ancestor in a direct line
- ❑ PROGENY — offspring, children
- ❑ PROGNOSIS — prediction of disease outcome; any prediction
- ❑ PROGRESSIVE — favoring progress or change; moving forward, going step-by-step
- ❑ PROLIFERATION — propagation, reproduction; enlargement, expansion
- ❑ PROLIFIC — productive, fertile
- ❑ PROLOGUE — introductory section of a literary work or play
- ❑ PROMONTORY — piece of land or rock higher than its surroundings
- ❑ PROMULGATE — to make known publicly
- ❑ PROPENSITY — inclination, tendency
- ❑ PROPINQUITY — nearness
- ❑ PROPITIATE — to win over, appease
- ❑ PROPITIOUS — favorable, advantageous
- ❑ PROPONENT — advocate, defender, supporter
- ❑ PROSAIC — relating to prose; dull, commonplace
- ❑ PROSCRIBE — to condemn; to forbid, outlaw
- ❑ PROSE — ordinary language used in everyday speech
- ❑ PROSECUTOR — person who initiates a legal action or suit
- ❑ PROSELYTIZE — to convert to a particular belief or religion

- PROSTRATE — lying face downward, lying flat on ground
- PROTAGONIST — main character in a play or story, hero
- PROTEAN — readily assuming different forms or characters
- PROTESTATION — declaration
- PROTOCOL — ceremony and manners observed by diplomats
- PROTRACT — to prolong, draw out, extend
- PROTRUSION — something that sticks out
- PROVINCIAL — rustic, unsophisticated, limited in scope
- PROVOCATION — cause, incitement to act or respond
- PROWESS — bravery, skill
- PROXIMITY — nearness
- PROXY — power to act as a substitute for another
- PRUDE — one who is excessively proper or modest
- PRUDENT — careful, cautious
- PRURIENT — lustful, exhibiting lewd desires
- PRY — to intrude into; force open
- PSEUDONYM — pen name; fictitious or borrowed name
- PSYCHIC (adj.) — perceptive of non-material, spiritual forces
- PUERILE — childish, immature, silly
- PUDGY — chubby, overweight
- PUGILISM — boxing
- PUGNACIOUS — quarrelsome, eager and ready to fight
- PULCHRITUDE — beauty
- PULVERIZE — to pound, crush, or grind into powder; destroy
- PUMMEL — to pound, beat
- PUNCTILIOUS — careful in observing rules of behavior or ceremony
- PUNGENT — strong or sharp in smell or taste
- PUNITIVE — having to do with punishment
- PURGATION — catharsis, purification
- PURGE — to cleanse or free from impurities
- PURITANICAL — adhering to a rigid moral code
- PURPORT — to profess, suppose, claim

Q

- QUACK — faker; one who falsely claims to have medical skill
- QUADRILATERAL — four-sided polygon
- QUADRUPED — animal having four feet
- QUAGMIRE — marsh; difficult situation
- QUALIFY — to provide with needed skills; modify, limit
- QUANDARY — dilemma, difficulty
- QUARANTINE — isolation period, originally 40 days, to prevent spread of disease
- QUATERNARY — consisting of or relating to four units or members
- QUELL — to crush or subdue
- QUERULOUS — inclined to complain, irritable
- QUERY (n.) — question
- QUIBBLE — to argue about insignificant and irrelevant details
- QUICKEN (v.) — to hasten, arouse, excite
- QUIESCENCE — inactivity, stillness
- QUINTESSENCE — most typical example; concentrated essence
- QUIVER — to shake slightly, tremble, vibrate
- QUIXOTIC — overly idealistic, impractical
- QUOTIDIAN — occurring daily; commonplace

R

- RACONTEUR — witty, skillful storyteller
- RADICAL — fundamental; drastic
- RAIL (v.) — to scold with bitter or abusive language
- RALLY (v.) — to assemble; recover, recuperate
- RAMBLE — to roam, wander; to babble, digress
- RAMIFICATION — an implication, outgrowth, or consequence
- RAMSHACKLE — likely to collapse
- RANCID — spoiled, rotten
- RANCOR — bitter hatred
- RANT — to harangue, rave, forcefully scold
- RAPPORT — relationship of trust and respect
- RAPT — deeply absorbed
- RAREFY — to make thinner, purer, or more refined
- RASH (adj.) — careless, hasty, reckless
- RATIFY — to approve formally, confirm
- RATIOCINATION — methodical, logical reasoning

❑ RATION (n.) — portion, share

❑ RATION (v.) — to supply; to restrict consumption of

❑ RATIONAL — logical, reasonable

❑ RAUCOUS — harsh-sounding; boisterous

❑ RAVAGE — to destroy, devastate

❑ RAVENOUS — extremely hungry

❑ RAVINE — deep, narrow gorge

❑ RAZE — to tear down, demolish

❑ REACTIONARY — marked by extreme conservatism, esp. in politics

❑ REBUFF (n.) — blunt rejection

❑ REBUKE — to reprimand, scold

❑ REBUT — to refute by evidence or argument

❑ RECALCITRANT — resisting authority or control

❑ RECANT — to retract a statement, opinion, etc.

❑ RECAPITULATE — to review by a brief summary

❑ RECEPTIVE — open to others' ideas; congenial

❑ RECLUSIVE — shut off from the world

❑ RECONDITE — relating to obscure learning; known to only a few

❑ RECOUNT — to describe facts or events

❑ RECRUIT (v.) — to draft, enlist; to seek to enroll

❑ RECTIFY — to correct

❑ RECTITUDE — moral uprightness

❑ RECURRENCE — repetition

❑ REDRESS — relief from wrong or injury

❑ REDUNDANCY — unnecessary repetition

❑ REFECTORY — room where meals are served

❑ REFLECTION — image, likeness; opinion, thought, impression

❑ REFORM — to change, correct

❑ REFRACT — to deflect sound or light

❑ REFUGE — escape, shelter

❑ REFURBISH — to renovate

❑ REFUTE — to contradict, discredit

❑ REGIMEN — government rule; systematic plan

❑ REGRESS — to move backward; revert to an earlier form or state

❑ REHABILITATE — to restore to good health or condition; reestablish a person's good reputation

❑ REITERATE — to say or do again, repeat

❑ REJOINDER — response

❑ REJUVENATE — to make young again; renew

❑ RELEGATE — to assign to a class, especially an inferior one

❑ RELINQUISH — to renounce or surrender something

❑ RELISH (v.) — to enjoy greatly

❑ REMEDIABLE — capable of being corrected

❑ REMEDY (v.) — to cure, correct

❑ REMINISCENCE — remembrance of past events

❑ REMISSION — lessening, relaxation

❑ REMIT — to send (usually money) as payment

❑ REMOTE — distant, isolated

❑ REMUNERATION — pay or reward for work, trouble, etc.

❑ RENASCENT — reborn, coming into being again

❑ RENEGE — to go back on one's word

❑ RENEGADE — traitor, person abandoning a cause

❑ RENOUNCE — to give up or reject a right, title, person, etc.

❑ RENOWN — fame, widespread acclaim

❑ REPAST — meal or mealtime

❑ REPEAL — to revoke or formally withdraw (often a law)

❑ REPEL — to rebuff, repulse; disgust, offend

❑ REPENT — to regret a past action

❑ REPENTANT — apologetic, guilty, remorseful

❑ REPLETE — abundantly supplied

❑ REPLICATE — to duplicate, repeat

❑ REPOSE — relaxation, leisure

❑ REPRESS — to restrain or hold in

❑ REPRESSION — act of restraining or holding in

❑ REPREHENSIBLE — blameworthy, disreputable

❑ REPRISE — repetition, esp. of a piece of music

❑ REPROACH — to find fault with; blame

❑ REPROBATE — morally unprincipled person

❑ REPROVE — to criticize or correct

❑ REPUDIATE — to reject as having no authority

❑ REPULSE — repel, fend off; sicken, disgust

❑ REQUIEM — hymns or religious service for the dead

❑ REQUITE — to return or repay

❑ RESCIND — to repeal, cancel

❑ RESIDUE — remainder, leftover, remnant

❑ RESILIENT — able to recover quickly after illness or bad luck; able to bounce back to shape

❑ RESOLUTE — determined; with a clear purpose

❑ RESOLVE (n.) — determination, firmness of purpose

❑ RESOLVE (v.) — to conclude, determine

❑ RESONATE — to echo

❑ RESPIRE — to breathe

❑ RESPITE — interval of relief

❑ RESPLENDENT — splendid, brilliant

❑ RESTITUTION — act of compensating for loss or damage

❑ RESTIVE — impatient, uneasy, restless

- ❏ RESTORATIVE — having the power to renew or revitalize
- ❏ RESTRAINED — controlled, repressed, restricted
- ❏ RESUSCITATE — to revive, bring back to life
- ❏ RETAIN — to hold, keep possession of
- ❏ RETARD (v.) — to slow, hold back
- ❏ RETICENT — not speaking freely; reserved
- ❏ RETINUE — group of attendants with an important person
- ❏ RETIRING — shy, modest, reserved
- ❏ RETORT — cutting response
- ❏ RETRACT — to draw in or take back
- ❏ RETRENCH — to regroup, reorganize
- ❏ RETRIEVE — to bring, fetch; reclaim
- ❏ RETROACTIVE — applying to an earlier time
- ❏ RETROGRADE — having a backward motion or direction
- ❏ RETROSPECTIVE — review of the past
- ❏ REVELRY — boisterous festivity
- ❏ REVERE — to worship, regard with awe
- ❏ REVERT — to backslide, regress
- ❏ REVILE — to criticize with harsh language, verbally abuse
- ❏ REVITALIZE — to renew; give new energy to
- ❏ REVOKE — to annul, cancel, call back
- ❏ REVULSION — strong feeling of repugnance or dislike
- ❏ RHAPSODY — emotional literary or musical work
- ❏ RHETORIC — persuasive use of language
- ❏ RHYTHM — regular pattern or variation of sounds and stresses
- ❏ RIBALD — humorous in a vulgar way
- ❏ RIDDLE (v.) — to make many holes in; permeate
- ❏ RIFE — widespread, prevalent; abundant
- ❏ RISQUE (accent on E) — bordering on being inappropriate or indecent
- ❏ ROBUST — strong and healthy; hardy
- ❏ ROCOCO — very highly ornamented
- ❏ ROOT (v.) — to dig with a snout (like a pig)
- ❏ ROSTRUM — stage for public speaking
- ❏ ROTUND — round in shape; fat
- ❏ RUE — to regret
- ❏ RUMINATE — to contemplate, reflect upon
- ❏ RUSTIC — rural

S

- ❏ SACCHARINE — excessively sweet or sentimental
- ❏ SACROSANCT — extremely sacred; beyond criticism
- ❏ SAGACIOUS — shrewd
- ❏ SALIENT — prominent or conspicuous
- ❏ SALLOW — sickly yellow in color
- ❏ SALUBRIOUS — healthful
- ❏ SALUTATION — greeting
- ❏ SANCTION — permission, support; law; penalty
- ❏ SANCTUARY — haven, retreat
- ❏ SANGUINE — ruddy; cheerfully optimistic
- ❏ SARDONIC — cynical, scornfully mocking
- ❏ SATIATE — to satisfy
- ❏ SAUNTER — to amble; walk in a leisurely manner
- ❏ SAVANT — learned person
- ❏ SAVORY — agreeable in taste or smell
- ❏ SCABBARD — sheath for sword or dagger
- ❏ SCALE (v.) — to climb to the top of
- ❏ SCATHING — harshly critical; painfully hot
- ❏ SCENARIO — plot outline; possible situation
- ❏ SCINTILLA — trace amount
- ❏ SCINTILLATE — to sparkle, flash
- ❏ SCOFF — to deride, ridicule
- ❏ SCORE (n.) — notation for a musical composition
- ❏ SCORE (v.) — to make a notch or scratch
- ❏ SCRIVENER — professional copyist
- ❏ SCRUPULOUS — restrained; careful and precise
- ❏ SCRUTINY — careful observation
- ❏ SCURRILOUS — vulgar, low, indecent
- ❏ SECANT — straight line intersecting a curve at two points
- ❏ SECEDE — to withdraw formally from an organization
- ❏ SECLUDED — isolated and remote
- ❏ SECTARIAN — narrow-minded; relating to a group or sect
- ❏ SECULAR — not specifically pertaining to religion
- ❏ SEDENTARY — inactive, stationary; sluggish
- ❏ SEDITION — behavior promoting rebellion
- ❏ SEISMOLOGY — science of earthquakes
- ❏ SEMINAL — relating to the beginning or seeds of something
- ❏ SENESCENT — aging, growing old
- ❏ SENSUAL — satisfying or gratifying the senses; suggesting sexuality
- ❏ SENTENTIOUS — having a moralizing tone
- ❏ SENTIENT — aware, conscious, able to perceive

- SEQUEL — anything that follows
- SEQUESTER — to remove or set apart; put into seclusion
- SERAPHIC — angelic, pure, sublime
- SERENDIPITY — habit of making fortunate discoveries by chance
- SERENITY — calm, peacefulness
- SERPENTINE — serpent-like; twisting, winding
- SERRATED — saw-toothed, notched
- SERVILE — submissive, obedient
- SHARD — piece of broken glass or pottery
- SHEEPISH — timid, meek or bashful
- SHIRK — to avoid a task due to laziness or fear
- SIGNIFY — denote, indicate; symbolize
- SIMIAN — ape-like; relating to apes
- SIMPER — to smirk, smile foolishly
- SINECURE — well-paying job or office that requires little or no work
- SINGE — to burn slightly, scorch
- SINUOUS — winding; intricate, complex
- SKEPTICAL — doubtful, questioning
- SKULK — to move in a stealthy or cautious manner; sneak
- SLIGHT — to treat as unimportant; insult
- SLIPSHOD — careless, hasty
- SLOTH — sluggishness, laziness
- SLOUGH — to discard or shed
- SLOVENLY — untidy, messy
- SLUGGARD — lazy, inactive person
- SMELT (v.) — to melt metal in order to refine it
- SNIPPET — tiny part, tidbit
- SOBRIETY — seriousness
- SOBRIQUET — nickname
- SODDEN — thoroughly soaked; saturated
- SOJOURN — visit, stay
- SOLACE — comfort in distress; consolation
- SOLARIUM — room or glassed-in area exposed to the sun
- SOLECISM — grammatical mistake
- SOLICITOUS — concerned, attentive; eager
- SOLIDARITY — unity based on common aims or interests
- SOLILOQUY — literary or dramatic speech by one character, not addressed to others
- SOLIPSISM — belief that the self is the only reality
- SOLSTICE — shortest and longest day of the year
- SOLUBLE — capable of being solved or dissolved

- SOMBER — dark and gloomy; melancholy, dismal
- SOMNAMBULIST — sleepwalker
- SOMNOLENT — drowsy, sleepy; inducing sleep
- SONIC — relating to sound
- SONOROUS — producing a full, rich sound
- SOPHIST — person good at arguing deviously
- SOPHISTRY — deceptive reasoning or argumentation
- SOPHOMORIC — immature and overconfident
- SOPORIFIC — sleepy or tending to cause sleep
- SORDID — filthy; contemptible and corrupt
- SOVEREIGN — having supreme power
- SPARTAN — austere, severe, grave; simple, bare
- SPAWN — to generate, produce
- SPECULATION — contemplation; act of taking business risks for financial gain
- SPECULATIVE — involving assumption; uncertain; theoretical
- SPONTANEOUS — on the spur of the moment, impulsive
- SPORADIC — infrequent, irregular
- SPORTIVE — frolicsome, playful
- SPRIGHTLY — lively, animated, energetic
- SPUR (v.) — to prod
- SPURIOUS — lacking authenticity; counterfeit, false
- SPURN — to reject or refuse contemptuously; scorn
- SQUALID — filthy; morally repulsive
- SQUANDER — to waste
- STACCATO — marked by abrupt, clear-cut sounds
- STAGNANT — immobile, stale
- STAID — self-restrained to the point of dullness
- STAND (n.) — group of trees
- STALK (v.) — to hunt, pursue
- STARK — bare, empty, vacant
- STASIS — motionless state; standstill
- STIFLE — to smother or suffocate; suppress
- STIGMA — mark of disgrace or inferiority
- STILTED — stiff, unnatural
- STINT (n.) — period of time spent doing something
- STINT (v.) — to be sparing or frugal
- STIPEND — allowance; fixed amount of money paid regularly
- STOCKADE — enclosed area forming defensive wall
- STOIC — indifferent to or unaffected by emotions
- STOLID — having or showing little emotion
- STRATAGEM — trick designed to deceive an enemy
- STRATIFY — to arrange into layers

❑ STRICTURE — something that restrains; negative criticism

❑ STRIDENT — loud, harsh, unpleasantly noisy

❑ STRINGENT — imposing severe, rigorous standards

❑ STULTIFY — to impair or reduce to uselessness

❑ STUNTED — having arrested growth or development

❑ STUPEFY — to dull the senses of; stun, astonish

❑ STYLIZE — to fashion, formalize

❑ STYMIE — to block or thwart

❑ SUAVE — smoothly gracious or polite; blandly ingratiating

❑ SUBDUED — suppressed, stifled

❑ SUBJECTION — dependence, obedience, submission

❑ SUBJUGATE — to conquer, subdue; enslave

❑ SUBLIME — awe-inspiring; of high spiritual or moral value

❑ SUBLIMINAL — subconscious; imperceptible

❑ SUBMISSIVE — tending to be meek and submit

❑ SUBPOENA — notice ordering someone to appear in court

❑ SUBSEQUENT — following in time or order

❑ SUBTERFUGE — trick or tactic used to avoid something

❑ SUBTERRANEAN — hidden, secret; underground

❑ SUBTLE — hard to detect or describe; perceptive

❑ SUBVERT — to undermine or corrupt

❑ SUCCINCT — terse, brief, concise

❑ SUCCULENT — juicy; full of vitality or freshness

❑ SUFFERABLE — bearable

❑ SUFFRAGIST — one who advocates extended voting rights

❑ SULLEN — brooding, gloomy

❑ SULLY — to soil, stain, tarnish; taint

❑ SUMPTUOUS — lavish, splendid

❑ SUPERANNUATED — too old, obsolete, outdated

❑ SUPERCILIOUS — arrogant, haughty, overbearing, condescending

❑ SUPERFLUOUS — extra, more than necessary

❑ SUPERSEDE — to take the place of; replace

❑ SUPERVISE — to direct or oversee the work of others

❑ SUPPLANT — replace, substitute

❑ SUPPLE — flexible, pliant

❑ SUPPLICANT — one who asks humbly and earnestly

❑ SURFEIT — excessive amount

❑ SURLY — rude and bad-tempered

❑ SURMISE — to make an educated guess

❑ SURMOUNT — to conquer, overcome

❑ SURPASS — to do better than, be superior to

❑ SUPERFICIAL — hasty; shallow and phony

❑ SURPLUS — excess

❑ SURREPTITIOUS — characterized by secrecy

❑ SURVEY (v.) — to examine in a comprehensive way

❑ SUSCEPTIBLE — vulnerable, unprotected

❑ SUSPEND — to defer, interrupt; dangle, hang

❑ SUSTAIN — support, uphold; endure, undergo

❑ SWARTHY — having a dark complexion

❑ SYBARITE — person devoted to pleasure and luxury

❑ SYCOPHANT — self-serving flatterer, yes-man

❑ SYLLABUS — outline of a course

❑ SYMBIOSIS — cooperation, mutual helpfulness

❑ SYMPOSIUM — meeting with short presentations on related topics

❑ SYNCOPATION — temporary irregularity in musical rhythm

❑ SYNOPSIS — plot summary

❑ SYNTHESIS — blend, combination

❑ SYNTHETIC — artificial, imitation

T

❑ TABLEAU — vivid description, striking incident or scene

❑ TACIT — silently understood or implied

❑ TACITURN — uncommunicative, not inclined to speak much

❑ TACTILE — relating to the sense of touch

❑ TAINT — to spoil or infect; to stain honor

❑ TAINTED — stained, tarnished; corrupted, poisoned

❑ TALON — claw of an animal, esp. a bird of prey

❑ TANG — sharp flavor or odor

❑ TANGENTIAL — digressing, diverting

❑ TANGIBLE — able to be sensed; perceptible, measurable

❑ TANTAMOUNT — equivalent in value or significance; amounting to

❑ TARNISHED — corroded, discolored; discredited, disgraced

❑ TAWDRY — gaudy, cheap, showy

❑ TAXONOMY — science of classification

❑ TECHNOCRAT — strong believer in technology; technical expert

❑ TEMPERANCE — restraint, self-control, moderation

❑ TEMPERED — moderated, restrained

❑ TEMPESTUOUS — stormy, raging, furious

❑ TENABLE — defensible, reasonable

❑ TENACIOUS — stubborn, holding firm

❑ TENET — belief, doctrine

❑ TENSILE — capable of withstanding physical stress

❑ TENUOUS — weak, insubstantial

❑ TEPID — lukewarm; showing little enthusiasm

❑ TERMINAL (adj.) — concluding, final; fatal

❑ TERMINAL (n.) — depot, station

❑ TERRESTRIAL — earthly; down-to-earth, commonplace

❑ TERSE — concise, brief, free of extra words

❑ TESTAMENT — statement of belief; will

❑ TESTIMONIAL — statement testifying to a truth; something given in tribute to a person's achievement

❑ TETHER — to bind, tie

❑ THEOCRACY — government by priests representing a god

❑ THEOLOGY — study of God and religion

❑ THEORETICAL — abstract

❑ THERAPEUTIC — medicinal

❑ THESAURUS — book of synonyms and antonyms

❑ THESIS — theory or hypothesis; dissertation or long written composition

❑ THWART — to block or prevent from happening; frustrate

❑ TIDINGS — news

❑ TIMOROUS — timid, shy, full of apprehension

❑ TINGE — to color slightly; slight amount

❑ TIRADE — long violent speech; verbal assault

❑ TITAN — person of colossal stature or achievement

❑ TOADY — flatterer, hanger-on, yes-man

❑ TOLERANCE — capacity to respect different values; capacity to endure or resist something

❑ TOME — book, usually large and academic

❑ TONAL — relating to pitch or sound

❑ TOPOGRAPHY — art of making maps or charts

❑ TORPID — lethargic; unable to move; dormant

❑ TORRID — burning hot; passionate

❑ TORSION — act of twisting and turning

❑ TORTUOUS — having many twists and turns; highly complex

❑ TOTTERING — barely standing

❑ TOXIN — poison

❑ TRACTABLE — obedient, yielding

❑ TRANSCEND — to rise above, go beyond

❑ TRANSCENDENT — rising above, going beyond

❑ TRANSCRIPTION — copy, reproduction; record

❑ TRANSGRESS — to trespass, violate a law

❑ TRANSIENT — temporary, short lived, fleeting

❑ TRANSITORY — short-lived, existing only briefly

❑ TRANSLUCENT — partially transparent

❑ TRANSMUTE — to change in appearance or shape

❑ TRANSPIRE — to happen, occur; become known

❑ TRAVESTY — parody, exaggerated imitation, caricature

❑ TREMULOUS — trembling, quivering; fearful, timid

❑ TRENCHANT — acute, sharp, incisive; forceful, effective

❑ TREPIDATION — fear and anxiety

❑ TRIFLING — of slight worth, trivial, insignificant

❑ TRITE — shallow, superficial

❑ TROUNCE — to beat severely, defeat

❑ TROUPE — group of actors

❑ TRUNCATE — to cut off, shorten by cutting

❑ TRYING — difficult to deal with

❑ TRYST — agreement between lovers to meet; rendezvous

❑ TUMULT — state of confusion; agitation

❑ TUNDRA — treeless plain found in arctic or subarctic regions

❑ TURBULENCE — commotion, disorder

❑ TURGID — swollen, bloated

❑ TURPITUDE — inherent vileness, foulness, depravity

❑ TYRO — beginner, novice

U

❑ UBIQUITOUS — being everywhere simultaneously

❑ UMBRAGE — offense, resentment

❑ UNADULTERATED — absolutely pure

❑ UNANIMITY — state of total agreement or unity

❑ UNAPPEALING — unattractive, unpleasant

❑ UNAVAILING — hopeless, useless

❑ UNCONSCIONABLE — unscrupulous; shockingly unfair or unjust

❑ UNCTUOUS — greasy, oily; smug and falsely earnest

❑ UNDERMINE — to sabotage, thwart

❑ UNDOCUMENTED — not certified, unsubstantiated

❑ UNDULATING — moving in waves

❑ UNEQUIVOCAL — absolute, certain

❑ UNFROCK — to strip of priestly duties

❑ UNHERALDED — unannounced, unexpected, not publicized

❑ UNIDIMENSIONAL — having one size or dimension, flat

- ❑ UNIFORM (adj.) — consistent and unchanging; identical
- ❑ UNIMPEACHABLE — beyond question
- ❑ UNINITIATED — not familiar with an area of study
- ❑ UNKEMPT — uncombed, messy in appearance
- ❑ UNOBTRUSIVE — modest, unassuming
- ❑ UNSCRUPULOUS — dishonest
- ❑ UNSOLICITED — unrequested
- ❑ UNWARRANTED — groundless, unjustified
- ❑ UNWITTING — unconscious; unintentional
- ❑ UNYIELDING — firm, resolute
- ❑ UPBRAID — to scold sharply
- ❑ UPROARIOUS — loud and forceful
- ❑ URBANE — courteous, refined, suave
- ❑ USURP — to seize by force
- ❑ USURY — practice of lending money at exorbitant rates
- ❑ UTILITARIAN — efficient, functional, useful
- ❑ UTOPIA — perfect place

V

- ❑ VACILLATE — to waver, show indecision
- ❑ VACUOUS — empty, void; lacking intelligence, purposeless
- ❑ VAGRANT — poor person with no home
- ❑ VALIDATE — to authorize, certify, confirm
- ❑ VANQUISH — to conquer, defeat
- ❑ VAPID — tasteless, dull
- ❑ VARIABLE — changeable, inconstant
- ❑ VARIEGATED — varied; marked with different colors
- ❑ VAUNTED — boasted about, bragged about
- ❑ VEHEMENTLY — strongly, urgently
- ❑ VENDETTA — prolonged feud marked by bitter hostility
- ❑ VENERABLE — respected because of age
- ❑ VENERATION — adoration, honor, respect
- ❑ VENT — to express, say out loud
- ❑ VERACIOUS — truthful, accurate
- ❑ VERACITY — accuracy, truth
- ❑ VERBATIM — word for word
- ❑ VERBOSE — wordy
- ❑ VERDANT — green with vegetation; inexperienced
- ❑ VERDURE — fresh, rich vegetation
- ❑ VERIFIED — proven true
- ❑ VERISIMILITUDE — quality of appearing true or real

- ❑ VERITY — truthfulness; belief viewed as true and enduring
- ❑ VERMIN — small creatures offensive to humans
- ❑ VERNACULAR — everyday language used by ordinary people; specialized language of a profession
- ❑ VERNAL — related to spring
- ❑ VERSATILE — adaptable, all-purpose
- ❑ VESTIGE — trace, remnant
- ❑ VETO — to reject formally
- ❑ VEX — to irritate, annoy; confuse, puzzle
- ❑ VIABLE — workable, able to succeed or grow
- ❑ VIADUCT — series of elevated arches used to cross a valley
- ❑ VICARIOUS — substitute, surrogate; enjoyed through imagined participation in another's experience
- ❑ VICISSITUDE — change or variation; ups and downs
- ❑ VIE — to compete, contend
- ❑ VIGILANT — attentive, watchful
- ❑ VIGNETTE — decorative design; short literary composition
- ❑ VILIFY — to slander, defame
- ❑ VIM — energy, enthusiasm
- ❑ VINDICATE — to clear of blame; support a claim
- ❑ VINDICATION — clearance from blame or suspicion
- ❑ VINDICTIVE — spiteful, vengeful, unforgiving
- ❑ VIRILE — manly, having qualities of an adult male
- ❑ VIRTUOSO — someone with masterly skill; expert musician
- ❑ VIRULENT — extremely poisonous; malignant; hateful
- ❑ VISCOUS — thick, syrupy and sticky
- ❑ VITRIOLIC — burning, caustic; sharp, bitter
- ❑ VITUPERATE — to abuse verbally
- ❑ VIVACIOUS — lively, spirited
- ❑ VIVID — bright and intense in color; strongly perceived
- ❑ VOCIFEROUS — loud, vocal and noisy
- ❑ VOID (adj.) — not legally enforceable; empty
- ❑ VOID (n.) — emptiness, vacuum
- ❑ VOID (v.) — to cancel, invalidate
- ❑ VOLITION — free choice, free will; act of choosing
- ❑ VOLLEY (n.) — flight of missiles, round of gunshots
- ❑ VOLUBLE — speaking much and easily, talkative; glib
- ❑ VOLUMINOUS — large, having great volume
- ❑ VORACIOUS — having a great appetite
- ❑ VULNERABLE — defenseless, unprotected; innocent, naive

W

☐ WAIVE — to refrain from enforcing a rule; to give up a legal right

☐ WALLOW — to indulge oneself excessively, luxuriate

☐ WAN — sickly pale

☐ WANTON — undisciplined, unrestrained, reckless

☐ WARRANTY — guarantee of a product's soundness

☐ WARY — careful, cautious

☐ WAYWARD — erratic, unrestrained, reckless

☐ WEATHER (v.) — to endure, undergo

☐ WHET — to sharpen, stimulate

☐ WHIMSY — playful or fanciful idea

☐ WILY — clever, deceptive

☐ WINDFALL — sudden, unexpected good fortune

☐ WINSOME — charming, happily engaging

☐ WITHDRAWN — unsociable, aloof; shy, timid

☐ WIZENED — withered, shriveled, wrinkled

☐ WRIT — written document, usually in law

☐ WRY — amusing, ironic

X

☐ XENOPHOBIA — fear or hatred of foreigners or strangers

Y

☐ YOKE (v.) — to join together

Z

☐ ZEALOT — someone passionately devoted to a cause

☐ ZENITH — highest point, summit

☐ ZEPHYR — gentle breeze

☐ ZOOLOGIST — scientist who studies animals

THE KAPLAN ROOT LIST

❏ A, AN — not, without
amoral, atrophy, asymmetrical, anarchy, anesthetic, anonymity, anomaly

❏ AB, A — from, away, apart
abnormal, abdicate, aberration, abhor, abject, abjure, ablution, abnegate, abortive, abrogate, abscond, absolve, abstemious, abstruse, annul, avert, aversion

❏ AC, ACR — sharp, sour
acid, acerbic, exacerbate, acute, acuity, acumen, acrid, acrimony

❏ AD, A — to, toward
adhere, adjacent, adjunct, admonish, adroit, adumbrate, advent, abeyance, abet, accede, accretion, acquiesce, affluent, aggrandize, aggregate, alleviate, alliteration, allude, allure, ascribe, aspersion, aspire, assail, assonance, attest

❏ ALI, ALTR — another
alias, alienate, inalienable, altruism

❏ AM, AMI — love
amorous, amicable, amiable, amity

❏ AMBI, AMPHI — both
ambiguous, ambivalent, ambidextrous, amphibious

❏ AMBL, AMBUL — walk
amble, ambulatory, perambulator, somnambulist

❏ ANIM — mind, spirit, breath
animal, animosity, unanimous, magnanimous

❏ ANN, ENN — year
annual, annuity, superannuated, biennial, perennial

❏ ANTE, ANT — before
antecedent, antediluvian, antebellum, antepenultimate, anterior, antiquity, antiquated, anticipate

❏ ANTHROP — human
anthropology, anthropomorphic, misanthrope, philanthropy

❏ ANTI, ANT — against, opposite
antidote, antipathy, antithesis, antacid, antagonist, antonym

❏ AUD — hear
audio, audience, audition, auditory, audible

❏ AUTO — self
autobiography, autocrat, autonomous

❏ BELLI, BELL — war
belligerent, bellicose, antebellum, rebellion

❏ BENE, BEN — good
benevolent, benefactor, beneficent, benign

❏ BI — two
bicycle, bisect, bilateral, bilingual, biped

❑ BIBLIO — book
Bible, bibliography, bibliophile

❑ BIO — life
biography, biology, amphibious, symbiotic, macrobiotics

❑ BURS — money, purse
reimburse, disburse, bursar

❑ CAD, CAS, CID — happen, fall
accident, cadence, cascade, deciduous

❑ CAP, CIP — head
captain, decapitate, capitulate, precipitous, precipitate

❑ CARN — flesh
carnal, carnage, carnival, carnivorous, incarnate

❑ CAP, CAPT, CEPT, CIP — take, hold, seize
capable, capacious, recapitulate, captivate, deception, intercept, precept, inception, anticipate, emancipation, incipient, percipient, cede, precede, accede, recede, antecedent, intercede, secede, cession

❑ CED, CESS — yield, go
cease, cessation, incessant, cede

❑ CHROM — color
chrome, chromatic, monochrome

❑ CHRON — time
chronology, chronic, anachronism

❑ CIDE — murder
suicide, homicide, regicide, patricide

❑ CIRCUM — around
circumference, circumlocution, circumnavigate, circumscribe, circumspect, circumvent

❑ CLIN, CLIV — slope
incline, declivity, proclivity

❑ CLUD, CLUS, CLAUS, CLOIS — shut, close
conclude, reclusive, claustrophobia, cloister, preclude, occlude

❑ CO, COM, CON — with, together
coeducation, coagulate, coalesce, coerce, cogent, cognate, collateral, colloquial, colloquy, commensurate, commodious, compassion, compatriot, complacent, compliant, complicity, compunction, concerto, conciliatory, concord, concur, condone, conflagration, congeal, congenial, congenital, conglomerate, conjure, conjugal, conscientious, consecrate, consensus, consonant, constrained, contentious, contrite, contusion, convalescence, convene, convivial, convoke, convoluted, congress

❑ COGN, GNO — know
recognize, cognition, cognizance, incognito, diagnosis, agnostic, prognosis, gnostic, ignorant

❑ CONTRA — against
controversy, incontrovertible, contravene

❑ CORP — body
corpse, corporeal, corpulence

❑ COSMO, COSM — world
cosmopolitan, cosmos, microcosm, macrocosm

❑ CRAC, CRAT — rule, power
democracy, bureaucracy, theocracy, autocrat, aristocrat, technocrat

❑ CRED — trust, believe
incredible, credulous, credence

❑ CRESC, CRET — grow
crescent, crescendo, accretion

❑ CULP — blame, fault
culprit, culpable, inculpate, exculpate

❑ CURR, CURS — run
current, concur, cursory, precursor, incursion

❑ DE — down, out, apart
depart, debase, debilitate, declivity, decry, deface, defamatory, defunct, delegate, demarcation, demean, demur, deplete, deplore, depravity, deprecate, deride, derivative, desist, detest, devoid

❑ DEC — ten, tenth
decade, decimal, decathlon, decimate

❑ DEMO, DEM — people
democrat, demographics, demagogue, epidemic, pandemic, endemic

❑ DI, DIURN — day
diary, diurnal, quotidian

❑ DIA — across
diagonal, diatribe, diaphanous

❑ DIC, DICT — speak
diction, interdict, predict, abdicate, indict, verdict

❑ DIS, DIF, DI — not, apart, away
disaffected, disband, disbar, disburse, discern, discordant, discredit, discursive, disheveled, disparage, disparate, dispassionate, dispirit, dissemble, disseminate, dissension, dissipate, dissonant, dissuade, distend, differentiate, diffidence, diffuse, digress, divert

❑ DOC, DOCT — teach
doctrine, docile, doctrinaire

❑ DOL — pain
condolence, doleful, dolorous, indolent

❑ DUC, DUCT — lead
seduce, induce, conduct, viaduct, induct

❑ EGO — self
ego, egoist, egocentric

❑ EN, EM — in, into
enter, entice, encumber, endemic, ensconce, enthrall, entreat, embellish, embezzle, embroil, empathy

❑ ERR — wander
erratic, aberration, errant

❑ EU — well, good
eulogy, euphemism, euphony, euphoria, eurythmics, euthanasia

❏ EX, E — out, out of
exit, exacerbate, excerpt, excommunicate, exculpate, execrable, exhume, exonerate, exorbitant, exorcise, expatriate, expedient, expiate, expunge, expurgate, extenuate, extort, extremity, extricate, extrinsic, exult, evoke, evict, evince, elicit, egress, egregious

❏ FAC, FIC, FECT, FY, FEA — make, do
factory, facility, benefactor, malefactor, fiction, fictive, beneficent, affect, confection, refectory, magnify, unify, rectify, vilify, feasible

❏ FAL, FALS — deceive
false, infallible, fallacious

❏ FERV — boil
fervent, fervid, effervescent

❏ FID — faith, trust
confident, diffidence, perfidious, fidelity

❏ FLU, FLUX — flow
fluent, flux, affluent, confluence, effluvia, superfluous

❏ FORE — before
forecast, foreboding, forestall

❏ FRAG, FRAC — break
fragment, fracture, diffract, fractious, refract

❏ FUS — pour
profuse, infusion, effusive, diffuse

❏ GEN — birth, class, kin
generation, congenital, homogeneous, heterogeneous, ingenious, engender, progenitor, progeny

❏ GRAD, GRESS — step
graduate, gradual, retrograde, centigrade, degrade, gradation, gradient, progress, congress, digress, transgress, ingress, egress

❏ GRAPH, GRAM — writing
biography, bibliography, epigraph, grammar, epigram

❏ GRAT — pleasing
grateful, gratitude, gratis, ingrate, congratulate, gratuitous, gratuity

❏ GRAV, GRIEV — heavy
grave, gravity, aggravate, grieve, aggrieve, grievous

❏ GREG — crowd, flock
segregate, gregarious, egregious, congregate, aggregate

❏ HABIT, HIBIT — have, hold
habit, inhibit, cohabit, habitat

❏ HAP — by chance
happen, haphazard, hapless, mishap

❏ HELIO, HELI — sun
heliocentric, helium, heliotrope, aphelion, perihelion

❏ HETERO — other
heterosexual, heterogeneous, heterodox

❏ HOL — whole
holocaust, catholic, holistic

❏ HOMO — same
homosexual, homogenize, homogeneous, **homonym**

❏ HOMO — man
homo sapiens, homicide, bonhomie

❏ HYDR — water
hydrant, hydrate, dehydration

❏ HYPER — too much, excess
hyperactive, hyperbole, hyperventilate

❏ HYPO — too little, under
hypodermic, hypothermia, hypochondria, **hypothesis, hypothetical**

❏ IN, IG, IL, IM, IR — not
incorrigible, indefatigable, indelible, indubitable, inept, inert, inexorable, insatiable, insentient, insolvent, insomnia, interminable, intractable, incessant, inextricable, infallible, infamy, **innumerable,** inoperable, insipid, intemperate, intrepid, inviolable, ignorant, ignominious, ignoble, illicit, illimitable, immaculate, **immutable,** impasse, impeccable, impecunious, impertinent, implacable, impotent, impregnable, improvident, impassioned, impervious, **irregular,** invade, inaugurate, incandescent, incarcerate, incense, indenture, induct, ingratiate, introvert, **incarnate, inception, incisive, infer**

❏ IN, IL, IM, IR — in, on, into
infusion, ingress, innate, inquest, inscribe, insinuate, inter, **illustrate, imbue, immerse,** implicate, irrigate, irritate

❏ INTER — between, among
intercede, intercept, interdiction, interject, **interlocutor, interloper, intermediary,** intermittent, interpolate, interpose, interregnum, interrogate, intersect, **intervene**

❏ INTRA, INTR — within
intrastate, intravenous, intramural, **intrinsic**

❏ IT, ITER — between, among
transit, itinerant, reiterate, transitory

❏ JECT, JET — throw
eject, interject, abject, trajectory, jettison

❏ JOUR — day
journal, adjourn, sojourn

❏ JUD — judge
judge, judicious, prejudice, adjudicate

❏ JUNCT, JUG — join
junction, adjunct, injunction, conjugal, **subjugate**

❏ JUR — swear, law
jury, abjure, adjure, conjure, perjure, **jurisprudence**

❏ LAT — side
lateral, collateral, unilateral, bilateral, **quadrilateral**

❏ LAV, LAU, LU — wash
lavatory, laundry, ablution, antediluvian

❏ LEG, LEC, LEX — read, speak
legible, lecture, lexicon

❏ LEV — light
elevate, levitate, levity, alleviate

❑ LIBER — free
liberty, liberal, libertarian, libertine

❑ LIG, LECT — choose, gather
eligible, elect, select

❑ LIG, LI, LY — bind
ligament, oblige, religion, liable, liaison, lien, ally

❑ LING, LANG — tongue
lingo, language, linguistics, bilingual

❑ LITER — letter
literate, alliteration, literal

❑ LITH — stone
monolith, lithograph, megalith

❑ LOQU, LOC, LOG — speech, thought
eloquent, loquacious, colloquial, colloquy, soliloquy, circumlocution, interlocutor, monologue, dialogue, eulogy, philology, neologism

❑ LUC, LUM — light
lucid, illuminate, elucidate, pellucid, translucent

❑ LUD, LUS — play
ludicrous, allude, delusion, allusion, illusory

❑ MACRO — great
macrocosm, macrobiotics

❑ MAG, MAJ, MAS, MAX — great
magnify, majesty, master, maximum, magnanimous, magnate, magnitude

❑ MAL — bad
malady, maladroit, malevolent, malodorous

❑ MAN — hand
manual, manuscript, emancipate, manifest

❑ MAR — sea
submarine, marine, maritime

❑ MATER, MATR — mother
maternal, matron, matrilineal

❑ MEDI — middle
intermediary, medieval, mediate

❑ MEGA — great
megaphone, megalomania, megaton, megalith

❑ MEM, MEN — remember
memory, memento, memorabilia, reminisce

❑ METER, METR, MENS — measure
meter, thermometer, perimeter, metronome, commensurate

❑ MICRO — small
microscope, microorganism, microcosm, microbe

❑ MIS — wrong, bad, hate
misunderstand, misanthrope, misapprehension, misconstrue, misnomer, mishap

❑ MIT, MISS — send
transmit, emit, missive

❑ MOLL — soft
mollify, emollient, mollusk

❑ MON, MONIT — warn
admonish, monitor, premonition

❑ MONO — one
monologue, monotonous, monogamy, monolith, monochrome

❑ MOR — custom, manner
moral, mores, morose

❑ MOR, MORT — dead
morbid, moribund, mortal, amortize

❑ MORPH — shape
amorphous, anthropomorphic, metamorphosis, morphology

❑ MOV, MOT, MOB, MOM — move
remove, motion, mobile, momentum, momentous

❑ MUT — change
mutate, mutability, immutable, commute

❑ NAT, NASC — born
native, nativity, natal, neonate, innate, cognate, nascent, renascent, renaissance

❑ NAU, NAV — ship, sailor
nautical, nauseous, navy, circumnavigate

❑ NEG — not, deny
negative, abnegate, renege

❑ NEO — new
neoclassical, neophyte, neologism, neonate

❑ NIHIL — none, nothing
annihilation, nihilism

❑ NOM, NYM — name
nominate, nomenclature, nominal, cognomen, misnomer, ignominious, antonym, homonym, pseudonym, synonym, anonymity

❑ NOX, NIC, NEC, NOC — harm
obnoxious, noxious, pernicious, internecine, innocuous

❑ NOV — new
novelty, innovation, novitiate

❑ NUMER — number
numeral, numerous, innumerable, enumerate

❑ OB — against
obstruct, obdurate, obfuscate, obnoxious, obsequious, obstinate, obstreperous, obtrusive

❏ OMNI — all
omnipresent, omnipotent, omniscient, omnivorous

❏ ONER — burden
onerous, onus, exonerate

❏ OPER — work
operate, cooperate, inoperable

❏ PAC — peace
pacify, pacifist, pacific

❏ PALP — feel
palpable, palpitation

❏ PAN — all
panorama, panacea, panegyric, pandemic, panoply

❏ PATER, PATR — father
paternal, paternity, patriot, compatriot, expatriate, patrimony, patricide, patrician

❏ PATH, PASS — feel, suffer
sympathy, antipathy, empathy, apathy, pathos, impassioned

❏ PEC — money
pecuniary, impecunious, peculation

❏ PED, POD — foot
pedestrian, pediment, expedient, biped, quadruped, tripod

❏ PEL, PULS — drive
compel, compelling, expel, propel, compulsion

❏ PEN — almost
peninsula, penultimate, penumbra

❏ PEND, PENS — hang
pendant, pendulous, compendium, suspense, propensity

❏ PER — through, by, for, throughout
perambulator, percipient, perfunctory, permeable, perspicacious, pertinacious, perturbation, perusal, perennial, peregrinate

❏ PER — against, destruction
perfidious, pernicious, perjure

❏ PERI — around
perimeter, periphery, perihelion, peripatetic

❏ PET — seek, go toward
petition, impetus, impetuous, petulant, centripetal

❏ PHIL — love
philosopher, philanderer, philanthropy, bibliophile, philology

❏ PHOB — fear
phobia, claustrophobia, xenophobia

❏ PHON — sound
phonograph, megaphone, euphony, phonetics, phonics

❏ PLAC — calm, please
placate, implacable, placid, complacent

❑ PON, POS — put, place
postpone, proponent, exponent, preposition, posit, interpose, juxtaposition, depose

❑ PORT — carry
portable, deportment, rapport

❑ POT — drink
potion, potable

❑ POT — power
potential, potent, impotent, potentate, omnipotence

❑ PRE — before
precede, precipitate, preclude, precocious, precursor, predilection, predisposition, preponderance, prepossessing, presage, prescient, prejudice, predict, premonition, preposition

❑ PRIM, PRI — first
prime, primary, primal, primeval, primordial, pristine

❑ PRO — ahead, forth
proceed, proclivity, procrastinator, profane, profuse, progenitor, progeny, prognosis, prologue, promontory, propel, proponent, propose, proscribe, protestation, provoke

❑ PROTO — first
prototype, protagonist, protocol

❑ PROX, PROP — near
approximate, propinquity, proximity

❑ PSEUDO — false
pseudoscientific, pseudonym

❑ PYR — fire
pyre, pyrotechnics, pyromania

❑ QUAD, QUAR, QUAT — four
quadrilateral, quadrant, quadruped, quarter, quarantine, quaternary

❑ QUES, QUER, QUIS, QUIR — question
quest, inquest, query, querulous, inquisitive, inquiry

❑ QUIE — quiet
disquiet, acquiesce, quiescent, requiem

❑ QUINT, QUIN — five
quintuplets, quintessence

❑ RADI, RAMI — branch
radius, radiate, radiant, eradicate, ramification

❑ RECT, REG — straight, rule
rectangle, rectitude, rectify, regular

❑ REG — king, rule
regal, regent, interregnum

❑ RETRO — backward
retrospective, retroactive, retrograde

❑ RID, RIS — laugh
ridiculous, deride, derision

❑ ROG — ask
interrogate, derogatory, abrogate, arrogate, arrogant

❑ RUD — rough, crude
rude, erudite, rudimentary

❑ RUPT — break
disrupt, interrupt, rupture

❑ SACR, SANCT — holy
sacred, sacrilege, consecrate, sanctify, sanction, sacrosanct

❑ SCRIB, SCRIPT, SCRIV — write
scribe, ascribe, circumscribe, inscribe, proscribe, script, manuscript, scrivener

❑ SE — apart, away
separate, segregate, secede, sedition

❑ SEC, SECT, SEG — cut
sector, dissect, bisect, intersect, segment, secant

❑ SED, SID — sit
sedate, sedentary, supersede, reside, residence, assiduous, insidious

❑ SEM — seed, sow
seminar, seminal, disseminate

❑ SEN — old
senior, senile, senescent

❑ SENT, SENS — feel, think
sentiment, nonsense, assent, sentient, consensus, sensual

❑ SEQU, SECU — follow
sequence, sequel, subsequent, obsequious, obsequy, non sequitur, consecutive

❑ SIM, SEM — similar, same
similar, semblance, dissemble, verisimilitude

❑ SIGN — mark, sign
signal, designation, assignation

❑ SIN — curve
sine curve, sinuous, insinuate

❑ SOL — sun
solar, parasol, solarium, solstice

❑ SOL — alone
solo, solitude, soliloquy, solipsism

❑ SOMN — sleep
insomnia, somnolent, somnambulist

❑ SON — sound
sonic, consonance, dissonance, assonance, sonorous, resonate

❑ SOPH — wisdom
philosopher, sophistry, sophisticated, sophomoric

❑ SPEC, SPIC — see, look
spectator, circumspect, retrospective, perspective, perspicacious

❑ SPER — hope
prosper, prosperous, despair, desperate

❑ SPERS, SPAR — scatter
disperse, sparse, aspersion, disparate

❑ SPIR — breathe
respire, inspire, spiritual, aspire, transpire

❑ STRICT, STRING — bind
strict, stricture, constrict, stringent, astringent

❑ STRUCT, STRU — build
structure, construe, obstruct

❑ SUB — under
subconscious, subjugate, subliminal, subpoena, subsequent, subterranean, subvert

❑ SUMM — highest
summit, summary, consummate

❑ SUPER, SUR — above
supervise, supercilious, supersede, superannuated, superfluous, insurmountable, surfeit

❑ SURGE, SURRECT — rise
surge, resurgent, insurgent, insurrection

❑ SYN, SYM — together
synthesis, sympathy, synonym, syncopation, synopsis, symposium, symbiosis

❑ TACIT, TIC — silent
tacit, taciturn, reticent

❑ TACT, TAG, TANG — touch
tact, tactile, contagious, tangent, tangential, tangible

❑ TEN, TIN, TAIN — hold, twist
detention, tenable, tenacious, pertinacious, retinue, retain

❑ TEND, TENS, TENT — stretch
intend, distend, tension, tensile, ostensible, contentious

❑ TERM — end
terminal, terminus, terminate, interminable

❑ TERR — earth, land
terrain, terrestrial, extraterrestrial, subterranean

❑ TEST — witness
testify, attest, testimonial, testament, detest, protestation

❑ THE — god
atheist, theology, apotheosis, theocracy

❑ THERM — heat
thermometer, thermal, thermonuclear, hypothermia

❑ TIM — fear, frightened
timid, intimidate, timorous

❑ TOP — place
topic, topography, utopia

❑ TORT — twist
distort, extort, tortuous

❑ TORP — stiff, numb
torpedo, torpid, torpor

❑ TOX — poison
toxic, toxin, intoxication

❑ TRACT — draw
tractor, intractable, protract

❑ TRANS — across, over, through, beyond
transport, transgress, transient, transitory, translucent, transmutation

❑ TREM, TREP — shake
tremble, tremor, tremulous, trepidation, intrepid

❑ TURB — shake
disturb, turbulent, perturbation

❑ UMBR — shadow
umbrella, umbrage, adumbrate, penumbra

❑ UNI, UN — one
unify, unilateral, unanimous

❑ URB — city
urban, suburban, urbane

❑ VAC — empty
vacant, evacuate, vacuous

❑ VAL, VAIL — value, strength
valid, valor, ambivalent, convalescence, avail, prevail, countervail

❑ VEN, VENT — come
convene, contravene, intervene, venue, convention, circumvent, advent, adventitious

❑ VER — true
verify, verity, verisimilitude, veracious, aver, verdict

❑ VERB — word
verbal, verbose, verbiage, verbatim

❑ VERT, VERS — turn
avert, convert, pervert, revert, incontrovertible, divert, subvert, versatile, aversion

❑ VICT, VINC — conquer
victory, conviction, evict, evince, invincible

❑ VID, VIS — see
evident, vision, visage, supervise

❑ VIL — base, mean
vile, vilify, revile

❑ VIV, VIT — life
vivid, vital, convivial, vivacious

❏ VOC, VOK, VOW — call, word
vocal, equivocate, vociferous, convoke, evoke, invoke, avow

❏ VOL — wish
voluntary, malevolent, benevolent, volition

❏ VOLV, VOLUT — turn, roll
revolve, evolve, convoluted

❏ VOR — eat
devour, carnivore, omnivorous, voracious

WORD FAMILIES

Note: These are samples of the kinds of word groups you can create to memorize words more efficiently.

❏ **Talkative**
- garrulous
- glib
- loquacious
- voluble
- verbose
- raconteur

❏ **Secret/Hidden**
- abscond
- incognito
- arcane
- covert
- furtive
- subterranean
- surreptitious
- clandestine
- lurk
- inconspicuous
- cryptic
- enigma
- skulk
- obscure
- alias

❏ **Not Talkative**
- laconic
- pithy
- concise
- taciturn
- reticent
- curt
- succinct

❏ **Praise**
- commend
- accolade
- eulogize
- laud
- extol
- exalt
- lionize
- revere
- adulation
- plaudit

❏ **Criticize/Scold**
- chastise
- censure
- admonish
- reprimand
- reproach
- revile
- reprove
- rebuke
- defame
- disparage
- disdain
- excoriate
- castigate
- upbraid
- obloquy
- vilify
- malign
- berate
- denigrate
- rail

❏ **Stubborn**
- obstinate
- obdurate
- refractory
- pertinacious
- recalcitrant
- mulish
- intractable
- tenacious

❑ Lazy/lacking energy

indolent
lethargic
lassitude
phlegmatic
torpid
laggard
listless
lackadaisical
languid
sluggard
loiter
somnolent

❑ Cowardly

craven
diffident
pusillanimous
timorous

❑ Inexperienced

callow
fledgling
novice
neophyte
ingenuous
tyro
infantile

❑ Obedient

pliant
tractable
amenable
assent
compliant
deferential
docile
submissive

❑ Haughty/Pretentious

aloof
affected
grandiose
grandiloquent
magniloquent
bombastic
supercilious
ostentatious
pontificate
mannered

❑ Friendly

affable
amiable
convivial
amicable
gregarious
bonhomie

❑ Lucky

fortuitous
opportune
auspicious
serendipity
windfall

❑ Soothe

anodyne
mollify
assuage
palliate
pacify
placate
alleviate
allay
mitigate
liniment

❑ Hostility/Hatred

antipathy
anathema
abhor
aversion
animosity
antagonism
contentious
odious
rancor
deplore

❑ Stupid

imbecilic
vacuous
vapid
inane
dupe
insipid
simpleton
fatuous
dupe
obtuse
buffoon
dolt

❑ Subservient

fawn
grovel
obsequious
toady
servile
subjection
sycophant

❑ Argumentative

adversarial
bellicose
belligerent
pugnacious
quibble
fractious
irascible
obstreperous

❑ Cautious

wary
chary
circumspect
prudent
discretion
leery

❑ Impermanent

ephemeral
transient
transitory
evanescent
fleeting

❑ Ability/Intelligence

acumen
adept
lucidity
adroit
sagacious
trenchant
deft
agile
erudite
dexterous
astute
cogent
lithe
literate

❑ Kind/Generous

magnanimous
philanthropic
benevolent
beneficent
altruistic
bestow
largess
liberal
munificent

MATH REFERENCE

The math on the SAT covers a lot of ground—from basic algebra to symbols problems to geometry.

Don't let yourself be intimidated. We've highlighted the 75 most important concepts that you'll need for SAT Math and listed them in this appendix.

You've probably been taught most of these in school already, so this list is a great way to refresh your memory.

NEED MORE HELP?

The math reference list comes from Kaplan's Math Workbook. For more help with the Math section of the SAT, the workbook is a great place to start.

A MATH STUDY PLAN

Use this list to remind yourself of the key areas you'll need to know. Do three concepts a day, and you'll be ready within a month. If a concept continually causes you trouble, circle it and refer back to it as you try to do the questions.

SAT MATH REFERENCE
A CATALOG OF THE MATH YOU NEED TO KNOW

SAT Math tests your understanding of a relatively limited number of mathematical concepts. It is possible to learn all the math you need to know for the SAT in a short time. In fact, you've seen it all before. The test-makers limit themselves to the math that just about every college-bound student sees by junior year. Listed on the following pages are **75 Things You Need to Know for the SAT**, divided into 3 levels.

Level 1 is the most basic. You couldn't answer any SAT Math questions if you didn't know Level 1 Math. Most people preparing to take the SAT are already pretty good at Level 1 Math. Look over the Level 1 list below just to make sure you're comfortable with the basics.

Level 2 is the place for most people to start their review of SAT Math. These skills and formulas come into play quite frequently on the SAT, especially in the medium and hard questions. If you're like a lot of students, your Level 2 Math is probably rusty. You need to master Level 2 if you want to get into the 600s.

Level 3 is the hardest math you'll find on the SAT. These are skills and formulas that you might find difficult. Don't spend a lot of time on Level 3 if you still have gaps in Level 2. But once you've about mastered Level 2, then tackling Level 3 can put you over the top.

LEVEL 1 *(Math you probably already know)*

1. How to add, subtract, multiply, and divide WHOLE NUMBERS

2. How to add, subtract, multiply, and divide FRACTIONS

3. How to add, subtract, multiply, and divide DECIMALS

4. How to convert FRACTIONS TO DECIMALS and DECIMALS TO FRACTIONS

5. How to add, subtract, multiply, and divide POSITIVE AND NEGATIVE NUMBERS

6. How to plot points on the NUMBER LINE

7. How to plug a number into an ALGEBRAIC EXPRESSION

8. How to SOLVE a simple EQUATION

9. How to add and subtract LINE SEGMENTS

10. How to find the THIRD ANGLE of a TRIANGLE, given the other two angles

LEVEL 2 *(Math you might need to review)*

11. How to use the PERCENT FORMULA

Identify the part, the percent, and the whole.

$$Part = \frac{percent}{100} \times whole$$

> ☞ HINT — You'll usually find the Part near the word "is" and the Whole near the word "of."

Example: (Find the part):

What is 12 percent of 25 ?

Set-up: $Part = \frac{12}{100} \times 25 = 3$

Example: (Find the percent):

45 is what percent of 9?

Set-up: $45 = \frac{Percent}{100} \times 9$

Percent = 500

Example: (Find the whole): 15 is $\frac{3}{5}$ percent of what number?

Set-up: $15 = \frac{\frac{3}{5}}{100} \times whole$

Whole = 2,500

12. How to use the PERCENT INCREASE/ DECREASE FORMULAS

Identify the Original Whole and the Amount of Increase/Decrease.

$$Percent\ increase = \frac{amount\ of\ increase}{original\ whole} \times 100\%$$

$$Percent\ decrease = \frac{amount\ of\ decrease}{original\ whole} \times 100\%$$

Example: The price goes up from \$80 to \$100. What is the percent increase?

Set-up: Percent increase = $\frac{20}{80} \times 100\% = 25\%$

☞ HINT — Be sure to use the original Whole — not the new whole — for the base.

13. How to predict whether a sum, difference, or product will be ODD or EVEN

Don't bother memorizing the rules. Just take simple numbers like 1 and 2 and see what happens.

Example: If m is even and n is odd, is the product mn odd or even?

Set-up: Say $m = 2$ and $n = 1$.

2×1 is even, so mn is even.

14. How to recognize MULTIPLES of 2, 3, 4, 5, 6, 9, and 10

2: Last digit is even.
3: Sum of digits is multiple of 3.
4: Last two digits are a multiple of 4.
5: Last digit is 5 or 0.
6: Sum of digits is multiple of 3 AND last digit is even.
9: Sum of digits is multiple of 9.
10: Last digit is 0.

15. How to find a COMMON FACTOR

Break both numbers down to their prime factors to see what they have in common.

Example: What factors greater than 1 do 135 and 225 have in common?

Set-up: $135 = 3 \times 3 \times 3 \times 5$, and $225 = 3 \times 3 \times 5 \times 5$. They share two 3's and a 5. The common factors, then, are 3, 5, $3 \times 3 = 9$, $3 \times 5 = 15$, and $3 \times 3 \times 5 = 45$.

16. How to find a COMMON MULTIPLE

The product is the easiest common multiple to find. If the two numbers have any factors in common, you can divide them out of the product to get a lower common multiple.

Example: What is the least common multiple of 28 and 42 ?

Set-up: The product $28 \times 42 = 1176$ is a common multiple, but not the least. $28 = 2 \times 2 \times 7$, and $42 = 2 \times 3 \times 7$. They share a 2 and a 7, so divide the product by 2 and then by 7. $1176 \div 2 = 588$. $588 \div 7 = 84$. The least common multiple is 84.

17. How to find the AVERAGE

$$Average = \frac{sum\ of\ terms}{number\ of\ terms}$$

18. How to use the AVERAGE to find the SUM

$$Sum = (average) \times (number\ of\ terms)$$

Example: The average (arithmetic mean) of 24 numbers is 17.5. What is the sum?

Set-up: Sum = $17.5 \times 24 = 420$

19. How to find the AVERAGE of CONSECUTIVE NUMBERS

The average of evenly spaced numbers is simply the average of the smallest number and the largest number.

20. How to COUNT CONSECUTIVE NUMBERS

The number of integers from A to B inclusive is
$$B - A + 1$$

Example: How many integers are there from 73 through 419, inclusive?

Set-up: $419 - 73 + 1 = 347$

☞ HINT — Don't forget to add 1.

21. How to find the SUM of CONSECUTIVE NUMBERS

Sum = (average) × (number of terms)

Example: What is the sum of the integers from 10 through 50 inclusive?

Set-up: Average = (10 + 50) ÷ 2 = 30; number of terms = 50 – 10 + 1 = 41

Sum = 30 × 41 = 1,230

22. How to find the MEDIAN

Put the numbers in numerical order and take the middle number. (If there's an even number of numbers, take the average of the two numbers in the middle.)

23. How to find the MODE

Take the number that appears most often. (If there's a tie for most often, then there's more than one mode.)

24. How to use actual numbers to determine a RATIO

Identify the quantities to be compared. Either two parts, or a part and a whole.

$$Ratio = \frac{"of"}{"to"}$$

25. How to use a ratio to determine an ACTUAL NUMBER

Set up a proportion.

Example: The ratio of boys to girls is 3 to 4. If there are 135 boys, how many girls are there?

Set-up: $\frac{3}{4} = \frac{135}{x}$

$x = 180$

26. How to use actual numbers to determine a RATE

Identify the quantities and the units to be compared. Keep the units straight.

Example: Anders typed 9,450 words in $3\frac{1}{2}$ hours. What was his rate in words per minute?

Set-up: First convert $3\frac{1}{2}$ hours to 210 minutes.

Then set up the rate with "words" on top and "minutes" on bottom:

$$\frac{9,450 \text{ words}}{210 \text{ minutes}} = 45 \text{ words per minute}$$

☞ HINT — The unit before "per" goes on top, and the unit after "per" goes on the bottom.

27. How to deal with TABLES, GRAPHS, and CHARTS

Read the question and all labels extra carefully. Ignore extraneous information and zero in on what's asked for.

28. How to count the NUMBER OF POSSIBILITIES

Forget about combinations and permutations formulas. You won't need them on the SAT. The number of possibilities is generally so small that the best approach is just to write them out systematically and count them.

Example: How many 3-digit numbers can be formed with the digits 1, 3, and 5?

Set-up: Write them out. Be systematic so you don't miss any: 135, 153, 315, 351, 513, 531. Count 'em: 6 possibilities.

29. How to calculate a simple PROBABILITY

$$Probability = \frac{number\ of\ favorable\ outcomes}{total\ number\ of\ possible\ outcomes}$$

30. How to work with new SYMBOLS

If you see a symbol you've never seen before, don't freak out: It's a made-up symbol. Everything you need to know is in the question stem. Just follow the instructions.

31. How to SIMPLIFY POLYNOMIALS

First multiply to eliminate all parentheses. Then combine like terms.

32. How to FACTOR certain POLYNOMIALS

Learn to spot these classic factorables:

$$ab + ac = a(b + c)$$
$$a^2 + 2ab + b^2 = (a + b)^2$$
$$a^2 - 2ab + b^2 = (a - b)^2$$
$$a^2 - b^2 = (a - b)(a + b)$$

33. How to solve for one variable IN TERMS OF another

To find x "in terms of" y: isolate x on one side, leaving y as the only variable on the other.

34. How to solve an INEQUALITY

Treat it much like an equation — adding, subtracting, multiplying, and dividing both sides by the same thing. Just remember to reverse the inequality sign if you multiply or divide by a negative.

35. How to TRANSLATE English into algebra

Look for the key words and systematically turn phrases into algebraic expressions and sentences into equations.

☞ HINT— Be extra careful of order when subtraction is called for.

36. How to find an ANGLE formed by INTERSECTING LINES

Vertical angles are equal. Adjacent angles add up to 180°.

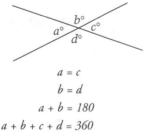

$$a = c$$
$$b = d$$
$$a + b = 180$$
$$a + b + c + d = 360$$

37. How to find an angle formed by a TRANSVERSAL across PARALLEL LINES

All the acute angles are equal. All the obtuse angles are equal. An acute plus an obtuse equals 180°.

Example:

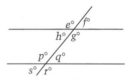

$$e = g = p = r$$
$$f = h = q = s$$
$$e + q = g + s = 180$$

☞ HINT — Forget about the terms "alternate interior," "alternate exterior," and "corresponding" angles. The SAT never uses them.

38. How to find the AREA of a TRIANGLE

$$Area = \frac{1}{2}(base)(height)$$

Example:

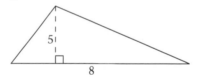

Set-up:

$$Area = \frac{1}{2}(5)(8) = 20$$

☞ HINT — You may have to construct an altitude.

39. How to work with ISOSCELES TRIANGLES

Isosceles triangles have two equal sides and two equal angles.

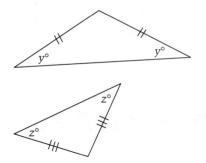

40. How to work with EQUILATERAL TRIANGLES

Equilateral triangles have three equal sides and three 60° angles.

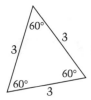

41. How to work with SIMILAR TRIANGLES

Corresponding sides are proportional.
Corresponding angles are equal.

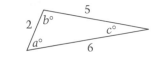

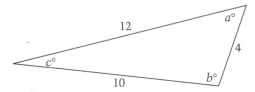

42. How to find the HYPOTENUSE or a LEG of a RIGHT TRIANGLE

Pythagorean theorem:
$$a^2 + b^2 = c^2$$

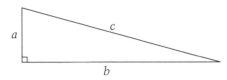

☞ HINT — Most right triangles on the SAT are "special" right triangles (see below), so you can often bypass the Pythagorean theorem.

43. How to spot SPECIAL RIGHT TRIANGLES

3-4-5
5-12-13
30-60-90
45-45-90

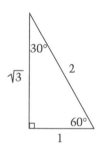

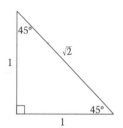

44. How to find the PERIMETER of a RECTANGLE

Perimeter = 2(length + width)

Example:

Set-up: Perimeter = 2(2 + 5) = 14

45. How to find the AREA of a RECTANGLE

Area = (length)(width)

Example:

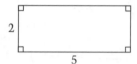

Set-up: Area = 2 × 5 = 10

46. How to find the AREA of a SQUARE

Area = (side)^2

Example:

Set-up: Area = 3^2 = 9

47. How to find the CIRCUMFERENCE of a CIRCLE

Circumference = 2πr

Example:

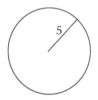

Set-up: *Circumference* = 2π(5) = 10π

48. How to find the AREA of a CIRCLE

Area = πr^2

Example:

Set-up: *Area* = π × 5^2 = 25π

49. How to find the DISTANCE BETWEEN POINTS on the coordinate plane

If the points have the same x's or the same y's — that is, they make a line segment that is parallel to an axis — all you have to do is subtract the numbers that are different.

Example: What is the distance from (2, 3) to (–7, 3) ?

Set-up: The y's are the same, so just subtract the x's.

$2 - (-7) = 9$.

If the points have different x's and different y's, make a right triangle and use the Pythagorean theorem.

Example: What is the distance from (2, 3) to (–1, –1)?

Set-up:

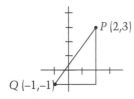

It's a 3-4-5 triangle!

$PQ = 5$

☞ HINT — Look for "special" right triangles.

50. How to find the SLOPE of a LINE

$$Slope = \frac{rise}{run} = \frac{change\ in\ y}{change\ in\ x}$$

Example: What is the slope of the line that contains points (1, 2) and (4, –5) ?

Set-up: Slope $= \dfrac{2-(-5)}{1-4} = -\dfrac{7}{3}$

LEVEL 3 *(Math you might find difficult)*

51. How to determine COMBINED PERCENT INCREASE/DECREASE

Start with 100 and see what happens.

> **Example:** Price rises 10 percent one year and 20 percent the next. What's the combined percent increase?
>
> **Set-up:** Say the original price is $100.
>
> First year: $100 + (10% of 100)
>
> = 100 + 10 = 110.
>
> Second year: 110 + (20% of 110)
>
> = 110 + 22 = 132.
>
> From 100 to 132 — That's a 32 percent increase.

52. How to find the ORIGINAL WHOLE before percent increase/decrease

Think of a 15% increase over x as $1.15x$ and set up an equation.

> **Example:** After decreasing 5 percent, the population is now 57,000. What was the original population?
>
> **Set-up:** $.95 \times$ (Original Population) = 57,000
>
> Original Population = $57,000 \div .95 = 60,000$

53. How to solve a REMAINDERS problem

Pick a number that fits the given conditions and see what happens.

> **Example:** When n is divided by 7, the remainder is 5. What is the remainder when $2n$ is divided by 7 ?
>
> **Set-up:** Find a number that leaves a remainder of 5 when divided by 7. A good choice would be 12. If $n = 12$, then $2n = 24$, which when divided by 7 leaves a remainder of 3.

54. How to solve a DIGITS problem

Use a little logic — and some trial and error.

> **Example:** If A, B, C, and D represent distinct digits in the addition problem below, what is the value of D ?

$$AB$$
$$+ BA$$
$$\overline{CDC}$$

> **Set-up:** Two 2-digit numbers will add up to at most something in the 100's, so $C = 1$. B plus A in the units' column gives a 1, and since it can't simply be that $B + A = 1$, it must be that $B + A = 11$, and a 1 gets carried. In fact, A and B can be just about any pair of digits that add up to 11 (3 and 8, 4 and 7, etc.), but it doesn't matter what they are, they always give you the same thing for D:

47	83
+74	+38
121	121

55. How to find a WEIGHTED AVERAGE

Give each term the appropriate "weight."

> **Example:** The girls' average score is 30. The boys' average score is 24. If there are twice as many boys as girls, what is the overall average?
>
> **Set-up:**
>
> $$\text{Weighted Avg.} = \frac{1 \times 30 + 2 \times 24}{3} = \frac{78}{3} = 26$$

> ☞ HINT — Don't just average the averages.

56. How to find the NEW AVERAGE when a number is added or deleted

Use the sum.

> **Example:** Michael's average score after 4 tests is 80. If he scores 100 on the fifth test, what is his new average?
>
> **Set-up:** Convert the original average to the original sum:
>
> Original sum $= 4 \times 80 = 320$
>
> Add the fifth score to make the New Sum:
>
> New sum $= 320 + 100 = 420$
>
> Convert new sum to new average:
>
> New average $= \dfrac{420}{5} = 84$

57. How to use the ORIGINAL AVERAGE and NEW AVERAGE to figure out WHAT WAS ADDED OR DELETED

Use the sums.

Number added = (new sum) – (original sum)

Number deleted = (original sum) – (new sum)

Example: The average of 5 numbers is 2. After 1 number is deleted, the new average is –3. What number was deleted?

Set-up: Convert the original average to the original sum:

Original sum = $5 \times 2 = 10$

Convert the new average to the new sum:

New sum = $4 \times (-3) = -12$

The difference is the answer.

Number deleted = $10 - (-12) = 22$

58. How to find an AVERAGE RATE

Convert to totals.

$$Average\ A\ per\ B = \frac{Total\ A}{Total\ B}$$

Example: If the first 500 pages have an average of 150 words per page, and the remaining 100 pages have an average of 450 words per page, what is the average number of words per page for the entire 600 pages?

Set-up: Total pages = $500 + 100 = 600$

Total words = $500 \times 150 + 100 \times 450$

$= 120,000$

Average words per page = $\frac{120,000}{600} = 200$

$$Average\ speed = \frac{total\ distance}{total\ time}$$

Example: Rosa drove 120 miles one way at an average speed of 40 miles per hour and returned by the same 120-mile route at an average speed of 60 miles per hour. What was Rosa's average speed for the entire 240-mile round trip?

Set-up: To drive 120 miles at 40 mph takes 3 hours. To return at 60 mph takes 2 hours. The total time, then, is 5 hours.

$$Average\ speed = \frac{240\ miles}{5\ hours} = 48\ mph$$

☞ HINT — Don't just average the rates.

59. How to determine a COMBINED RATIO

Multiply one or both ratios by whatever you need to in order to get the terms they have in common to match.

Example: The ratio of a to b is 7:3 . The ratio of b to c is 2:5. What is the ratio of a to c?

Set-up: Multiply $a{:}b$ by 2:2 and multiply $b{:}c$ by 3:3 and you get $a{:}b$ = 14:6 and $b{:}c$ = 6:15. Now that the b's match, you can just take a and c and say $a{:}c$ = 14:15.

60. How to MULTIPLY/DIVIDE POWERS

Add/subtract the exponents.

$$x^a \times x^b = x^{(a+b)} \qquad 2^3 \times 2^4 = 2^7$$

$$\frac{x^c}{x^d} = x^{(c-d)} \qquad \frac{5^6}{5^2} = 5^4$$

61. How to RAISE A POWER TO A POWER

Multiply the exponents.

$$(x^a)^b = x^{ab} \qquad (3^4)^5 = 3^{20}$$

62. How to ADD, SUBTRACT, MULTIPLY, and DIVIDE ROOTS

You can add/subtract roots only when the parts inside the $\sqrt{}$ are identical.

Example:. $\sqrt{2} + 3\sqrt{2} = 4\sqrt{2}$

$\sqrt{2} - 3\sqrt{2} = -2\sqrt{2}$

$\sqrt{2} + \sqrt{3}$ — cannot be combined.

To multiply/divide, deal with what's inside the $\sqrt{}$ and outside the $\sqrt{}$ separately.

Example:

$$(2\sqrt{3})(7\sqrt{5}) = (2 \times 7)(\sqrt{3 \times 5}) = 14\sqrt{15}$$

$$\frac{10\sqrt{21}}{5\sqrt{3}} = \frac{10}{5}\sqrt{\frac{21}{3}} = 2\sqrt{7}$$

63. How to SIMPLIFY A SQUARE ROOT

Look for perfect squares (4, 9, 16, 25, 36,...) inside the $\sqrt{}$. Factor them out and "unsquare" them.

Example: $\sqrt{48} = \sqrt{16} \times \sqrt{3} = 4\sqrt{3}$

$\sqrt{180} = \sqrt{36} \times \sqrt{5} = 6\sqrt{5}$

64. How to solve certain QUADRATIC EQUATIONS

Forget the quadratic formula. Manipulate the equation (if necessary) into the "____ = 0" form, factor the left side, and break the quadratic into two simple equations.

Example:
$$x^2 + 6 = 5x$$
$$x^2 - 5x + 6 = 0$$
$$(x - 2)(x - 3) = 0$$
$$x - 2 = 0 \text{ or } x - 3 = 0$$
$$x = 2 \text{ or } 3$$

☞ **HINT** — Watch out for x^2. There can be two solutions.

Example: $x^2 = 9$

$x = 3 \text{ or} - 3$

65. How to solve MULTIPLE EQUATIONS

When you see two equations with two variables on the SAT, they're probably easy to combine in such a way that you get something closer to what you're looking for.

Example: If $5x - 2y = -9$ and $3y - 4x = 6$, what is the value of $x + y$?

Set-up: The question doesn't ask for x and y separately, so don't solve for them separately if you don't have to. Look what happens if you just rearrange a little and "add" the equations:

$$5x - 2y = -9$$
$$-4x + 3y = 6$$
$$\overline{}$$
$$x + y = -3$$

☞ **HINT** — Don't do more work than you have to. Look for the shortcut.

66. How to find the MAXIMUM and MINIMUM lengths for a SIDE of a TRIANGLE

If you know two sides of a triangle, then you know that the third side is somewhere between the difference and the sum.

Example: The length of one side of a triangle is 7. The length of another side is 3. What is the range of possible lengths for the third side?

Set-up: The third side is greater than the difference (7 – 3 = 4) and less than the sum (7 + 3 = 10).

67. How to find one angle or the sum of all the ANGLES of a REGULAR POLYGON

Sum of the angles in a polygon with n sides =
$$(n - 2) \times 180$$

Measure of one angle in a Regular Polygon with n sides =
$$\frac{(n-2) \times 180}{n}$$

Example: What is the measure of one angle of a regular pentagon?

Set-up: Plug $n = 5$ into the formula:

Measure of One Angle =
$$\frac{(5-2) \times 180}{5} = \frac{540}{5} = 108$$

68. How to find the LENGTH of an ARC

Think of an arc as a fraction of the circle's circumference.

$$Length\ of\ arc = \frac{n}{360} \times 2\pi r$$

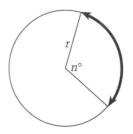

69. How to find the AREA of a SECTOR

Think of a sector as a fraction of the circle's area.

$$Area\ of\ sector = \frac{n}{360} \times \pi r^2$$

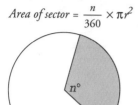

70. How to find the dimensions or area of an INSCRIBED or CIRCUMSCRIBED FIGURE

Look for the connection. Is the diameter the same as a side or a diagonal?

Example: If the area of the square is 36, what is the circumference of the circle?

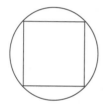

Set-up: To get the circumference, you need the diameter or radius. The circle's diameter is also the square's diagonal, which (it's a 45-45-90 triangle!) is $6\sqrt{2}$

Circumference = π(diameter) = $6\pi\sqrt{2}$

71. How to find the VOLUME of a RECTANGULAR SOLID

$$Volume = length \times width \times height$$

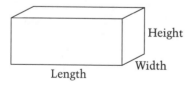

72. How to find the SURFACE AREA of a RECTANGULAR SOLID

$$Surface\ area =$$
$$2(length \times width + length \times height + width \times height)$$

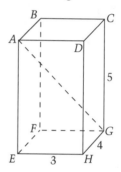

73. How to find the DIAGONAL of a RECTANGULAR SOLID

Use the Pythagorean theorem twice.

Example: What is the length of AG?

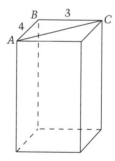

Set-up: Draw diagonal AC.

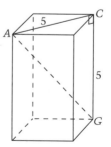

ABC is a 3-4-5 triangle, so $AC = 5$. Now look at triangle ACG:

It's a 45-45-90, so $AG = 5\sqrt{2}$

74. How to find the VOLUME of a CYLINDER

$Volume = \pi r^2 h$

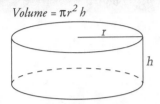

75. How to find the VOLUME of a SPHERE

$Volume = \dfrac{4}{3}\pi r^3$

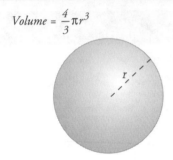

Start with number 1 for each new section. If a section has fewer questions than answer spaces, leave the extra spaces blank.

SECTION 1

1	Ⓐ Ⓑ Ⓒ Ⓓ Ⓔ	11	Ⓐ Ⓑ Ⓒ Ⓓ Ⓔ	21	Ⓐ Ⓑ Ⓒ Ⓓ Ⓔ	31	Ⓐ Ⓑ Ⓒ Ⓓ Ⓔ
2	Ⓐ Ⓑ Ⓒ Ⓓ Ⓔ	12	Ⓐ Ⓑ Ⓒ Ⓓ Ⓔ	22	Ⓐ Ⓑ Ⓒ Ⓓ Ⓔ	32	Ⓐ Ⓑ Ⓒ Ⓓ Ⓔ
3	Ⓐ Ⓑ Ⓒ Ⓓ Ⓔ	13	Ⓐ Ⓑ Ⓒ Ⓓ Ⓔ	23	Ⓐ Ⓑ Ⓒ Ⓓ Ⓔ	33	Ⓐ Ⓑ Ⓒ Ⓓ Ⓔ
4	Ⓐ Ⓑ Ⓒ Ⓓ Ⓔ	14	Ⓐ Ⓑ Ⓒ Ⓓ Ⓔ	24	Ⓐ Ⓑ Ⓒ Ⓓ Ⓔ	34	Ⓐ Ⓑ Ⓒ Ⓓ Ⓔ
5	Ⓐ Ⓑ Ⓒ Ⓓ Ⓔ	15	Ⓐ Ⓑ Ⓒ Ⓓ Ⓔ	25	Ⓐ Ⓑ Ⓒ Ⓓ Ⓔ	35	Ⓐ Ⓑ Ⓒ Ⓓ Ⓔ
6	Ⓐ Ⓑ Ⓒ Ⓓ Ⓔ	16	Ⓐ Ⓑ Ⓒ Ⓓ Ⓔ	26	Ⓐ Ⓑ Ⓒ Ⓓ Ⓔ	36	Ⓐ Ⓑ Ⓒ Ⓓ Ⓔ
7	Ⓐ Ⓑ Ⓒ Ⓓ Ⓔ	17	Ⓐ Ⓑ Ⓒ Ⓓ Ⓔ	27	Ⓐ Ⓑ Ⓒ Ⓓ Ⓔ	37	Ⓐ Ⓑ Ⓒ Ⓓ Ⓔ
8	Ⓐ Ⓑ Ⓒ Ⓓ Ⓔ	18	Ⓐ Ⓑ Ⓒ Ⓓ Ⓔ	28	Ⓐ Ⓑ Ⓒ Ⓓ Ⓔ	38	Ⓐ Ⓑ Ⓒ Ⓓ Ⓔ
9	Ⓐ Ⓑ Ⓒ Ⓓ Ⓔ	19	Ⓐ Ⓑ Ⓒ Ⓓ Ⓔ	29	Ⓐ Ⓑ Ⓒ Ⓓ Ⓔ	39	Ⓐ Ⓑ Ⓒ Ⓓ Ⓔ
10	Ⓐ Ⓑ Ⓒ Ⓓ Ⓔ	20	Ⓐ Ⓑ Ⓒ Ⓓ Ⓔ	30	Ⓐ Ⓑ Ⓒ Ⓓ Ⓔ	40	Ⓐ Ⓑ Ⓒ Ⓓ Ⓔ

 # correct in section 1

 # wrong in section 1

SECTION 2

1	Ⓐ Ⓑ Ⓒ Ⓓ Ⓔ	11	Ⓐ Ⓑ Ⓒ Ⓓ Ⓔ	21	Ⓐ Ⓑ Ⓒ Ⓓ Ⓔ	31	Ⓐ Ⓑ Ⓒ Ⓓ Ⓔ
2	Ⓐ Ⓑ Ⓒ Ⓓ Ⓔ	12	Ⓐ Ⓑ Ⓒ Ⓓ Ⓔ	22	Ⓐ Ⓑ Ⓒ Ⓓ Ⓔ	32	Ⓐ Ⓑ Ⓒ Ⓓ Ⓔ
3	Ⓐ Ⓑ Ⓒ Ⓓ Ⓔ	13	Ⓐ Ⓑ Ⓒ Ⓓ Ⓔ	23	Ⓐ Ⓑ Ⓒ Ⓓ Ⓔ	33	Ⓐ Ⓑ Ⓒ Ⓓ Ⓔ
4	Ⓐ Ⓑ Ⓒ Ⓓ Ⓔ	14	Ⓐ Ⓑ Ⓒ Ⓓ Ⓔ	24	Ⓐ Ⓑ Ⓒ Ⓓ Ⓔ	34	Ⓐ Ⓑ Ⓒ Ⓓ Ⓔ
5	Ⓐ Ⓑ Ⓒ Ⓓ Ⓔ	15	Ⓐ Ⓑ Ⓒ Ⓓ Ⓔ	25	Ⓐ Ⓑ Ⓒ Ⓓ Ⓔ	35	Ⓐ Ⓑ Ⓒ Ⓓ Ⓔ
6	Ⓐ Ⓑ Ⓒ Ⓓ Ⓔ	16	Ⓐ Ⓑ Ⓒ Ⓓ Ⓔ	26	Ⓐ Ⓑ Ⓒ Ⓓ Ⓔ	36	Ⓐ Ⓑ Ⓒ Ⓓ Ⓔ
7	Ⓐ Ⓑ Ⓒ Ⓓ Ⓔ	17	Ⓐ Ⓑ Ⓒ Ⓓ Ⓔ	27	Ⓐ Ⓑ Ⓒ Ⓓ Ⓔ	37	Ⓐ Ⓑ Ⓒ Ⓓ Ⓔ
8	Ⓐ Ⓑ Ⓒ Ⓓ Ⓔ	18	Ⓐ Ⓑ Ⓒ Ⓓ Ⓔ	28	Ⓐ Ⓑ Ⓒ Ⓓ Ⓔ	38	Ⓐ Ⓑ Ⓒ Ⓓ Ⓔ
9	Ⓐ Ⓑ Ⓒ Ⓓ Ⓔ	19	Ⓐ Ⓑ Ⓒ Ⓓ Ⓔ	29	Ⓐ Ⓑ Ⓒ Ⓓ Ⓔ	39	Ⓐ Ⓑ Ⓒ Ⓓ Ⓔ
10	Ⓐ Ⓑ Ⓒ Ⓓ Ⓔ	20	Ⓐ Ⓑ Ⓒ Ⓓ Ⓔ	30	Ⓐ Ⓑ Ⓒ Ⓓ Ⓔ	40	Ⓐ Ⓑ Ⓒ Ⓓ Ⓔ

 # correct in section 2

 # wrong in section 2

SECTION 3

1	Ⓐ Ⓑ Ⓒ Ⓓ Ⓔ	11	Ⓐ Ⓑ Ⓒ Ⓓ Ⓔ	21	Ⓐ Ⓑ Ⓒ Ⓓ Ⓔ	31	Ⓐ Ⓑ Ⓒ Ⓓ Ⓔ
2	Ⓐ Ⓑ Ⓒ Ⓓ Ⓔ	12	Ⓐ Ⓑ Ⓒ Ⓓ Ⓔ	22	Ⓐ Ⓑ Ⓒ Ⓓ Ⓔ	32	Ⓐ Ⓑ Ⓒ Ⓓ Ⓔ
3	Ⓐ Ⓑ Ⓒ Ⓓ Ⓔ	13	Ⓐ Ⓑ Ⓒ Ⓓ Ⓔ	23	Ⓐ Ⓑ Ⓒ Ⓓ Ⓔ	33	Ⓐ Ⓑ Ⓒ Ⓓ Ⓔ
4	Ⓐ Ⓑ Ⓒ Ⓓ Ⓔ	14	Ⓐ Ⓑ Ⓒ Ⓓ Ⓔ	24	Ⓐ Ⓑ Ⓒ Ⓓ Ⓔ	34	Ⓐ Ⓑ Ⓒ Ⓓ Ⓔ
5	Ⓐ Ⓑ Ⓒ Ⓓ Ⓔ	15	Ⓐ Ⓑ Ⓒ Ⓓ Ⓔ	25	Ⓐ Ⓑ Ⓒ Ⓓ Ⓔ	35	Ⓐ Ⓑ Ⓒ Ⓓ Ⓔ
6	Ⓐ Ⓑ Ⓒ Ⓓ Ⓔ	16	Ⓐ Ⓑ Ⓒ Ⓓ Ⓔ	26	Ⓐ Ⓑ Ⓒ Ⓓ Ⓔ	36	Ⓐ Ⓑ Ⓒ Ⓓ Ⓔ
7	Ⓐ Ⓑ Ⓒ Ⓓ Ⓔ	17	Ⓐ Ⓑ Ⓒ Ⓓ Ⓔ	27	Ⓐ Ⓑ Ⓒ Ⓓ Ⓔ	37	Ⓐ Ⓑ Ⓒ Ⓓ Ⓔ
8	Ⓐ Ⓑ Ⓒ Ⓓ Ⓔ	18	Ⓐ Ⓑ Ⓒ Ⓓ Ⓔ	28	Ⓐ Ⓑ Ⓒ Ⓓ Ⓔ	38	Ⓐ Ⓑ Ⓒ Ⓓ Ⓔ
9	Ⓐ Ⓑ Ⓒ Ⓓ Ⓔ	19	Ⓐ Ⓑ Ⓒ Ⓓ Ⓔ	29	Ⓐ Ⓑ Ⓒ Ⓓ Ⓔ	39	Ⓐ Ⓑ Ⓒ Ⓓ Ⓔ
10	Ⓐ Ⓑ Ⓒ Ⓓ Ⓔ	20	Ⓐ Ⓑ Ⓒ Ⓓ Ⓔ	30	Ⓐ Ⓑ Ⓒ Ⓓ Ⓔ	40	Ⓐ Ⓑ Ⓒ Ⓓ Ⓔ

 # correct in section 3

 # wrong in section 3

Remove this scoresheet and use it to complete the practice test.

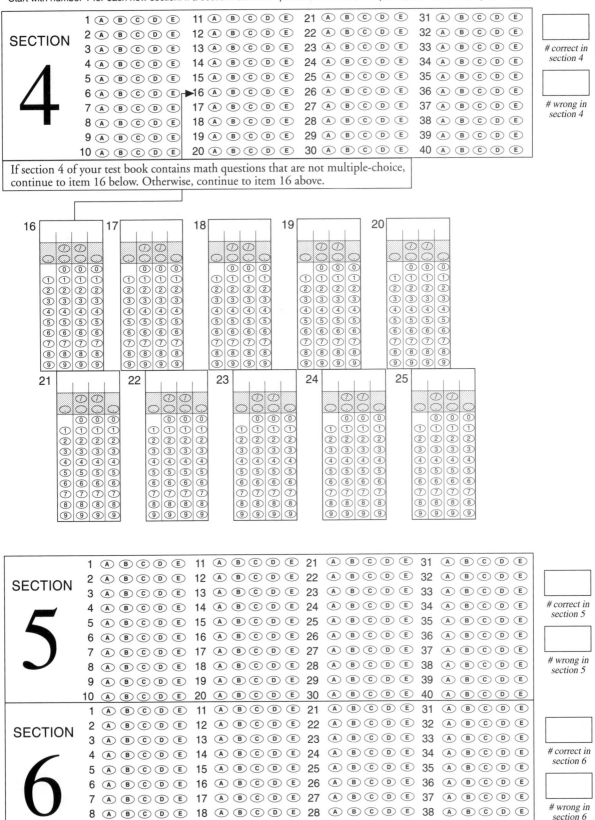

Remove this scoresheet and use it to complete the practice test.

PRACTICE TEST

Before taking this practice test, find a quiet room where you can work uninterrupted for 2 and a half hours. Make sure you have a comfortable desk, your calculator and several #2 pencils.

Use the answer grid on the previous page to record your answers.

Once you start this practice test, don't stop until you've finished. Remember—you can review any questions within a section, but you may not go back or forward a section.

You'll find the answer key and score converter following the test.

Good luck.

Time–30 Minutes
35 Questions

For each of the following questions, choose the best answer and darken the corresponding oval on the answer sheet.

Select the lettered word or set of words that best completes the sentence.

Example:

Today's small, portable computers contrast markedly with the earliest electronic computers, which were - - - - .

(A) effective
(B) invented
(C) useful
(D) destructive
(E) enormous

1 More insurers are limiting the sale of property insurance in coastal areas and other regions ---- natural disasters.

(A) safe from
(B) according to
(C) despite
(D) which include
(E) prone to

2 Roman legions ---- the mountain ---- of Masada for three years before they were able to seize it.

(A) dissembled..bastion
(B) assailed..symbol
(C) besieged..citadel
(D) surmounted..dwelling
(E) honed..stronghold

3 Unlike his calmer, more easy-going colleagues, the senator was ----, ready to quarrel at the slightest provocation.

(A) whimsical
(B) irascible
(C) gregarious
(D) ineffectual
(E) benign

4 Although historians have long thought of Genghis Khan as a ---- potentate, new research has shown he was ---- by many of his subjects.

(A) tyrannical..abhorred
(B) despotic..revered
(C) redundant..venerated
(D) jocular..esteemed
(E) peremptory..invoked

5 Jill was ---- by her employees because she often ---- them for not working hard enough.

(A) deified..goaded
(B) loathed..berated
(C) disregarded...eulogized
(D) cherished..derided
(E) execrated..lauded

6 Reconstructing the skeletons of extinct species like dinosaurs is ---- process that requires much patience and effort by paleontologists.

(A) a nascent
(B) an aberrant
(C) a disheveled
(D) a worthless
(E) an exacting

7 Nearly ---- by disease and the destruction of their habitat, koalas are now found only in isolated parts of eucalyptus forests.

(A) dispersed
(B) compiled
(C) decimated
(D) infuriated
(E) averted

8 Deep ideological ---- and internal power struggles ---- the government.

(A) disputes..facilitated
(B) similarities..protracted
(C) distortions..accelerated
(D) agreements..stymied
(E) divisions..paralyzed

9 Medical experts have viewed high doses of vitamins as a popular remedy whose value is, as yet, ----.

(A) medicinal
(B) prescribed
(C) recommended
(D) unproven
(E) beneficial

GO ON TO THE NEXT PAGE

Choose the lettered pair of words that is related in the same way as the pair in capital letters.

Example:

FLAKE:SNOW::

(A) storm:hail
(B) drop:rain
(C) field:wheat
(D) stack:hay
(E) cloud:fog

10 TROUT:FISH::

(A) grain:sand
(B) human:mammal
(C) river:stream
(D) chicken:egg
(E) frog:toad

11 INHALE:LUNGS::

(A) swallow:stomach
(B) attack:heart
(C) ache:head
(D) pump:blood
(E) travel:foot

12 BRAGGART:BOAST

(A) laggard:tarry
(B) hypocrite:speak
(C) extrovert:brood
(D) mendicant:compromise
(E) boor:gratify

13 ALLEVIATE:PAIN::

(A) soothe:antidote
(B) depreciate:value
(C) contract:job
(D) deviate:standard
(E) officiate:safety

14 INFURIATE:ANNOY::

(A) admire:respect
(B) indulge:lure
(C) terrify:frighten
(D) satiate:deprive
(E) vex:startle

15 MISERLY:MAGNANIMITY::

(A) greedy:mirth
(B) transient:stupefaction
(C) admirable:fastidiousness
(D) innocent:culpability
(E) offensive:avarice

GO ON TO THE NEXT PAGE ➡

Answer the questions below based on the information in the accompanying passages.

Questions 16-23 are based on the following passage.

In this excerpt, a Nobel Prize-winning scientist discusses ways of thinking about extremely long periods of time.

There is one fact about the origin of life which is reasonably certain. Whenever and wherever it happened, it started a very long time ago, so long
Line ago that it is extremely difficult to form any
(5) realistic idea of such vast stretches of time. The shortness of human life necessarily limits the span of direct personal recollection.

Human culture has given us the illusion that our memories go further back than that. Before
(10) writing was invented, the experience of earlier generations, embodied in stories, myths and moral precepts to guide behavior, was passed down verbally or, to a lesser extent, in pictures, carvings and statues. Writing has made more precise and
(15) more extensive the transmission of such information and, in recent times, photography has sharpened our images of the immediate past. Even so, we have difficulty in contemplating steadily the march of history, from the beginnings of
(20) civilization to the present day, in such a way that we can truly experience the slow passage of time. Our minds are not built to deal comfortably with periods as long as hundreds or thousands of years.

Yet when we come to consider the origin of life,
(25) the time scales we must deal with make the whole span of human history seem but the blink of an eyelid. There is no simple way to adjust one's thinking to such vast stretches of time. The immensity of time passed is beyond our ready
(30) comprehension. One can only construct an impression of it from indirect and incomplete descriptions, just as a blind man laboriously builds up, by touch and sound, a picture of his immediate surroundings.

(35) The customary way to provide a convenient framework for one's thoughts is to compare the age of the universe with the length of a single earthly day. Perhaps a better comparison, along the same lines, would be to equate the age of our earth with a
(40) single week. On such a scale the age of the universe, since the Big Bang, would be about two or three weeks. The oldest macroscopic fossils (those from the start of the Cambrian Period*) would have been alive just one day ago. Modern man would
(45) have appeared in the last ten seconds and agriculture in the last one or two. Odysseus** would have lived only half a second before the present time.

Even this comparison hardly makes the longer

(50) time scale comprehensible to us. Another alternative is to draw a linear map of time, with the different events marked on it. The problem here is to make the line long enough to show our own experience on a reasonable scale, and yet short
(55) enough for convenient reproduction and examination. But perhaps the most vivid method is to compare time to the lines of print themselves. Let us make a 200-page book equal in length to the time from the start of the Cambrian to the present;
(60) that is, about 600 million years. Then each full page will represent roughly 3 million years, each line about ninety thousand years and each letter or small space about fifteen hundred years. The origin of the earth would be about seven books ago and
(65) the origin of the universe (which has been dated only approximately) ten or so books before that. Almost the whole of recorded human history would be covered by the last two or three letters of the book.

(70) If you now turn back the pages of the book, slowly reading *one letter at a time* — remember, each letter is fifteen hundred years — then this may convey to you something of the immense stretches of time we shall have to consider. On this scale the
(75) span of your own life would be less than the width of a comma.

*Cambrian: the earliest period in the Paleozoic era, beginning about 600 million years ago.
**Odysseus: the most famous Greek hero of antiquity; he is the hero of Homer's *The Odyssey*, which describes the aftermath of the Trojan War (ca. 1200 B.C.).

16 The word "span" in line 6 most nearly means

(A) rate of increase
(B) value
(C) bridge
(D) extent
(E) accuracy

17 The phrase "to a lesser extent" in line 13, indicates that, before the invention of writing, the wisdom of earlier generations was

(A) rejected by recent generations when portrayed in pictures, carvings or statues
(B) passed down orally, or not at all
(C) transmitted more effectively by spoken word than by other means
(D) based on illusory memories that turned fact into fiction
(E) more strongly grounded in science than in the arts

GO ON TO THE NEXT PAGE ➥

18 The author most likely describes the impact of writing (lines 14-17) in order to

(A) illustrate the limitations of the human memory
(B) provide an example of how cultures transmit information
(C) indicate how primitive preliterate cultures were
(D) refute an opinion about the origin of human civilization
(E) explain the difference between historical facts and myth

19 The word "ready" in line 29 most nearly means

(A) set
(B) agreeable
(C) immediate
(D) apt
(E) willing

20 The analogy of the "blind man" (line 32) is presented primarily to show that

(A) humans are unable to comprehend long periods of time
(B) myths and legends fail to give an accurate picture of the past
(C) human history is only a fraction of the time since life began
(D) humans refuse to learn the lessons of the past
(E) long periods of time can only be understood indirectly

21 In lines 40-44, the author mentions the Big Bang and the Cambrian Period in order to demonstrate which point?

(A) The age of the earth is best understood using the time scale of a week.
(B) Agriculture was a relatively late development in human history.
(C) No fossil record exists before the Cambrian Period.
(D) Convenient time scales do not adequately represent the age of the earth.
(E) The customary framework for thinking about the age of the universe should be discarded permanently.

22 According to lines 52-56, one difficulty of using a linear representation of time is that

(A) linear representations of time do not meet accepted scientific standards of accuracy
(B) prehistoric eras overlap each other, making linear representation deceptive
(C) the more accurate the scale, the more difficult the map is to copy and study
(D) there are too many events to represent on a single line
(E) our knowledge of pre-Cambrian time is insufficient to construct an accurate linear map

23 The author of this passage discusses several kinds of time scales primarily in order to illustrate the

(A) difficulty of assigning precise dates to past events
(B) variety of choices faced by scientists investigating the origin of life
(C) evolution of efforts to comprehend the passage of history
(D) immensity of time since life began on earth
(E) development of the technology of communication

Questions 24–30 are based on the following passage.

The following excerpt is from a speech delivered in 1873 by Susan B. Anthony, a leader in the women's rights movement of the 19th century.

Friends and fellow-citizens: I stand before you tonight under indictment for the alleged crime of having voted at the last Presidential election,
Line without having a lawful right to vote. It shall be my
(5) work this evening to prove to you that in thus voting, I not only committed no crime, but, instead, simply exercised my citizen's rights, guaranteed to me and all United States citizens by the National Constitution, beyond the power of
(10) any State to deny.
The preamble of the Federal Constitution says:
"We, the people of the United States, in order to form a more perfect union, establish justice, insure domestic tranquillity, provide for the common
(15) defense, promote the general welfare, and secure the blessings of liberty to ourselves and our posterity, do ordain and establish this Constitution for the United States of America."
It was we, the people; not we, the white male
(20) citizens; nor yet we, the male citizens; but we, the whole people, who formed the Union. And we formed it, not to give the blessings of liberty, but to secure them; not to the half of ourselves and the half of our posterity, but to the whole people —
(25) women as well as men. And it is a downright mockery to talk to women of their enjoyment of the blessings of liberty while they are denied the use of the only means of securing them provided by this democratic-republican government — the
(30) ballot.
For any State to make sex a qualification that must ever result in the disfranchisement* of one entire half of the people is a violation of the supreme law of the land. By it the blessings of
(35) liberty are forever withheld from women and their female posterity. To them this government had no just powers derived from the consent of the governed. To them this government is not a democracy. It is not a republic. It is an odious
(40) aristocracy; a hateful oligarchy of sex; this oligarchy of sex, which makes father, brothers, husband, sons, the oligarchs over the mother and sisters, the wife and daughters of every household —which ordains all men sovereigns, all women
(45) subjects, carries dissension, discord and rebellion into every home of the nation.
Webster, Worcester and Bouvier all define a citizen to be a person in the United States, entitled to vote and hold office.
(50) The one question left to be settled now is: Are women persons? And I hardly believe any of our opponents will have the hardihood to say they are not. Being persons, then, women are citizens; and no State has a right to make any law, or to enforce
(55) any old law, that shall abridge their privileges or immunities. Hence, every discrimination against women in the constitutions and laws of the several States is today null and void, precisely as is every one against Negroes.

*disfranchisement: to deprive of the right to vote.

24 In the first paragraph, Anthony states that her action in voting was

(A) illegal, but morally justified
(B) the result of her keen interest in national politics
(C) legal, if the Constitution is interpreted correctly
(D) an illustration of the need for a women's rights movement
(E) illegal, but worthy of leniency

25 Which best captures the meaning of the word "promote" in line 15?

(A) further
(B) organize
(C) publicize
(D) commend
(E) motivate

26 By saying "we, the people...the whole people, who formed the Union" (lines 19-21), Anthony means that

(A) the founders of the nation conspired to deprive women of their rights
(B) some male citizens are still being denied basic rights
(C) the role of women in the founding of the nation is generally ignored
(D) society is endangered when women are deprived of basic rights
(E) all people deserve to enjoy the rights guaranteed by the Constitution

GO ON TO THE NEXT PAGE ➡

27 By "the half of our posterity" (line 23-24), Anthony means

(A) the political legacy passed down from her era

(B) future generations of male United States citizens

(C) those who wish to enjoy the blessings of liberty

(D) current and future opponents of the women's rights movement

(E) future members of the democratic-republican government

28 In the fifth paragraph, lines 31-46, Anthony's argument rests mainly on the strategy of convincing her audience that

(A) any state which denies women the vote undermines its status as a democracy

(B) women deprived of the vote will eventually raise a rebellion

(C) the nation will remain an aristocracy if the status of women does not change

(D) women's rights issues should be debated in every home

(E) even an aristocracy cannot survive without the consent of the governed

29 The word "hardihood" in line 52 could best be replaced by

(A) endurance

(B) vitality

(C) nerve

(D) opportunity

(E) stupidity

30 When Anthony warns that "no State...shall abridge their privileges" (line 54-56), she means that

(A) women should be allowed to live a life of privilege

(B) women on trial cannot be forced to give up their immunity

(C) every state should repeal its outdated laws

(D) governments may not deprive citizens of their rights

(E) the rights granted to women must be decided by the people, not the state

This page intentionally left blank.

Time—30 Minutes 25 Questions	Solve each of the following problems, decide which is the best answer choice, and darken the corresponding oval on the answer sheet. Use available space in the test booklet for scratchwork.*

Notes:

(1) Calculator use is permitted.

(2) All numbers used are real numbers.

(3) Figures are provided for some problems. All figures are drawn to scale and lie in a plane UNLESS otherwise indicated.

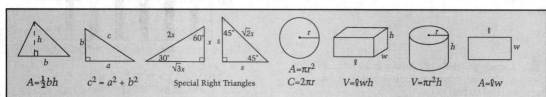

$A=\frac{1}{2}bh$ $c^2 = a^2 + b^2$ Special Right Triangles $A=\pi r^2$ $C=2\pi r$ $V=\ell wh$ $V=\pi r^2 h$ $A=\ell w$

The sum of the degree measures of the angles of a triangle is 180.
The number of degrees of arc in a circle is 360.
A straight angle has a degree measure of 180.

1 Which of the following must be equal to 30 percent of x?

(A) $30x$

(B) $3x$

(C) $\frac{3x}{10}$

(D) $\frac{3x}{100}$

(E) $\frac{3x}{1000}$

2 $(2 \times 10^4) + (5 \times 10^3) + (6 \times 10^2) + (4 \times 10^1) =$

(A) 2,564
(B) 20,564
(C) 25,064
(D) 25,604
(E) 25,640

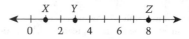

3 On the number line shown above, the length of YZ is how much greater than the length of XY?

(A) 3
(B) 4
(C) 5
(D) 6
(E) 7

4 If $2^{x+1} = 16$, what is the value of x?

(A) 2
(B) 3
(C) 4
(D) 5
(E) 6

*The directions on the actual SAT will vary slightly

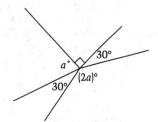

Note: Figure not drawn to scale

5 In the figure above, what is the value of *a*?

(A) 50
(B) 55
(C) 60
(D) 65
(E) 70

6 A machine labels 150 bottles in 20 minutes. At this rate, how many minutes does it take to label 60 bottles?

(A) 2
(B) 4
(C) 6
(D) 8
(E) 10

7 If $x - 1$ is a multiple of 3, which of the following must be the next greater multiple of 3?

(A) x
(B) $x + 2$
(C) $x + 3$
(D) $3x$
(E) $3x - 3$

8 When x is divided by 5, the remainder is 4. When x is divided by 9, the remainder is 0. Which of the following is a possible value for x?

(A) 24
(B) 45
(C) 59
(D) 109
(E) 144

9 In triangle *ABC*, $AB = 6$, $BC = 12$, and $AC = x$. Which of the following cannot be a value of x?

(A) 6
(B) 7
(C) 8
(D) 9
(E) 10

10 The average of 20, 70, and x is 40. If the average of 20, 70, x, and y is 50, then $y =$

(A) 100
(B) 80
(C) 70
(D) 60
(E) 30

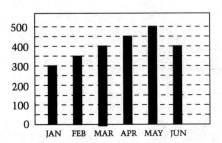

NUMBER OF BOOKS BORROWED
FROM MIDVILLE LIBRARY

11 According to the graph above, the number of books borrowed during the month of January was what fraction of the total number of books borrowed during the first six months of the year?

(A) $\frac{1}{8}$

(B) $\frac{1}{7}$

(C) $\frac{1}{6}$

(D) $\frac{3}{16}$

(E) $\frac{5}{12}$

12 If 40 percent of r is equal to s, then which of the following is equal to 10 percent of r?

(A) $4s$

(B) $2s$

(C) $\frac{s}{2}$

(D) $\frac{s}{4}$

(E) $\frac{s}{8}$

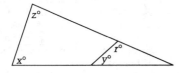

13 In the figure above, which of the following must be true?

(A) $x + r = z + y$
(B) $x + r = z - y$
(C) $x - y = z + r$
(D) $x - r = y - z$
(E) $x + y = z + r$

14 If a "prifact number" is a nonprime integer such that each factor of the integer other than 1 and the integer itself is a prime number, which of the following is a "prifact number"?

(A) 12
(B) 18
(C) 21
(D) 24
(E) 28

15 If $3x + y = 14$, and x and y are positive integers, each of the following could be the value of $x + y$ EXCEPT

(A) 12
(B) 10
(C) 8
(D) 6
(E) 4

16 A certain deck of cards contains r cards. After the cards are distributed evenly among s people, 8 cards are left over. In terms of r and s, how many cards did each person receive?

(A) $\frac{s}{8-r}$

(B) $\frac{r-s}{8}$

(C) $\frac{r-8}{s}$

(D) $s - 8r$

(E) $rs - 8$

17 If d is an integer, which of the following CANNOT be an integer?

(A) $\frac{d}{2}$

(B) $\frac{\sqrt{d}}{2}$

(C) $2d$

(D) $d\sqrt{2}$

(E) $d + 2$

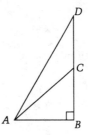

18 In the figure above, the area of triangle ABC is 6. If $BC = CD$, what is the area of triangle ACD?

(A) 6
(B) 8
(C) 9
(D) 10
(E) 12

19 The ratio of x to y to z is 3 to 6 to 8. If $y = 24$, what is the value of $x + z$?

(A) 11
(B) 33
(C) 44
(D) 66
(E) 88

20 What is the minimum number of rectangular tiles, each 12 centimeters by 18 centimeters, needed to completely cover 5 flat rectangular surfaces, each 60 centimeters by 180 centimeters?

(A) 50
(B) 100
(C) 150
(D) 200
(E) 250

GO ON TO THE NEXT PAGE ➡

21 If $x + y = 11$, $y + z = 14$, and $x + z = 13$, what is the value of $x + y + z$?

(A) 16
(B) 17
(C) 18
(D) 19
(E) 20

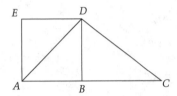

22 In the figure above, side AB of square $ABDE$ is extended to point C. If $BC = 8$ and $CD = 10$, what is the perimeter of triangle ACD?

(A) $18 + 6\sqrt{2}$
(B) $24 + 6\sqrt{2}$
(C) $26 + 6\sqrt{2}$
(D) 30
(E) 36

23 If $r < 0$ and $(4r - 4)^2 = 36$, what is the value of r?

(A) -2
(B) -1
(C) $-\frac{1}{2}$
(D) $-\frac{1}{4}$
(E) $-\frac{1}{8}$

24 Five liters of water were poured from tank A into tank B, and ten liters of water were then poured from tank A into tank C. If tank A originally had 10 more liters of water than tank C, how many more liters of water does tank C now have than tank A?

(A) 0
(B) 5
(C) 10
(D) 15
(E) 20

25 If a cube has a surface area of $36n^2$ square feet, what is its volume in cubic feet, in terms of n?

(A) $n^3\sqrt{6}$
(B) $6n^3\sqrt{6}$
(C) $36n^3$
(D) $36n^3\sqrt{6}$
(E) $216n^3$

IF YOU FINISH BEFORE TIME IS CALLED, YOU MAY CHECK YOUR WORK ON THIS SECTION ONLY. DO NOT TURN TO ANY OTHER SECTION IN THE TEST.

STOP

This page intentionally left blank.

Time–30 Minutes
35 Questions

For each of the following questions, choose the best answer and darken the corresponding oval on the answer sheet.

Select the lettered word or set of words that best completes the sentence.

Example:

Today's small, portable computers contrast markedly with the earliest electronic computers, which were - - - - .

(A) effective
(B) invented
(C) useful
(D) destructive
(E) enormous

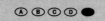

1 The rain is so rare and the land is so ---- that few of the men who work there see much ---- in farming.

(A) plentiful..hope
(B) barren..difficulty
(C) productive..profit
(D) infertile..future
(E) dry..danger

2 The principal declared that the students were not simply ignoring the rules, but openly ---- them.

(A) accepting
(B) redressing
(C) reviewing
(D) flouting
(E) discussing

3 Some critics believe that the ---- of modern art came with Dadaism, while others insist that the movement was a ----.

(A) zenith..sham
(B) pinnacle..triumph
(C) decline..disaster
(D) acceptance..success
(E) originality..fiasco

4 She would never have believed that her article was so ---- were it not for the ---- of correspondence which followed its publication.

(A) interesting..dearth
(B) inflammatory..lack
(C) controversial..spate
(D) commonplace..influx
(E) insignificant..volume

5 The writings of the philosopher Descartes are ----; many readers have difficulty following his complex, intricately woven arguments.

(A) generic
(B) trenchant
(C) reflective
(D) elongated
(E) abstruse

6 The prisoner was ---- even though he presented evidence clearly proving that he was nowhere near the scene of the crime.

(A) abandoned
(B) indicted
(C) exculpated
(D) exhumed
(E) rescinded

7 Many biologists are critical of the film's ---- premise that dinosaurs might one day return.

(A) scientific
(B) tacit
(C) speculative
(D) unwitting
(E) ambiguous

8 Mozart composed music with exceptional ----; he left no rough drafts because he was able to write out his compositions in ---- form.

(A) audacity..original
(B) facility..finished
(C) incompetence..ideal
(D) prestige..orchestral
(E) independence..concise

9 Known for their devotion, dogs were often used as symbols of ---- in Medieval and Renaissance painting.

(A) resistance
(B) benevolence
(C) generosity
(D) fidelity
(E) antagonism

10 It is ---- that a people so capable of treachery and brutality should also exhibit such a tremendous capacity for heroism.

(A) unfortunate
(B) explicable
(C) paradoxical
(D) distressing
(E) appalling

GO ON TO THE NEXT PAGE ➡

Choose the lettered pair of words that is related in the same way as the pair in capital letters.

Example:

FLAKE:SNOW::

(A) storm:hail
(B) drop:rain
(C) field:wheat
(D) stack:hay
(E) cloud:fog

11 CHARLATAN:SCRUPULOUS::

(A) confidant:virtuous
(B) laborer:stalwart
(C) officer:mutinous
(D) dullard:irritable
(E) tyrant:just

12 GREED:ACQUIRE::

(A) fear:disguise
(B) inertia:persuade
(C) gluttony:eat
(D) conformity:agree
(E) ignorance:speak

13 PARRY:BLOW::

(A) counter:argument
(B) sidestep:offense
(C) defer:ruling
(D) stumble:pitfall
(E) shine:light

14 MALIGN:SLURS::

(A) satisfy:treaties
(B) persecute:complaints
(C) torment:whispers
(D) court:debates
(E) flatter:compliments

15 LENTIL:LEGUME::

(A) rice:cereal
(B) nutrition:food
(C) horseshoe:pony
(D) husk:corn
(E) baker:cake

16 INDULGE:APPETITE::

(A) filter:impurity
(B) infuriate:anger
(C) coddle:emotion
(D) humor:whim
(E) liberate:freedom

17 MELLIFLUOUS:SOUND

(A) musical:entertainment
(B) fragrant:smell
(C) pale:color
(D) raucous:discussion
(E) auspicious:occasion

18 GUFFAW:LAUGH

(A) sniffle:sneeze
(B) whoop:cough
(C) yell:talk
(D) snore:sleep
(E) chuckle:sigh

19 CELESTIAL:HEAVENS

(A) planetary:orbit
(B) scientific:experiment
(C) nautical:ships
(D) solar:heat
(E) viscous:matter

20 ENERVATE:VITALITY

(A) consolidate:power
(B) energize:action
(C) daunt:courage
(D) estimate:worth
(E) admit:guilt

21 OLIGARCHY:FEW

(A) government:majority
(B) authority:consent
(C) constitution:country
(D) monarchy:one
(E) discrimination:minority

22 UNTRUTHFUL:MENDACIOUSNESS

(A) circumspect:caution
(B) timid:behavior
(C) agile:physique
(D) sensitive:patient
(E) trusting:honesty

23 INEXCUSABLE:JUSTIFY

(A) isolated:abandon
(B) unassailable:attack
(C) affable:like
(D) famous:admire
(E) splendid:revere

GO ON TO THE NEXT PAGE ➡

Answer the questions below based on the information in the accompanying passages.

Questions 24–35 are based on the following passage.

*In the following passage, a nineteenth-century
American writer recalls his boyhood in a small town
along the Mississippi River.*

My father was a justice of the peace, and I
supposed he possessed the power of life and death
over all men and could hang anybody that offended
him. This was distinction enough for me as a
(5) general thing; but the desire to be a steamboatman
kept intruding, nevertheless. I first wanted to be a
cabin boy, so that I could come out with a white
apron on and shake a tablecloth over the side,
where all my old comrades could see me. Later I
(10) thought I would rather be the deck hand who stood
on the end of the stage plank with a coil of rope in
his hand, because he was particularly conspicuous.
But these were only daydreams — too heavenly
to be contemplated as real possibilities. By and by
(15) one of the boys went away. He was not heard of for
a long time. At last he turned up as an apprentice
engineer or "striker" on a steamboat. This thing
shook the bottom out of all my Sunday-school
teachings. That boy had been notoriously worldly
(20) and I had been just the reverse — yet he was
exalted to this eminence, and I was left in obscurity
and misery. There was nothing generous about this
fellow in his greatness. He would always manage to
have a rusty bolt to scrub while his boat was
(25) docked at our town, and he would sit on the inside
guard and scrub it, where we could all see him and
envy him and loathe him.
He used all sorts of steamboat technicalities in
his talk, as if he were so used to them that he forgot
(30) common people could not understand them. He
would speak of the "labboard" side of a horse in an
easy, natural way that would make you wish he
was dead. And he was always talking about "St.
Looy" like an old citizen. Two or three of the boys
(35) had long been persons of consideration among us
because they had been to St. Louis once and had a
vague general knowledge of its wonders, but the
day of their glory was over now. They lapsed into a
humble silence, and learned to disappear when the
(40) ruthless "cub" engineer approached. This fellow had
money, too, and hair oil, and he wore a showy brass
watch chain, a leather belt, and used no suspenders.
No girl could withstand his charms. He "cut out"
every boy in the village. When his boat blew up at
(45) last, it diffused a tranquil contentment among us
such as we had not known for months. But when
he came home the next week, alive, renowned, and
appeared in church all battered up and bandaged, a
shining hero, stared at and wondered over by

(50) everybody, it seemed to us that the partiality of
Providence for an undeserving reptile had reached a
point where it was open to criticism.
This creature's career could produce but one
result, and it speedily followed. Boy after boy
(55) managed to get on the river. Four sons of the chief
merchant, and two sons of the county judge became
pilots, the grandest position of all. But some of us
could not get on the river — at least our parents
would not let us.
(60) So by and by I ran away. I said I would never
come home again till I was a pilot and could return
in glory. But somehow I could not manage it. I
went meekly aboard a few of the boats that lay
packed together like sardines at the long St. Louis
(65) wharf, and very humbly inquired for the pilots, but
got only a cold shoulder and short words from
mates and clerks. I had to make the best of this sort
of treatment for the time being, but I had
comforting daydreams of a future when I should be
(70) a great and honored pilot, with plenty of money,
and could kill some of these mates and clerks and
pay for them.

24 The author makes the statement that "I
supposed he...offended him" (lines 1-4)
primarily to suggest the

(A) power held by a justice of the peace in a
frontier town
(B) naive view that he held of his father's
importance
(C) respect in which the townspeople held his
father
(D) possibility of miscarriages of justice on the
American frontier
(E) harsh environment in which he was
brought up

25 As used in line 4, the word "distinction" most
nearly means

(A) difference
(B) variation
(C) prestige
(D) desperation
(E) clarity

26 The author decides that he would rather
become a deck hand than a cabin boy (lines 6-
12) because

(A) the job offers higher wages
(B) he believes that the work is easier
(C) he wants to avoid seeing his older friends
(D) deck hands often go on to become pilots
(E) the job is more visible to passersby

GO ON TO THE NEXT PAGE ➡

27 The author most likely mentions his "Sunday-school teachings" in lines 18-19 in order to emphasize

(A) the influence of his early education in later life
(B) his sense of injustice at the engineer's success
(C) his disillusionment with longstanding religious beliefs
(D) his determination to become an engineer at all costs
(E) the unscrupulous nature of the engineer's character

28 The author most likely concludes that the engineer is not "generous" (lines 22) because he

(A) has no respect for religious beliefs
(B) refuses to share his wages with friends
(C) flaunts his new position in public
(D) takes a pride in material possessions
(E) ignores the disappointment of other people's ambitions

29 The author most probably mentions the use of "steamboat technicalities" (lines 28-30) in order to emphasize the engineer's

(A) expertise after a few months on the job
(B) fascination for trivial information
(C) ignorance on most other subjects
(D) desire to appear sophisticated
(E) inability to communicate effectively

30 The word "consideration" in line 35 most nearly means

(A) generosity
(B) deliberation
(C) contemplation
(D) unselfishness
(E) reputation

31 According to the passage, the "glory" of having visited St. Louis (lines 36-38) was over because

(A) the boys' knowledge of St. Louis was much less detailed than the engineer's
(B) St. Louis had changed so much that the boys' stories were no longer accurate
(C) the boys realized that traveling to St. Louis was not a mark of sophistication
(D) the engineer's account revealed that the boys' stories were lies
(E) travel to St. Louis had become too commonplace to be envied

32 The author describes the engineer's appearance (lines 41-42) primarily in order to

(A) suggest one reason why many people found the engineer impressive
(B) convey the way steamboatmen typically dressed
(C) emphasize the inadequacy of his own wardrobe
(D) contrast the engineer's behavior with his appearance
(E) indicate his admiration for fashionable clothes

33 In lines 50-52, the author's response to the engineer's survival is one of

(A) thankfulness for what he believes is God's providence
(B) astonishment at the engineer's miraculous escape
(C) reflection on the occupational hazards of a steamboating career
(D) outrage at his rival's undeserved good fortune
(E) sympathy for the extent of the engineer's wounds

34 The major purpose of the passage is to

(A) sketch the peaceful life of a frontier town
(B) relate the events that led to a boy's first success in life
(C) portray the unsophisticated ambitions of a boy
(D) describe the characteristics of a small town boaster
(E) give a humorous portrayal of a boy's conflicts with his parents

35 At the end of the passage, the author reflects about

(A) his new ambition to become either a mate or a clerk
(B) the wisdom of seeking a job in which advancement is easier
(C) the prospect of abandoning a hopeless search for fame
(D) the impossibility of returning home and asking his parents' pardon
(E) his determination to keep striving for success in a glorious career

IF YOU FINISH BEFORE TIME IS CALLED, YOU MAY CHECK YOUR WORK ON THIS SECTION ONLY. DO NOT TURN TO ANY OTHER SECTION IN THE TEST. **STOP**

| **Time—30 Minutes**
25 Questions | Solve each of the following problems, decide which is the best answer choice, and darken the corresponding oval on the answer sheet. Use available space in the test booklet for scratchwork. |

Notes:

(1) Calculator use is permitted.

(2) All numbers used are real numbers.

(3) Figures are provided for some problems. All figures are drawn to scale and lie in a plane UNLESS otherwise indicated.

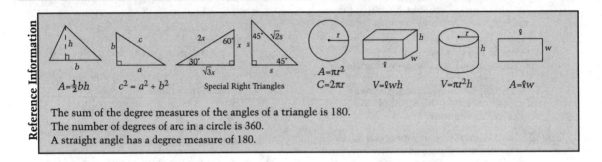

$A=\frac{1}{2}bh$ $c^2 = a^2 + b^2$ Special Right Triangles $A=\pi r^2$
$C=2\pi r$ $V=\ell wh$ $V=\pi r^2 h$ $A=\ell w$

The sum of the degree measures of the angles of a triangle is 180.
The number of degrees of arc in a circle is 360.
A straight angle has a degree measure of 180.

DIRECTIONS FOR QUANTITATIVE COMPARISON QUESTIONS

Compare the boxed quantity in Column A with the boxed quantity in Column B. Select answer choice

  A if Column A is greater;
  B if Column B is greater;
  C if the columns are equal; or
  D if more information is needed to determine the relationship.
An E response will be treated as an omission.

Notes:

1. Some questions include information about one or both quantities. That information is centered and unboxed.
2. A symbol that appears in both Column A and Column B stands for the same thing in both columns.
3. All numbers used are real numbers.

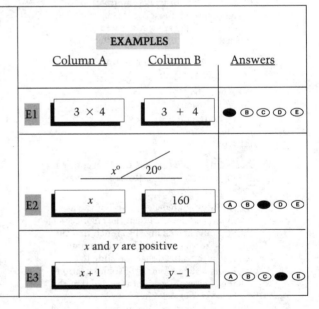

	Column A	Column B
1	$\frac{3}{8} + \frac{2}{5}$	1
2	The cost of 6 pens at 2 for 22 cents	The cost of 5 pens at 22 cents each

$$2a + b = 17$$
$$b - 3 = 2$$

	Column A	Column B
3	a	b
4	$x - 2(y + z)$	$x - 2y - 2z$

a, b, and c are positive integers such that $a + b + c = 150$.

	Column A	Column B
5	The mean of a, b, and c	The median of a, b, and c

For all numbers x and y, let $x \circledast y = (x + y)^3$.

	Column A	Column B
6	$4 \circledast 5$	$0 \circledast 9$

Column A   **Column B**

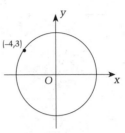

$(-4, 3)$

	Column A	Column B
7	The circumference of circle O	30

Jimmy owns a plant he waters every other day.

	Column A	Column B
8	The number of times Jimmy waters the plant during a certain week	The number of times Jimmy waters the plant during the following week

A certain line in the rectangular coordinate plane contains the points $(1,1)$, $(3,r)$, $(s,9)$, and $(6,11)$.

	Column A	Column B
9	r	s

$$r^2 + 4 = 21$$

	Column A	Column B
10	r	4

GO ON TO THE NEXT PAGE ➡

| Column A | Column B | | Column A | Column B |

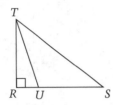

In right triangle *RST*,
RT = *US* = 6 and *RU* < 2.

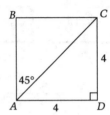

Note: Figure not drawn to scale.

| 11 | The perimeter of RST | 24 |

| 14 | The length of *AB* | 4 |

At a science fair, 5 students are semifinalists for 1st and 2nd place prizes.

| 12 | The total number of ways to select the two science fair prize winners | 10 |

t is a positive integer.

| 15 | The number of distinct prime factors of $2t$ | The number of distinct prime factors of $8t$ |

$$x > 0$$
$$0 < x^2 < 1$$

| 13 | $1 - x^2$ | $1 - x$ |

GO ON TO THE NEXT PAGE ➡

DIRECTIONS FOR STUDENT-PRODUCED RESPONSE QUESTIONS

For each of the questions below (16-25), solve the problem and indicate your answer by darkening the ovals in the special grid. For example:

Answer: 1.25 or $\frac{5}{4}$ or 5/4

Write answer in boxes. →

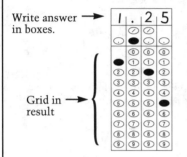

Grid in → result

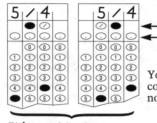

Fraction line

Decimal point

You may start your answers in any column, space permitting. Columns not needed should be left blank.

Either position is correct.

- It is recommended, though not required, that you write your answer in the boxes at the top of the columns. However, you will receive credit only for darkening the ovals correctly.

- Grid only one answer to a question, even though some problems have more than one correct answer.

- Darken no more than one oval in a column.

- No answers are negative.

- Mixed numbers cannot be gridded. For example: the number $1\frac{1}{4}$ must be gridded as 1.25 or 5/4.

  (If |1|1|/|4| is gridded, it will be interpreted as $\frac{11}{4}$, not $1\frac{1}{4}$.)

- Decimal Accuracy: Decimal answers must be entered as accurately as possible. For example, if you obtain an answer such as 0.1666..., you should record the result as .166 or .167. **Less accurate values such as .16 or .17 are not acceptable.**

  Acceptable ways to grid $\frac{1}{6}$ = .1666...

---

16 If $A = 2.54$ and $20B = A$, what is the value of B?

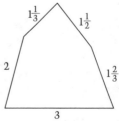

17 What is the perimeter of the figure shown above?

GO ON TO THE NEXT PAGE ➡

18 If $\frac{h}{3}$ and $\frac{h}{4}$ are integers, and if $75 < h < 100$, what is one possible value of h?

19 A retailer buys 16 shirts at $4.50 each and she sells all 16 shirts for $6.75 each. If the retailer purchases more of these shirts at $4.50 each, what is the greatest number of these shirts that she can buy with the profit she made on the 16 shirts?

20 Lines ℓ and m intersect at a point to form four angles. If one of the angles formed is 15 times as large as an adjacent angle, what is the measure, in degrees, of the smaller angle?

21 If $x = -4$ when $x^2 + 2xr + r^2 = 0$, what is the value of r?

22 Let $n\ast = n^2 - n$ for all positive numbers n.

What is the value of $\frac{1}{4}\ast - \frac{1}{2}\ast$?

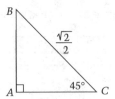

23 What is the area of $\triangle ABC$ shown above?

24 If x is a factor of 8,100 and if x is an odd integer, what is the greatest possible value of x?

25 In a certain class, $\frac{1}{2}$ of the male students and $\frac{2}{3}$ of the female students speak French. If there are $\frac{3}{4}$ as many girls as boys in the class, what fraction of the entire class speaks French?

IF YOU FINISH BEFORE TIME IS CALLED, YOU MAY CHECK YOUR WORK ON THIS SECTION ONLY. DO NOT TURN TO ANY OTHER SECTION IN THE TEST. **STOP**

This page intentionally left blank.

| Time–15 Minutes 12 Questions | Answer the questions below based on the information in the accompanying passages. |

Questions 1-12 are based on the following passages.

The controversy over the authorship of Shakespeare's plays began in the 18th century and continues to this day. Here, the author of Passage 1 embraces the proposal that Francis Bacon actually wrote the plays, while the author of Passage 2 defends the traditional attribution to Shakespeare himself.

Passage 1

Anyone with more than a superficial knowledge of Shakespeare's plays must necessarily entertain some doubt concerning their true authorship. Can
Line scholars honestly accept the idea that such
(5) masterworks were written by a shadowy actor with limited formal education and a social position that can most charitably be called "humble"? Obviously, the author of the plays must have traveled widely, yet there is no record that Shakespeare ever left his
(10) native England. Even more obviously, the real author had to have intimate knowledge of life within royal courts and palaces, yet Shakespeare was a commoner, with little firsthand experience of the aristocracy. No, common sense tells us that the
(15) plays must have been written by someone with substantial expertise in the law, the sciences, classics, foreign languages, and the fine arts — someone, in other words, like Shakespeare's eminent contemporary, Sir Francis Bacon.
(20)   The first person to suggest that Bacon was the actual author of the plays was Reverend James Wilmot. Writing in 1785, Wilmot argued that someone of Shakespeare's educational background could hardly have produced works of such erudition
(25) and insight. But a figure like Bacon, a scientist and polymath* of legendary stature, would certainly have known about, for instance, the circulation of the blood as alluded to in *Coriolanus*. And as an aristocrat, Bacon would have possessed the
(30) familiarity with court life required to produce a *Love's Labour's Lost*.
    Delia Bacon (no relation to Sir Francis) was next to make the case for Francis Bacon's authorship. In 1856, in collaboration with Nathaniel Hawthorne,
(35) she insisted that it was ridiculous to look for the creator of Hamlet among "that dirty, doggish group of players, who come into the scene [of the play Hamlet] summoned like a pack of hounds to his service." Ultimately, she concluded that the plays
(40) were actually composed by a committee consisting of Bacon, Edmund Spenser, Walter Raleigh, and several others.
    Still, some might wonder why Bacon, if indeed the plays were wholly or partly his work, would not
(45) put his own name on them. But consider the political climate of England in Elizabethan times. Given that it would have been politically and personally damaging for a man of Bacon's position to associate himself with such controversial plays,

(50) it is quite understandable that Bacon would hire a lowly actor to take the credit — and the consequences.
    But perhaps the most convincing evidence of all comes from the postscript of a 1624 letter sent to
(55) Bacon by Sir Tobie Matthew. "The most prodigious wit that I ever knew...is your lordship's name," Matthew wrote, "though he be known by another." That name, of course, was William Shakespeare.

*polymath — a person of wide and varied learning

Passage 2

Over the years, there have been an astonishing
(60) number of persons put forth as the "true author" of Shakespeare's plays. Some critics have even gone so far as to claim that only a "committee" could have possessed the abundance of talent and energy necessary to produce Shakespeare's thirty-seven
(65) plays. Among the individual figures most seriously promoted as "the real Shakespeare" is Sir Francis Bacon. Apparently, the fact that Bacon wrote most of his own work in academic Latin does nothing to deter those who would crown him the premier
(70) stylist in the English language.
    Although the entire controversy reeks of scholarly gamesplaying, the issue underlying it is worth considering: how could an uneducated actor create such exquisite works? But the answer to that
(75) is easy. Shakespeare's dramatic gifts had little to do with encyclopedic knowledge, complex ideas, or a fluency with great systems of thought. Rather, Shakespeare's genius was one of common sense and perceptive intuition — a genius that grows not out
(80) of book-learning, but out of a deep understanding of human nature and a keen grasp of basic emotions, passions, and jealousies.
    One of the most common arguments advanced by skeptics is that the degree of familiarity with the
(85) law exhibited in a *Hamlet* or a *Merchant of Venice* can only have been achieved by a lawyer or other man of affairs. The grasp of law evidenced in these plays, however, is not a detailed knowledge of formal law, but a more general understanding of so-
(90) called "country law". Shakespeare was a landowner — an extraordinary achievement in itself for an ill-paid Elizabethan actor — and so would have been knowledgeable about legal matters related to the buying, selling, and renting of real estate. Evidence

GO ON TO THE NEXT PAGE ➡

(95) of such a common understanding of land regulations can be found, for instance, in the gravedigging scene of *Hamlet*.

So no elaborate theories of intrigue and secret identity are necessary to explain the accomplish-
(100) ment of William Shakespeare. Scholars who have made a career of ferreting out "alternative bards" may be reluctant to admit it, but literary genius can flower in any socioeconomic bracket. Shakespeare, in short, was Shakespeare — an observation that
(105) one would have thought was obvious to everyone.

1 In line 2, "entertain" most nearly means

(A) amuse
(B) harbor
(C) occupy
(D) cherish
(E) engage

2 In Passage 1, the author draws attention to Shakespeare's social standing as a "commoner" (line 13) in order to cast doubt on the Elizabethan actor's

(A) aptitude for writing poetically
(B) knowledge of foreign places and habits
(C) ability to support himself by playwriting
(D) familiarity with life among persons of high rank
(E) understanding of the problems of government

3 *Coriolanus* and *Love's Labour's Lost* are mentioned in lines 28-31 as examples of works that

(A) only Francis Bacon could have written
(B) exhibit a deep understanding of human nature
(C) resemble works written by Francis Bacon under his own name
(D) portray a broad spectrum of Elizabethan society
(E) reveal expertise more likely held by Bacon than Shakespeare

4 In Passage 1, the quotation from Delia Bacon (lines 36-39) conveys a sense of

(A) disdain for the disreputable vulgarity of Elizabethan actors
(B) resentment at the way Shakespeare's characters were portrayed
(C) regret that conditions for Elizabethan actors were not better
(D) doubt that Shakespeare could actually have created such unsavory characters
(E) disappointment at the incompetence of Elizabethan actors

5 The author of Passage 1 maintains that Bacon did not put his own name on the plays attributed to Shakespeare because he

(A) regarded writing as an unsuitable occupation for an aristocrat
(B) wished to protect himself from the effects of controversy
(C) preferred being known as a scientist and politician rather than as a writer
(D) did not want to associate himself with lowly actors
(E) sought to avoid the attention that fame brings

6 In the first paragraph of Passage 2, the author calls into question Bacon's likely ability to

(A) write in a language with which he was unfamiliar
(B) make the transition between scientific writing and playwriting
(C) produce the poetic language evident in the plays
(D) cooperate with other members of a committee
(E) singlehandedly create thirty-seven plays

7 The word "premier" in line 69 most nearly means

(A) earliest
(B) influential
(C) inaugural
(D) greatest
(E) original

8 In line 76, the word "encyclopedic" most nearly means

(A) technical
(B) comprehensive
(C) abridged
(D) disciplined
(E) specialized

9 The author of Passage 2 cites Shakespeare's status as a landowner in order to

(A) prove that Shakespeare was a success as a playwright
(B) refute the claim that Shakespeare had little knowledge of aristocratic life
(C) prove that Shakespeare didn't depend solely on acting for his living
(D) dispute the notion that Shakespeare was a commoner
(E) account for Shakespeare's apparent knowledge of the law

GO ON TO THE NEXT PAGE ➡

10 In lines 99-103, the author maintains that literary genius

(A) is not dependent on a writer's external circumstances

(B) must be based on an inborn comprehension of human nature

(C) is enhanced by the suffering that poverty brings

(D) frequently goes unrecognized among those of modest means and position

(E) can be stifled by too much book-learning and academic training

11 The author of Passage 2 would probably respond to the speculation in the fourth paragraph of Passage 1 by pointing out that

(A) Shakespeare's plays would not have seemed particularly controversial to Elizabethan audiences

(B) The extent and range of Bacon's learning has been generally exaggerated

(C) such scenarios are farfetched and unnecessary if one correctly understands Shakespeare's genius

(D) Bacon would not have had the knowledge of the lower classes required to produce the plays

(E) the claim implies that Shakespeare was disreputable when in fact he was a respectable landowner

12 The author of Passage 1 would probably respond to the skepticism expressed in lines 67-70 by making which of the following statements?

(A) The similarities between English and Latin make it plausible that one person could write well in both languages.

(B) Plays written in Latin would not have been likely to attract a wide audience in Elizabethan England.

(C) The premier stylist in the English language is more likely to have been an eminent scholar than an uneducated actor.

(D) Writing the plays in Latin would have shielded Bacon from much of the political damage he wanted to avoid.

(E) The style of the plays is notable mostly for the clarity of thought behind the lines rather than their musicality or beauty.

This page intentionally left blank.

<table>
<tr><td>Time—15 Minutes
10 Questions</td><td>Solve each of the following problems, decide which is the best answer choice, and darken the corresponding oval on the answer sheet. Use available space in the test booklet for scratchwork.</td></tr>
</table>

Notes:

(1)   Calculator use is permitted.

(2)   All numbers used are real numbers.

(3)   Figures are provided for some problems. All figures are drawn to scale and lie in a plane UNLESS otherwise indicated.

Reference Information

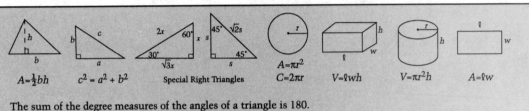

$A=\frac{1}{2}bh$ $c^2 = a^2 + b^2$ Special Right Triangles $A=\pi r^2$ $C=2\pi r$ $V=\ell wh$ $V=\pi r^2 h$ $A=\ell w$

The sum of the degree measures of the angles of a triangle is 180.
The number of degrees of arc in a circle is 360.
A straight angle has a degree measure of 180.

---

1   If $p = -2$ and $q = 3$, then $p^3 q^2 + p^2 q =$

(A)   –84
(B)   –60
(C)   36
(D)   60
(E)   84

N	P
2	7
4	13
6	19
8	25

3   Which of the following equations describes the relationship of each pair of numbers (N,P) in the table above?

(A) $P = N + 5$
(B) $P = 2N + 3$
(C) $P = 2N + 5$
(D) $P = 3N + 1$
(E) $P = 3N - 1$

A   B   C D E

Note: Figure not drawn to scale.

2   In the figure above, B is the midpoint of AC and D is the midpoint of CE. If $AB = 5$ and $BD = 8$, what is the length of DE?

(A) 8
(B) 6
(C) 5
(D) 4
(E) 3

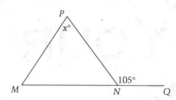

Note: Figure not drawn to scale.

4　In the figure above, *MQ* is a straight line. If *PM* = *PN*, what is the value of *x*?

(A) 30
(B) 45
(C) 60
(D) 75
(E) 90

5　Marty has exactly 5 blue pens, 6 black pens, and 4 red pens in his knapsack. If he pulls out one pen at random from his knapsack, what is the probability that the pen is either red or black?

(A) $\frac{11}{15}$

(B) $\frac{2}{3}$

(C) $\frac{1}{2}$

(D) $\frac{1}{3}$

(E) $\frac{1}{5}$

6　Two hot dogs and a soda cost $3.25. If three hot dogs and a soda cost $4.50, what is the cost of two sodas?

(A) $0.75
(B) $1.25
(C) $1.50
(D) $2.50
(E) $3.00

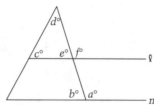

7　In the figure above, if $\ell \parallel m$, which of the following must be equal to *a*?

(A) $b + c$
(B) $b + e$
(C) $c + d$
(D) $d + e$
(E) $d + f$

8　A certain phone call cost 75 cents for the first 3 minutes plus 15 cents for each additional minute. If the call lasted *x* minutes and *x* is an integer greater than 3, which of the following expresses the cost of the call, in dollars?

(A) $0.75(3) + 0.15x$
(B) $0.75(3) + 0.15(x + 3)$
(C) $0.75 + 0.15(3 - x)$
(D) $0.75 + 0.15(x - 3)$
(E) $0.75 + 0.15x$

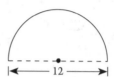

9　The figure above shows a piece of wire in the shape of a semicircle. If the piece of wire is bent to form a circle without any of the wire overlapping, what is the area of the circle?

(A)　6π
(B)　9π
(C)　12π
(D)　18π
(E)　36π

10　If $a^2 - a = 72$, and *b* and *n* are integers such that $b^n = a$, which of the following cannot be a value for *b*?

(A)　-8
(B)　-2
(C)　2
(D)　3
(E)　9

COMPUTE YOUR SCORE

Use this key to correct your test. Follow the instructions on the next page to convert your scores to the standard SAT scale.

SECTION 1

1......E
2......C
3......B
4......B
5......B
6......E
7......C
8......E
9......D
10.....B
11.....A
12.....A
13.....B
14.....C
15.....D
16.....D
17.....C
18.....B
19.....C
20.....E
21.....A
22.....C
23.....D
24.....C
25.....A
26.....E
27.....B
28.....A
29.....C
30.....D

SECTION 2

1......C
2......E
3......A
4......B
5......E
6......D
7......B
8......E
9......A
10.....B
11.....A
12.....D
13.....D
14.....C
15.....E
16.....C
17.....D
18.....A
19.....C
20.....E
21.....D
22.....B
23.....C
24.....D
25.....B

SECTION 3

1......D
2......D
3......A
4......C
5......E
6......B
7......C
8......B
9......D
10.....C
11.....E
12.....C
13.....A
14.....E
15.....A
16.....D
17.....B
18.....C
19.....C
20.....C
21.....D
22.....A
23.....B
24.....B
25.....C
26.....E
27.....B
28.....C
29.....D
30.....E
31.....A
32.....A
33.....D
34.....C
35.....E

SECTION 4

1......B
2......B
3......A
4......C
5......D
6......C
7......A
8......D
9......C
10.....D
11.....B
12.....A
13.....A
14.....D
15.....C
16..... .127
17..... 9.5 or 19/2
18..... 84 OR 96
19..... 8
20..... 45/4, 11.2 or 11.3
21..... 4
22..... 1/16, .062 or .063
23..... 1/8 or .125
24..... 2025
25..... 4/7 or .571

SECTION 5

1......B
2......D
3......E
4......A
5......B
6......C
7......D
8......B
9......E
10.....A
11.....C
12.....C

SECTION 6

1......B
2......E
3......D
4......A
5......B
6......C
7......C
8......D
9......B
10.....C

	NUMBER CORRECT		NUMBER WRONG		RAW SCORE
SECTION 1:	☐	− .25 x	☐	=	☐
SECTION 3:	☐	− .25 x	☐	=	☐
SECTION 5:	☐	− .25 x	☐	=	☐
VERBAL RAW SCORE:					☐
SECTION 4A: (Questions 1 to 15)	☐	− .33 x	☐	=	☐
SECTION 4B: (Questions 16 to 25)	☐	(No wrong answer penalty)		=	☐
SECTION 2:	☐	− .25 x	☐	=	☐
SECTION 6:	☐	− .25 x	☐	=	☐
MATH RAW SCORE:					☐

First, check your answers against the answer key and count up the number right and the number wrong for each section. Remember not to count omissions as wrong. You can use the chart on the previous page.

Then figure out your raw scores. The verbal raw score is equal to the total right in the three verbal sections minus one-fourth of the number wrong in those sections. The math raw score is equal to the total right in the three math sections minus one-fourth of the number wrong in the two Regular Math sections and minus one-third the number wrong in the QCs. (Remember: there is no deduction for wrong answers in the Grid-ins.) Round each raw score to the nearest whole number.

Finally, use the tables below to convert each raw score to a range of scaled scores.

VERBAL		MATH	
Raw Score	Scaled Score	Raw Score	Scaled Score
73-78	700-800	55-60	700-800
67-72	650-750	50-54	650-750
61-66	600-700	45-49	600-700
54-60	550-650	40-44	550-650
48-53	500-600	35-39	500-600
41-47	450-550	30-24	450-550
33-40	400-500	25-29	400-500
26-32	350-450	19-24	350-450
19-25	300-400	13-18	300-400
11-18	250-350	7-12	250-350
less than 11	200-300	less than 7	200-300

Don't take these scores too literally. Practice test conditions cannot precisely mirror real test conditions. Your actual SAT scores will almost certainly vary from your practice test scores.

Your score on the practice test gives you a rough idea of your range on the actual exam. Use this list to help you set a goal for the real SAT. This is a partial list of schools from around the country, together with the median scores of their incoming freshmen, based on available published data.

If you don't like your score, it's not too late to do something about it. Work your way way through this book again, and turn to Kaplan's Verbal and Math Workbooks for even more help.

MEDIAN SAT OVER 1250

Amherst College, MA

Barnard College, NY

Bates College, ME

Bowdoin College, ME

Brown University, RI

Bryn Mawr College, PA

California Institute of Technology, CA

Claremont McKenna College, CA

College of William and Mary, VA

Columbia University, NY

Cooper Union, NY

Cornell University, NY

Curtis Institute of Music, PA

Dartmouth College, NH

Davidson College, NC

Duke University, NC

Georgetown University, DC

Harvard & Radcliffe Colleges, MA

Harvey Mudd College, CA

Haverford College, PA

Johns Hopkins University, MD

Juilliard School, NY

Massachusetts Institute of Technology, MA

Northwestern University, IL

Oberlin College, OH

Pomona College, CA

Princeton University, NJ

Rice University, TX

Smith College, MA

Stanford University, CA

Swarthmore College, PA

Tufts University, MA

United States Air Force Academy, CO

United States Coast Guard Academy, CT

United States Military Academy, NY

United States Naval Academy, MD

University of Chicago, IL

University of Michigan, MI

University of Notre Dame, IN

University of Pennsylvania, PA

University of Virginia, VA

Vassar College, NY

Wake Forest University, NC

Washington and Lee University, VA

Webb Institute of Naval Architecture, NY

Wellesley College, MA

Wesleyan University, CT

Williams College, MA

Yale University, CT

MEDIAN SAT 1150-1250

Bard College, NY

Brandeis University, MA

Carleton College, MN

Carnegie Mellon University, PA

Case Western Reserve University, OH

Colorado State University, CO

Connecticut College, CT

Drew University, NJ

Emory University, GA

Fordham University, NY

George Washington University, DC

Gettysburg College, PA

Grinnell College, IA

Hamilton College, NY

Kenyon College, OH

Lawrence University, WI

Macalester College, MN

Miami University, OH

Middlebury College, VT

Mount Holyoke College, MA

New College of the University of S. Florida

New York University, NY

Reed College, OR

Rensselaer Polytechnic Institute, NY

Rhode Island School of Design, RI

Rose-Hulman Institute of Technology, IN

Rutgers College, NJ

Saint Olaf College, MN

Sarah Lawrence College, NY

Skidmore College, NY

Southwestern University, TX

State University of NY at Binghamton, NY

Syracuse University, NY

Trinity College, CT

Tulane University, LA

University of California at Berkeley, CA

University of California, Los Angeles, CA

University of Illinois at Urbana-Champaign, IL

University of Massachusetts at Amherst, MA

University of Missouri, Columbia, MO

University of North Carolina at Chapel Hill

Vanderbilt University, TN

Western International University, AZ

Wheaton College, IL

MEDIAN SAT 1050-1150

Alfred University, NY

American University, DC

Beloit College, WI

Birmingham-Southern College, AL

Boston University, MA

Brigham Young University, UT

City University of NY/Hunter College

Coe College, IA

Denison University, OH

DePauw University, IN

Earlham College, IN

Eckerd College, FL

Florida State University, FL

Goucher College, MD

Hampshire College, MA

Hillsdale College, MI

Hofstra University, NY

La Salle University, PA

Lewis and Clark College, OR

Loyola College, MD

Marlboro College, VT

Marquette University, WI

Mills College, CA

Mississippi State University, MS

Northeast Missouri State University, MO

Prescott College, AZ

Saint John's College, MD

Texas A & M University, TX

Transylvania University, KY

University of Connecticut, CT

University of Maryland at College Park, MD

University of Miami, FL

University of Missouri-Rolla, MO

University of Texas at Austin, TX

University of Vermont, VT

University of Wisconsin-Madison, WI

Valparaiso University, IN

MEDIAN SAT 900-1050

Adelphi University, NY

Auburn University, AL

Ball State University, IN

Bennington College, VT

Bethany College, WV

Calvin College, MI

Catholic University of America, DC

Christendom College, VA

Christian Brothers University, TN

College of Wooster, OH

Covenant College, GA

Drake University, IA

Drury College, MO

Fisk University, TN

Glassboro State College, NJ

Guilford College, NC

Hope College, MI

Howard University, DC

Indiana University of Pennsylvania, PA

Kent State University, OH

LeTourneau University, TX

Loyola University, LA

Manhattan College, NY

Millsaps College, MS

Monmouth College, IL

Morehouse College, GA

Niagara University, NY

Northwestern College, WI

Rockhurst College, MO

Seton Hall University, NJ

Sweet Briar College, VA

University of Illinois at Chicago, IL

University of Iowa, IA

University of Oregon, OR

University of Wisconsin-Milwaukee, WI

Washington College, MD

Wayne State University, MI

Wheaton College, MA

MEDIAN SAT UNDER 900

Albany State College, GA

Alcorn State University, MS

Bethel College, TN

Blue Mountain College, MS

Boise State University, ID

Central Missouri State University, MO

College of Santa Fe, NM

Cumberland College, KY

Fayetteville State University, NC

Franklin Pierce College, NH

Indiana University at Kokomo, IN

Jackson State University, MS

Johnson C. Smith University, NC

Lamar University, TX

Lane College, TN

Marshall University, WV

Methodist College, NC

Mississippi Valley State University, MS

New England College, NH

Nichols College, MA

Nyack College, NY

Pfeiffer College, NC

Piedmont College, GA

Saint Augustine's College, NC

Saint Leo College, FL

Saint Martin's College, WA

Simpson College, CA

Tuskegee University, AL

University of Nebraska at Omaha, NE

DISAPPOINTED?

Remember, this is just a partial list of the many colleges available to you. Ask your guidance counselor for more alternatives.

If you're aiming for a school that doesn't match your performance on the practice test, call 1–(800)-KAPTEST for information on one of Kaplan's courses.